ISLAMIC CORPORATE FINANCE

Most existing texts covering topics in Islamic finance discuss the potential of Islamic banking; very few talk about other forms of financing and the investment activities of Islamic firms from the standpoint of owners and managers. This book fills this gap by looking at the traditional as well as non-traditional financing and investment activities of *shariah*-compliant companies.

The chapters in this edited text offer a full range of topics in corporate finance for Islamic firms, including global comparisons of *shariah* screening, dividend policy and capital structure of Islamic firms, details of global Islamic equity markets, trends and performance of *sukuk* markets, and a brief account of derivative securities that can be used in Islamic finance. This is a useful reference for anyone who wishes to learn more about the performance of *shariah*-compliant companies vis-à-vis conventional firms. The book includes both technical and non-technical information that would be suitable for classroom teaching as well as a reference for postgraduate research students.

M. Kabir Hassan is Hibernia Professor of Economics and Finance, and Bank One Professor of Business at the University of New Orleans, Louisiana, USA.

Mamunur Rashid is Senior Assistant Professor of Finance at the Universiti Brunei Darussalam.

Sirajo Aliyu is Senior Lecturer at the Federal Polytechnic Bauchi-Nigeria, and a certified member of the International Council of Islamic Finance Educators and Chartered Institute of Islamic Finance Professionals.

Because they comply with *shariah* law, Islamic firms – financial as well as non-financial – behave differently from their conventional counterparts. While we know a lot about the structure and operation of Islamic financial institutions, information on Islamic non-financial corporations is very limited. This book combines technical as well as non-technical information on Islamic listed corporations and their structures and strategies, from several dimensions. The contents of this book will be particularly useful for academics to gain an in-depth view of Islamic corporate finance, with evidence garnered from around the globe.

—Professor Dr. Habib Ahmed
Durham University, UK

In recent years the Islamic financial services industry has seen astonishing, double-digit global growth, mostly in the form of financial firms (Islamic banks, microcredits, and others). However, the existing literature provides minimal coverage of the underlying corporate finance assumptions and relevant financing strategies of *non*-financial *shariah*-compliant corporations which engage in *halal* business – that permitted by *shariah* law. This book covers regular topics in corporate finance, such as performance matrix/ measures, capital structure, dividend policy, and pertinent corporate finance issues, from the perspective of Islamic corporations. The book will help both corporate leaders and academics to arrive at a deeper understanding of Islamic corporate financing, especially in emerging economies.

—Dr. Syed Musa Bin Syed Jaafar Alhabshi
Dean, International Islamic University Malaysia (IIUM)
Institute of Islamic Banking and Finance, Malaysia

ISLAMIC CORPORATE FINANCE

Edited by M. Kabir Hassan, Mamunur Rashid and Sirajo Aliyu

Routledge
Taylor & Francis Group
LONDON AND NEW YORK

First published 2019
by Routledge
2 Park Square, Milton Park, Abingdon, Oxon OX14 4RN

and by Routledge
52 Vanderbilt Avenue, New York, NY 10017

Routledge is an imprint of the Taylor & Francis Group, an informa business

British Library Cataloguing in Publication Data
A catalogue record for this book is available from the British Library

Library of Congress Cataloging in Publication Data
Names: Hassan, Kabir, editor. | Rashid, Mamunur
(Assistant Professor in Finance), editor. | Aliyu, Sirajo, editor.
Title: Islamic corporate finance / edited by M. Kabir Hassan,
Mamunur Rashid and Sirajo Aliyu.
Description: Abingdon, Oxon ; New York, NY : Routledge, 2019. |
Includes bibliographical references and index.
Identifiers: LCCN 2019004447 | ISBN 9781138480919 (hardback) |
ISBN 9781138480926 (pbk.) | ISBN 9781351061506 (ebook)
Subjects: LCSH: Corporations–Islamic countrires–Finance. |
Finance–Religious aspects–Islam. | Finance–Islamic countries.
Classification: LCC HG4259 .I85 2019 | DDC 338.6/041091767–dc23
LC record available at https://lccn.loc.gov/2019004447

ISBN: 978-1-138-48091-9 (hbk)
ISBN: 978-1-138-48092-6 (pbk)
ISBN: 978-1-351-06150-6 (ebk)

Typeset in Times New Roman
by Newgen Publishing UK

MIX
Paper from responsible sources
FSC™ C013985
FSC www.fsc.org

Printed in the United Kingdom
by Henry Ling Limited

CONTENTS

FIGURES

TABLES

CONTRIBUTORS

Md. Faruk Abdullah is Senior Lecturer at the School of Banking and Finance, Faculty of Economics and Management Sciences, University of Sultan Zainal Abidin, Kuala Terengganu, Terengganu, Malaysia.

Nasiru Abdullahi is Senior Lecturer in the Department of Business Administration, Ahmadu Bello University Business School, Zaria, Nigeria.

Mustapha Abubakar is Senior Lecturer in the Department of Banking and Finance, Ahmadu Bello University Business School, Zaria, Nigeria.

Sirajo Aliyu is Senior Lecturer at the Federal Polytechnic Bauchi, Nigeria and a certified member of the International Council of Islamic Finance Educators and Chartered Institute of Islamic Finance Professionals.

Zaheer Anwer is Director at the Lahore Centre of Excellence in Islamic Banking and Finance, The University of Lahore, Lahore, Pakistan.

Ali Ashraf is a financial economist and Associate Professor of Finance at Frostburg State University, Maryland, USA.

Lim Li Chern is a postgraduate student at the Nottingham University Business School, University of Nottingham Malaysia Campus.

Mohammad Ashraful Ferdous Chowdhury is Assistant Professor at the School of Management and Business Administration, Shahjalal University of Science and Technology, Bangladesh.

M. Kabir Hassan is Hibernia Professor of Economics and Finance, and Bank One Professor of Business, at the University of New Orleans, Louisiana, USA.

Md. Shafiul Islam is Head of Operations at AM Securities Financial Services Limited, Bangladesh.

Shamsher Mohamad Ramadili Mohamad is Professor at the International Centre of Education in Islamic Finance, Kuala Lumpur, Malaysia.

Rasidah Mohd-Rashid is Senior Lecturer at School of Economics, Finance and Banking, Universiti Utara Malaysia, Kedah, Malaysia.

Andrea Paltrinieri is Associate Professor at the University of Udine, Udine, Italy.

Ahsanur Rahman is Head of International Trade and Sales, BRAC EPL Stock Brokerage Limited, Dhaka, Bangladesh.

Asmak Ab Rahman is Senior Lecturer at the Department of Shariah and Economics, Academy of Islamic Studies, University of Malaya, Kuala Lumpur, Malaysia.

Mamunur Rashid is Senior Assistant Professor of Finance at the Universiti Brunei Darussalam.

Mohamed Eskandar Shah Mohd Rasid is Associate Professor at the International Centre of Education in Islamic Finance, Kuala Lumpur, Malaysia.

Varun K. Sibdoyal is Assistant Manager at Deloitte Mauritius.

Ahmad Hakimi Tajuddin is Lecturer at Taylor's Business School, Taylor's University, Selangor, Malaysia.

Andrew Saw Tek Wei is Lecturer of Finance at the Universiti Malaysia Sabah.

Ajim Uddin is PhD Candidate at the Martin Tuchman School of Management, New Jersey Institute of Technology, USA.

Cheong Jiunn Yan is a postgraduate student at the Nottingham University Business School, University of Nottingham Malaysia Campus.

1

SCREENING AND PERFORMANCE OF *SHARIAH*-COMPLIANT COMPANIES

Mamunur Rashid and Andrew Saw Tek Wei

Introduction to *shariah* screening

According to a Pew Research Centre study published in April 2017 (Lipka & Hackett, 2017), there were approximately 1.8 billion Muslims worldwide as at 2015. With regard to recent growth, Islam is the second largest religion in terms of total size and is often reported to be the fastest-growing religion in terms of its annual percentage growth. With this tremendous population growth follows the potential for more firms to adopt practices that adhere to Islamic *shariah* principles to satisfy this growing market. This is especially the case considering the fact that as more first-time Muslim customers become informed about their choices, they are likely to prefer banking with Islamic banks in addition to maintaining their accounts with conventional banks. This adherence is strictly maintained in some countries, while in others, Muslims still prefer having accounts in Islamic as well as conventional banks (Iqbal et al., 2018).

A key tenet of the Islamic faith is that Islam provides a perfect and all-encompassing guideline and law for all aspects and areas of life. This takes the form of *shariah* law, or Islamic jurisprudence, believed to be divine law revealed by Allah through His messengers and the Holy Book. The last prophet, Mohammad (peace be upon him), was an active businessman. The current day-trading-based banking or profit-and-loss sharing principles in the Islamic world come from the Prophet's practices from some 1,400 years ago. Consequently, national economic authorities around the world, preferentially in Islamic jurisdictions, have established laws and requirements for companies to conduct business activities in accordance with and in harmony with Islamic law. These guidelines on business activities are well documented, whether codified in national legislation or in other forms, such as interpretations of scripture by *shariah* courts.

Under *shariah* law, Islamic businesses are forbidden from obtaining financing from banks that deal with interest (*riba*), invest despite excessive uncertainty (*gharar*), gamble (*maysir*), or engage in other non-*shariah* compliant activities. Understandably, this will influence the decisions of more religiously concerned Muslim customers to prefer *shariah*-compliant businesses as opposed to conventional businesses, as the former would be less likely to have intentions that would actively violate *shariah* law through their banking choices. Although guidelines on Islamic business activity are well documented, as with any theology and religious law, the interpretation and implementation of *shariah* law differs across different governments and jurisdictions around the world. In order to achieve sustainable growth in Islamic finance, it is necessary to obtain a clear understanding of the differences in *shariah* rulings across these jurisdictions. *Shariah* rulings must be integrated, standardized, and harmonized on an international basis to achieve sustainable growth. The subsequent parts of this chapter will illustrate several similarities and differences between *shariah* rulings across various jurisdictions.

The start of the Islamic finance standard

"The truthful and honest merchant is associated with the Prophets, the upright and the martyrs." This mention by the Prophet (peace be upon him) of the 'truthful and honest merchant' in the seventh century, encouraging honesty and kindness when dealing with customers, is the earliest known form of Islamic finance (Haron et al., 2013). However, during its early conception and operation Islamic finance did not perform smoothly, as it met with many challenges at a time when other, mostly Western, countries had colonized Islamic countries. The revival of Islamic finance started sometime between the 1940s and 1950s when Islamic countries began pushing for independence and gaining international recognition. Even so, the establishment of modern Islamic banking, which started in Malaysia during the 1940s, is remembered as being unsuccessful, with a follow-up attempt in the form of the Myt Ghamir bank in Egypt being unfortunately also short-lived. Elsewhere, other oil-rich Islamic Middle Eastern countries started Islamic financial exercises to serve their growing Muslim populations.

Islamic finance gained momentum from 1999 onwards when Dow Jones attempted to create the world's first Islamic index in Bahrain. This was quickly followed up by other equity providers such as the Shariah Advisory Council (SAC) from Malaysia. From this point onwards, Islamic finance experienced rapid growth and has since been acknowledged as a competitive alternative investment to its counterparts offered by conventional finance institutions. While the supply side – Islamic banking – has been experiencing tremendous growth in the Middle East, South Asia, and Southeast Asian countries, stakeholders have been sharing their sentiments about the need to strengthen the demand side of Islamic finance, i.e. Islamic businesses. The world has yet to witness a global or truly transnational Islamic corporation, as the screening processes involved for such corporations remain highly diverse. Table 1.1 shows that at least six commonly

TABLE 1.1 Comparison of qualitative screening criteria for *shariah*-compliant companies

Business activities	*Index*					
	DJIM	*S&P*	*SAC*	*FTSE*	*MSCI*	*AAOIFI*
Alcohol	P	P	P	P	P	P
Advertisement and media	P	P	A	A	A	–
Cloning	P	–	–	–	–	–
Conventional financial services	P	P	P	P	P	P
Gambling and gaming	P	P	P	P	P	P
Pork-related products	P	P	P	P	P	P
Adult entertainment (pornography)	P	P	P	P	P	P
Tobacco	P	P	P	P	P	P
Public image	–	–	I	–	–	–
Maslaha (public interest)	–	–	I	–	–	–
Weapons and arms	P	P	P	P	A	P
Hotels	P	A	A	P	P	–
Trading of gold and silver as cash on deferred basis	–	P	–	–	–	–
Stem cell research	–	–	–	–	–	P

Dow Jones Islamic Market (DJIM) Index; Standard & Poor's (S&P); SAC, Shariah Advisory Council; Financial Times Stock Exchange (FTSE), Morgan Stanley Capital International (MSCI; Accounting and Audit Organization for Islamic Financial Institutions (AAOIFI); P, prohibited; A, acceptable; I, important aspect; (-) , no information.

Source: Created from Htay et al. (2013).

used screening exercises are available at the present time. Due to limitations of the existing screening exercises, newer screenings are expected to be introduced in the coming years. Even though these screenings show some differences with respect to some individual industries (e.g. weapons and defence), there still exist major gaps in the screening criteria. This chapter hopes to summarize these criteria, to offer a direction towards future screening exercises.

Shariah *screening*

Muslims are prohibited from investing in businesses involved in activities classified as being non-*shariah*-compliant. It is often difficult to differentiate the compliant set of factors from the non-compliant set, owing to several financial, scientific, and social factors involved. Often, due to social customs, compliance from one factor becomes strongly non-compliant in others. For instance, payment of *zakat* (the mandatory amount of alms-giving on wealth for Muslims) by corporations is subject to the regulation and accounting practices of their respective legal jurisdictions

(Rashid et al., 2017). However, when *shariah* screening is completed, the set of companies are passed based on rigorous procedures to ensure compliance to *shariah*. *Shariah* screening, in this respect, is illustrated as also assisting Muslims in their decisions regarding investment in compliant ventures.

Because of the importance of Islamic-compliant businesses to Muslims, the business community has witnessed continuous growth of Islamic funds (Islamic mutual funds, exchange traded funds, unit trusts, and other funds) all over the world (Sanusi, et al., 2015). Muslim investors should not solely prioritize profitability of their investments; the investment must equally be ethical and socially acceptable (Ulrich & Marzban, 2008). Since Islamic screening is based on best Islamic practice, the screening exercises can be employed to identify the best set of investment opportunities for Muslims. The investments are not only compliant in general, but are also said to be socially beneficial and ethically fit to ensure socio-economic justice (Hassan et al., 2019).

The Dow Jones Islamic Market (DJIM) Index was developed in conjunction with the rise of Islamic finance, becoming the world's first Islamic equity screen provider. Not long after its formation, other equity providers such as the SAC and Standard & Poor's (S&P) indices were developed to fulfil the growing demand for Islamic finance. Although these equity providers have different opinions on the factors determining good *shariah* screening criteria, there are several common principles that govern all equity providers engaged in the screening of *shariah*-compliant companies. Most importantly, the businesses must be permissible (*halal*) according to *shariah* (Natarajan & Dharani, 2012), as the prohibition of undesirable activities is believed to ensure social development and economic justice (Ibrahim & Ong, 2012).

All the screen providers follow a common two-stage method: qualitative followed by quantitative screening (Htay et al., 2013) (Figure 1.1). The qualitative

Qualitative/activity screening	*Quantitative/financial screening*
Qualitative screening is a process of screening out companies and business activities involved in prohibited activities. According to Standard & Poor's (2009), business activities which involve advertising and media, food and drinks containing alcohol, stem cell research, or financial services (except *shariah*-compliant financial services on deferred basis) are screened out because these business activities are deemed inappropriate to Muslim investors.	After selection of companies based on qualitative screening, quantitative screening is carried out on the companies' audited annual reports. In quantitative screening, three aspects will be considered: leverage compliance, cash compliance, and the percentage of non-permissible revenue from non-compliant activities (Standard & Poor's, 2009).

FIGURE 1.1 Definition of qualitative and quantitative screening

Source: Standard and Poor's (2009).

stage screens companies based on their core business activities (Ulrich & Marzban, 2009). Hence, the first stage of the qualitative screen is often called the "activity screen". The quantitative stage involves financial ratio benchmarks, i.e. cash and debt ratios (Securities Commission Malaysia, 2017). These financial ratios typically identify the extent of involvement of Islamic corporations with traditional financing, interest, and their investment in interest income. The primary sources of this information are updates shown by the stock market and annual reports.

Across several national jurisdictions, the Shariah Supervisory Board (SSB) of each country reserves full rights to issue different screening criteria. Certain index providers such as the Financial Times Stock Exchange (FTSE), Morgan Stanley Capital International (MSCI), S&P, and Dow Jones have developed their own screening processes to screen and determine which companies and businesses are *shariah*-compliant for investment. One such example developed by Malaysia's SAC is said to be an inappropriate model in Bosnia and Herzegovina because of its lack of consideration of companies' liquidity of assets and indebtedness (Meskovic et al., 2012). On a similar note, the Dow Jones's screening criteria utilizing market capitalization in the screening processes, which was meant to be replaced by balance sheet items, has instead attracted considerable scholarly criticism (Meskovic et al., 2012).

In this context, there are two major differences between existing screenings. Firstly, the classification of activities as compliant or not, in the first stage, is subject to expert opinion. Often, it is difficult to identify a core business activity, especially in cases where the company is highly diversified. Therefore, benchmarking is complex. Secondly, the threshold levels used for the financial ratios are subject to *shariah* explanations that are often criticized by several groups on at least two grounds. The first is that the one-third maximum debt level is not based on enough grounds for clear justification. The second is that the use of market capitalization, as opposed to total assets, to calculate some of the ratios has been criticised by experts (for this differentiation, see Table 1.2). It is important to note that unless they are listed on the stock market, according to some screen providers (e.g. AAOIFI, S&P, and DJIM), firms cannot be screened as they do not have market capitalization. This may limit the promotion of small non-listed firms that are being screened according to the *shariah* guidelines in place. This is particularly dangerous for countries like Bangladesh or Malaysia, where a major portion of manufacturing output is attributable to small and medium enterprises (SMEs).

Another major hurdle present in current screening exercises stems from the various accounting standards employed in different countries. While it is important to acknowledge the effort that Islamic countries put in to establish and comply with Islamic accounting practices, for the sake of maintaining greater harmonization in corporate reporting, the necessity for Islamic firms across the board to adopt common reporting formats, such as those in use by conventional firms, is non-negotiable. This lack of a common format has resulted in inconsistency in various stages in the aforementioned screening processes between different countries. Added to this is possible unreliability stemming from the fact that the SSB will only use the available audited statements as provided by the company (Hashim et al., 2017).

TABLE 1.2 Comparison of quantitative screening criteria for *shariah*-compliant companies

Screens	*DJIM*	*S&P*	*SAC*	*FTSE*	*MSCI*	*AAOIFI*
Leverage compliance	Total debt/ 12-month average market capitalization ≤33%	Debt/36 months average market capitalization ≤33%	Debt/total assets ≤33%	Debt/total assets ≤33%	Debt/total assets ≤33.33%	Interest bearing debt/ average market capitalization ≤30%
Cash compliance	Account receivable/ 12-months average market capitalization ≤33%	Account receivable + cash/36-month average market capitalization ≤49%	-	Account receivable + cash/ total assets ≤50%	Account receivable + cash/ total assets ≤70%	Cash + deposits + account receivable/ market capitalization ≤67%
Revenue from non-compliant activities and total interest	Revenue from haram+ total interest / average market capitalization ≤5%	Revenue from haram+ total interest /36-month average market capitalization ≤5%	Revenue from haram+ total interest / total assets ≤5%	Revenue from haram+ total interest / total assets ≤5%	Revenue from haram+ total interest / total assets ≤5%	Revenue from haram+ total interest / total assets ≤5%
Cash and interest-bearing items	Cash + interest bearing items /12 months average market capitalization ≤33%	Cash + interest bearing items /36-month average market capitalization ≤33%	Cash (excluding Islamic account)/total assets ≤33%	Cash + interest bearing items / total assets ≤33%	Cash + interest bearing items / total assets ≤33.33%	Cash + deposit + interest bearing items / total assets ≤30%

Source: Created using data from Htay et al. (2013) for S&P, FTSE, and MSCI, S&P Global (2017) for DJIM, Securities Commission Malaysia (2017) for SAC, and Thomson Reuters (2015) for AAOIFI.

Table 1.2 shows in greater detail the differing quantitative screening criteria from six providers of equity indices. For instance, according to the AAOIFI interest-based debt must be less than 30%, but the DJIM, FTSE, S&P, and MSCI allow up to 33% or 33.33% of interest-rate-based debt. While the DJIM makes it compulsory to review companies based on the level of debt, liquidity, and interest income, the SAC only focuses on reviewing the core activities and the level of interest-based income of a company. However, the SAC has recently updated its quantitative screening processes, in which financial ratios such as cash over total assets and debt over total assets are made compulsory for all *shariah*-compliant companies (Securities Commission Malaysia, 2017).

Shariah-*compliant corporate universe*

Several studies have attempted to find an estimate of the size of the *shariah*-compliant corporate universe. Derigs and Marzban (2008) considered the S&P 500 index and reported that for 28% of cases (for 387 stocks), screening methodologies are decidedly and significantly diverse. Their study not only illustrates the niche that *shariah*-compliant corporations inhabit as being miniature in size, but also the lack of harmonization among its screening providers. Using data obtained about Malaysian firms, Abdul Rahman et al. (2010) reported that only 21% of the SAC-screened firms are deemed to be *shariah*-compliant according to DJIM and SAC guidelines. These results indicate that SAC guidelines may not be compatible with other internationally accepted screening exercises. A study by Adedokun and Rashid in 2019 of compliant firms from Nigeria, using the financial ratios applied by several screen providers, reported significant dissimilarities between Nigerian standards and the standards set by the SAC and DJIM, among others. Using only the financial screening, the study also discovered the Malaysia-based *shariah* index to be less stringent than the likes of DJIM and FTSE.

Hassan et al. (2019) created an Islamic Business Scorecard and replaced the activity screening by factoring in social and ethical compliances. Their study on Malaysia, Pakistan, and Bangladesh reported around 50% compliance (70% in Malaysia) to *shariah* rules in these countries. However, after the financial screening was taken into account, compliancy rates dropped to almost 20%. Their study concluded that companies mostly fell short of compliancy primarily due to financial factors. Because Islamic capital market activities and opportunities are limited, Islamic firms are forced to engage with non-Islamic financing, driving them out of the compliancy zone.

Limitations of existing shariah *screening: ethical and social responsibility issues*

Equity index providers around the world provide guidelines for *shariah*-compliant companies based on *shariah* principles. However, these authorities only focus on transactions prohibited in *shariah* law such as the concept of *riba* (interest), *gharar* (uncertainty), and *maysir* (gambling), but show limited or no concern towards the ethical and social responsibilities which *shariah*-compliant companies should be engaged. Many Islamic scholars believe that equity index providers should not focus purely on screening *shariah*-complaint companies by means of financial ratios and examining their business activities, but should also include a separate ethical and social responsibility screening stage that strives to encourage companies to comply with this aspect of Islamic law. Priority must be given to how ethical and *shariah*-compliant companies contribute to society. The Ethical Identity Index (EII) by Haniffa and Hudaib (2007) offers a test by which to decide whether or not a company is compliant with Islamic ethical conduct. Adopting EII, several studies have conducted various ethical identity compliancy tests for Islamic firms (Rashid and Hassan, 2014; Hassan et al., 2010).

Islamic Business Scorecard

The Islamic Business Scorecard (IBS), proposed by Hassan et al. (2019), combines *shariah* screening processes, ethical identity scores, and corporate social responsibility indices into a single scorecard. The IBS marked the beginning of the introduction of a holistic *shariah* screening process, which can be employed to screen *shariah*-compliant firms. Figure 1.2 shows the components of the IBS.

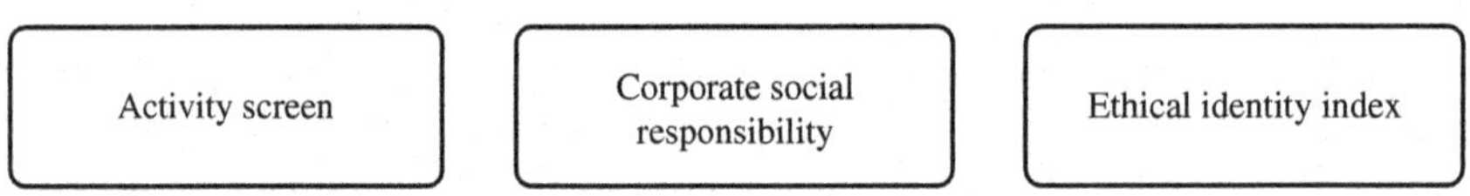

FIGURE 1.2 Components of the Islamic Business Scorecard
Source: See Hassan et al. (2019) for a detailed view of the IBS.

Ethical Identity Index

The EII was formulated as a tool to study the differences between the communicated ethical identity and the ideal ethical identity of *shariah*-compliant companies. Communicated ethical identities have a common problem in that absence of communication does not necessarily indicate absence of activity. EII is an ideal ethical identity benchmark that complies with the principles of *shariah*. An ideal ethical identity benchmark must also govern all aspects of Muslims' lives, promote justice (*al-adl*) and the welfare of society (*al-ihsan*), acquire God's blessings (*barakah*), and be successful in life (*al-falah*). The EII is founded upon eight dimensions, as follows:

1. Vision and mission statements,
2. Board of directors and top management,
3. Product and services,

4. *Zakat*,
5. Charity and benevolent loans,
6. Commitments towards debtors,
7. Commitments towards society, and
8. Shariah Supervisory Board (SSB).

Corporate social responsibility

Corporate social responsibility (CSR) is an umbrella term that defines and incorporates the tenets of a sustainable environment, ethics in business, corporate governance, public relations, and analysis of stakeholders and relationship marketing. CSR is also viewed as a medium for corporations'communications with their stakeholders.

Discussions concerning CSR became prominent in the wake of scandals involving major corporations such as Enron and Tyco. The earliest implementation of modern CSR started during the 1920s. However, records from the 1920s shows that at the time CSR was limited to the use of personal funds in social responsibility projects and issues, at the discretion of businessmen and in their own private time, usually after working hours. Today, CSR has developed into many categories, including public relations, services, trusteeship, and public welfare. The first known corporation that publicly disclosed its CSR activities was the Hongkong and Shanghai Banking Corporation (HSBC) back in 2003. HSBC disclosed its social initiatives in environmental protection, education support, and development of the arts.

Social ills such as poverty, unemployment, discrimination, and pollution have heightened awareness and public debate on the role of CSR (Barom, 2015). In Western countries, CSR is seen as a means of ingratiating capitalism with a public always suspicious about the overreaching exploitation of their individual interests by large corporations. By contrast, Islamic CSR gravitates towards a more holistic approach, as it is based on the teachings of the Quran and the Sunnah (the practices of the Prophet, *peace be upon him*) and focuses on human beings' interaction with nature and their fellow humans. CSR in the Islamic perspective can be traced to the concept of *ihsan* (benevolence) which requires Muslims to share and promote kindness to other people as part of their responsibility to society.

CSR in Islam follows the concept of *khalifah* (viceregency) under *shariah*. Under the concept of *khalifah*, "a company must act as a steward to its shareholders' financial resources, and society's economy, benefiting society and attaining the blessings of God" (Dusuki, 2008). Hence, *shariah*-compliant companies must achieve good CSR practices to ensure a sustainable environment, health and safety at work, philanthropic contributions, and activities that do not harm society. Figure 1.3 summarizes the concept of CSR in Islam.

Rashid et al. (2013) explain CSR using the model of a two-tiered social and ethical responsibility for Islamic banks, aptly named "customer-centric CSR for banks". Figure 1.4 shows their ethical efficiency framework. The framework also

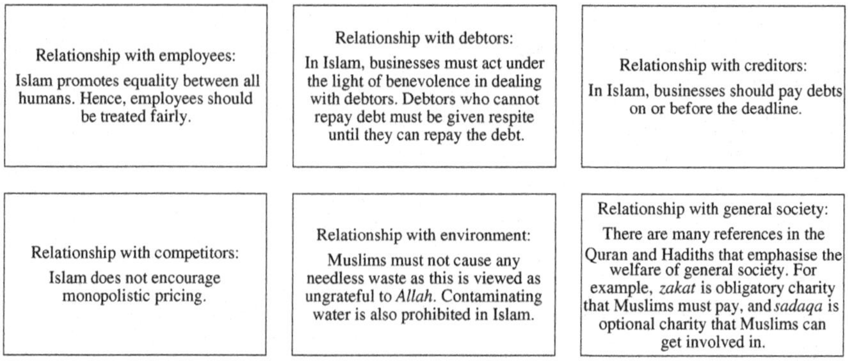

FIGURE 1.3 Concept of corporate social responsibility in Islam
Source: Based on Haniffa and Hudaib (2007) and Saw (2017).

functions as a learning ground for *shariah*-compliant firms and is compatible for integration with the proposed Islamic business scorecard by Hassan et al. (2018).

Summary

Shariah-compliant businesses are important to Muslim investors, since *shariah* compliance helps Muslims to avoid potential involvement in activities prohibited by Islam, such as *riba* (interest), *gharar* (uncertainty), and *maysir* (gambling). To guide Muslims with decisions relating to *shariah*-compliant businesses, equity index providers such as Dow Jones and the Shariah Advisory Council provide a set of *shariah* rules that serve as a guideline for defining *shariah*-compliant businesses. *Shariah* screening is the process of screening out *shariah*-compliant businesses from their conventional counterparts. In practice, however, *shariah* screening processes may vary depending on the equity index providers and legal jurisdictions involved. These differences result in inconsistencies in the *shariah* screening processes across countries. Furthermore, while the *shariah* screening process combines both qualitative and quantitative criteria, it ignores the ethical and social compliancy aspects that *shariah*-compliant businesses are meant to adhere to, as outlined by scripture. Islamic scholars have commented that ethical and social issues must be addressed by *shariah*-compliant businesses on top of the basic activity and financial screenings.

Multiple social and ethical models exist that can help to explain the role of ethics and CSR in screening exercises. The Ethical Identity Index (Haniffa and Hudaib, 2007) is a comprehensive ethical screening tool that can be employed for both Islamic and conventional firms to estimate the degree of their respective ethical practices. Several studies (Rashid and Hassan, 2014; Rashid et al., 2017; Hassan et al., 2010) have incorporated the Ethical Identity Index in different contexts, reporting it to have significant implications for Islamic firms. Barom (2015) explained three components of CSR that could be applied on the Islamic

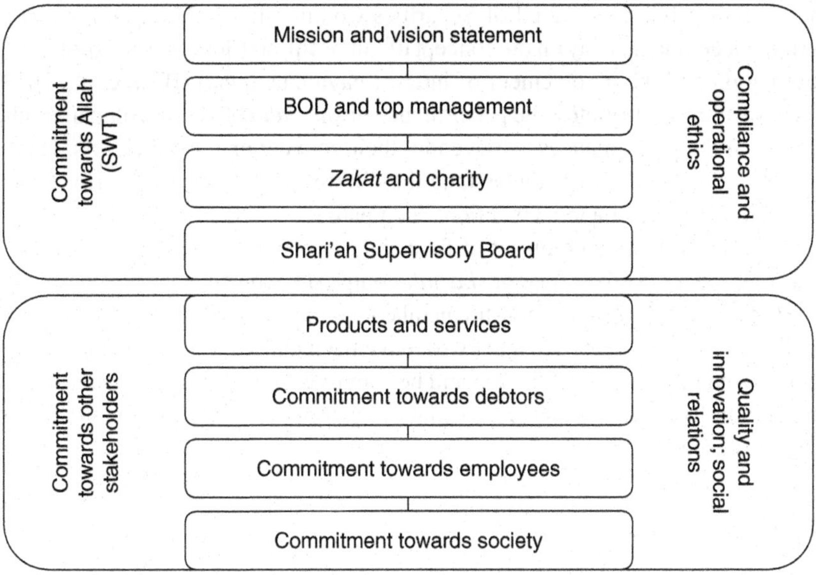

FIGURE 1.4 Ethical efficiency framework of Islamic banks
Source: Adopted from Rashid et al. (2013).

firms. These components are (1) contributions to the eradication of poverty, (2) contributions towards societal development, and (3) contributions to safeguarding the environment. Hassan et al. (2019) combined ethical and social components, as outlined by Haniffa and Hudaib (2007), and the CSR components explained by Barom (2015), alongside the basic activity screen offered by DJIM, to establish the first Islamic "business scorecard" for *shariah*-compliant firms. Their model not only offers a holistic view of Islamic business activities, but also presents a framework for the comprehensive screening out of *shariah*-compliant firms from their non-compliant counterparts. The future of Islamic investment largely depends on efforts regarding how these screening exercises are harmonized across disparate legal jurisdictions.

Performance of *shariah*-compliant firms

During the 1990s, Islamic funds experienced a boom due to growing awareness and demand for *shariah*-compliant capital by Muslims from around the world (Sanusi et al., 2015). For religiously informed Muslims, investment is not solely dependent on profitability; rather, it is understood as a channel to holistic socio-economic development. Hence, the performance of *shariah*-compliant firms can be imagined as a yardstick of the overall socio-economic performance within a selected country. *Shariah*-compliant companies are companies compliant with Islamic (*shariah*) principles and approved by an established advisory board (e.g.

the Shariah Advisory Council of Securities Commission in Malaysia). *Shariah*-compliant companies rely on the concept of fair profit-and-loss sharing, prohibiting speculation and the involvement of interest payments (*riba*) (Beck et al., 2013). Because of these attributes, the performance of *shariah*-compliant companies may vary from the performances achieved by their conventional counterparts. Hence, there exists a need to fully understand the differences between the performances of *shariah*-compliant and conventional companies.

In this section, a common set of financial ratios will be employed to evaluate and compare the performance of *shariah*-compliant and conventional companies. A list of selected Malaysian non-financial companies, *shariah*-compliant and conventional, from the years 2014 to 2016, have been chosen for this evaluation purpose. Based on total assets, the top and bottom five *shariah*-compliant and the top and bottom five conventional companies are compared. Table 1.3 gives details of the ratios used.

Liquidity ratios

Liquidity ratios are an important indication of a company's ability to meet its debt obligations. These ratios include the current ratio, quick ratio, and cash ratio. Referring to the trade-off hypothesis, firms and financial institutions that hold more in liquid assets will face lower default risk and bankruptcy costs while having higher debt raising capabilities (Bitar et al., 2017).

TABLE 1.3 Key financial ratios

Key financial ratios	*Ratio*	*Measurement*
Liquidity ratios	Current ratio	Current assets/current liability
	Quick ratio	(Current assets – inventory)/ current liabilities
	Cash ratio	Cash and cash equivalent/ current liabilities
Efficiency ratios	Inventory turnover ratio	Sales/average inventory
	Receivable turnover ratio	Sales/average receivable
	Asset turnover ratio	Sales/total asset
Debt management ratio	Debt to asset ratio	Total debt/total assets
	Long term debt to asset ratio	Long term debt/total assets
Profitability ratios	Profit margin ratio	Net income/sales
	Return on assets	Net income/total assets
	Return on equity	Net income/equity
Market value ratios	Earnings per share	Net income/common share outstanding
	Price earnings ratio	Market price/earnings per shares
	Market to book ratio	Market price/book value

Source: Based on Singh and Schmidgall (2002) and Linares-Mustarós et al. (2018).

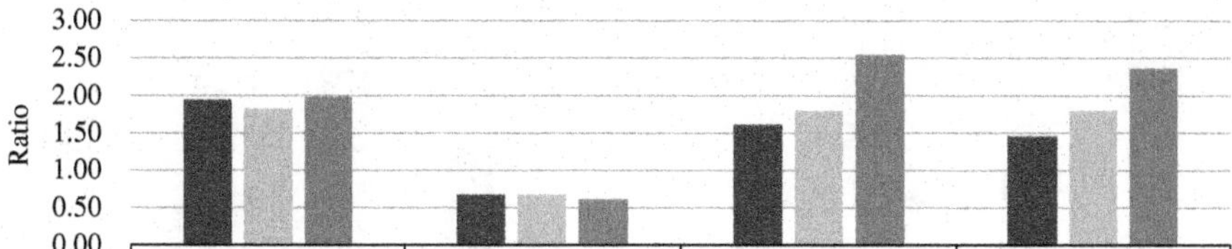

	Top 5 conventional firms	Top 5 *shariah*-compliant firms	Lowest 5 conventional firms	Lowest 5 *shariah*-compliant firms
2014	1.93	0.67	1.60	1.44
2015	1.82	0.68	1.80	1.80
2016	1.98	0.62	2.55	2.36

■2014 ■2015 ■2016

FIGURE 1.5 Conventional vs *shariah*-compliant firms, 2014–2016: Current ratio
Source: Authors' own.

Current ratio

The current ratio is used to measure the ability of a company to pay its short-term obligations and is measured by dividing its current assets by its current liabilities (Linares-Mustarós et al., 2018). When the current ratio is below 1, it indicates that a company's liabilities are greater than what the company holds in assets, thus suggesting that the company in question could have difficulty in meeting its short-term obligations. As can be seen from Figure 1.5, the current ratios for the top five conventional firms remained above 1 throughout the three years in question, while the current ratios for the top five *shariah*-compliant firms fell below 1 for the same period. The results indicate that the top five *shariah*-compliant firms were relatively less healthy in terms of meeting their short-term obligations compared to their conventional counterparts. Like the top five conventional firms, the lowest five conventional firms all had a current ratio above 1, indicating that the current assets of those firms were able to match the obligations of their current liabilities. However, unlike the top five *shariah*-compliant firms, the lowest five *shariah*-compliant firms had a current ratio above 1, indicating that the lowest five *shariah*-compliant firms were better able to meet their short obligations. Overall, the conventional firms are shown to have been more liquid than the selected Islamic firms.

Quick ratio

The quick ratio (also known as the acid test ratio) is a similar measure but based on the immediate liquid position of a company (Atieh, 2014). Unlike the current ratio, the quick ratio compares the most liquid assets to the company's current liabilities. The quick ratio is taken by dividing the company's current assets (excluding inventory) by its current liabilities (Linares-Mustarós et al., 2018). Figure 1.6 shows that the quick ratio of the top five conventional firms remained above 1 for

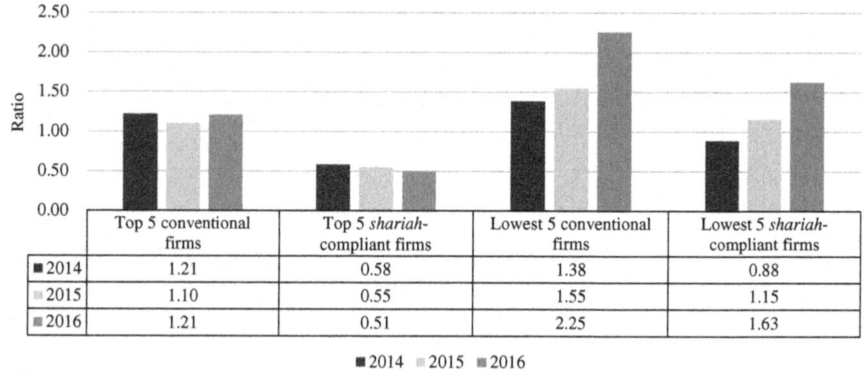

FIGURE 1.6 Conventional vs *shariah*-compliant firms, 2014–2016: Quick ratio
Source: Authors' own.

all three years, indicating that the proceeds from their most liquid current assets would be able to satisfy their short-term obligations. As before, compared to the *shariah* firms, the conventional firms enjoyed better quick liquidity.

Cash ratio

The cash ratio measures the extreme conservative point of a company's liquidity (Atieh, 2014). Unlike the current and quick ratios, the cash ratio only takes cash into account, omitting other current assets as used in calculating current and quick ratios, under the assumption that the cash held by the company represents the most liquid asset held relative to its other current assets. The cash ratio is measured by dividing cash and cash equivalents by the company's current liabilities. Figure 1.7 shows the cash ratios of the top five conventional firms to have been above 1 in 2014 and 2016, although dipping to slightly below 1 during the year, 2015. On the other hand, the results from the top five *shariah*-compliant firms indicate a poor cash ratio, below 0.3 in all three years. To compare, the lowest five conventional firms all have a cash ratio above 1 for the years 2015 and 2016, only falling slightly below 1 in 2014. While the lowest five *shariah*-compliant firms fared better than the top five *shariah*-compliant firms, their cash ratio remained below 1 in all three years.

The poor liquidity ratios of the top five *shariah*-compliant firms could be a result of the revised *shariah* screening methodology that was introduced in Malaysia, commencing on the 18 June 2012 (Zainudin et al., 2014). The revised *shariah* screening issued by the Shariah Advisory Council (SAC) of the Securities Commission (SC) of Malaysia is intended to measure *riba*-based elements by restricting the ratio of cash to total assets ratio to less than 33%. This restricts the amount of cash available to *shariah*-compliant companies. Although the top five *shariah*-compliant firms performed poorly in terms of liquidity ratios, as

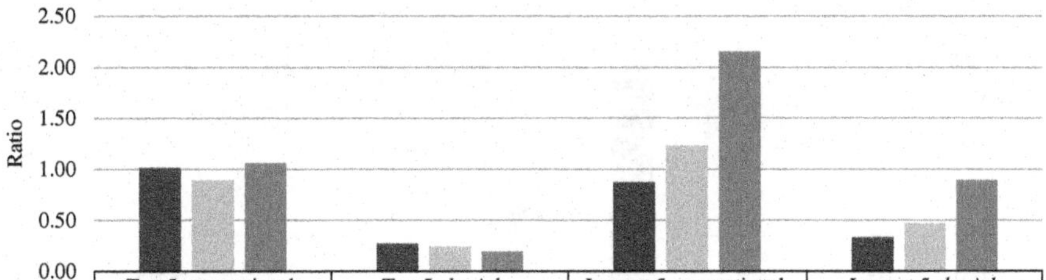

	Top 5 conventional firms	Top 5 *shariah*-compliant firms	Lowest 5 conventional firms	Lowest 5 *shariah*-compliant firms
2014	1.01	0.27	0.87	0.33
2015	0.89	0.24	1.23	0.47
2016	1.06	0.19	2.15	0.90

FIGURE 1.7 Conventional vs *shariah*-compliant firms, 2014–2016: Cash ratio
Source: Authors' own.

stated above, the revised *shariah* screening requirement for the debt over total assets ratio of *shariah*-compliant companies to not exceed 33% still stands. This ensures that the debt obligations of *shariah*-compliant companies are sustainable (Zainudin et al., 2014).

Efficiency ratios

Efficiency ratios measure a company's ability to utilize its assets and liabilities efficiently. Efficiency ratios include the inventory turnover ratio, the receivables turnover ratio, and the asset turnover ratio.

Inventory turnover ratio

The inventory turnover ratio shows how many times a company has sold and replaced its inventory in a given period. The inventory turnover ratio is measured by dividing the cost of goods sold by its average inventory. Figure 1.8 shows that the top five conventional firms reported inventory turnover ratios of 4.10, 3.58, and 3.27 for the years 2014, 2015, and 2016 respectively. In comparison, the top five *shariah*-compliant firms performed better in terms of their inventory ratios, with ratios of 11.78, 7.49 and 7.41 for the years 2014, 2015, and 2016 respectively. Similarly, the lowest five *shariah*-compliant firms outperformed the lowest five conventional firms in terms of their inventory turnover ratios.

Receivables turnover ratio

The receivables turnover ratio is a measure of a firm's efficiency in collecting debts on credit. A high receivables ratio indicates greater efficiency in a company's ability to collect receivables and suggests a high chance that the firm in question

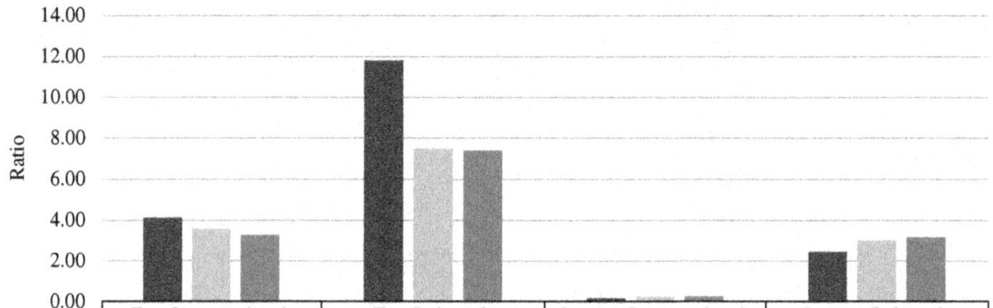

	Top 5 conventional firms	Top 5 *shariah*-compliant firms	Lowest 5 conventional firms	Lowest 5 *shariah*-compliant firms
2014	4.10	11.78	0.15	2.44
2015	3.58	7.49	0.27	3.02
2016	3.27	7.41	0.26	3.18

FIGURE 1.8 Conventional vs *shariah*-compliant firms, 2014–2016: Inventory turnover ratio
Source: Authors' own.

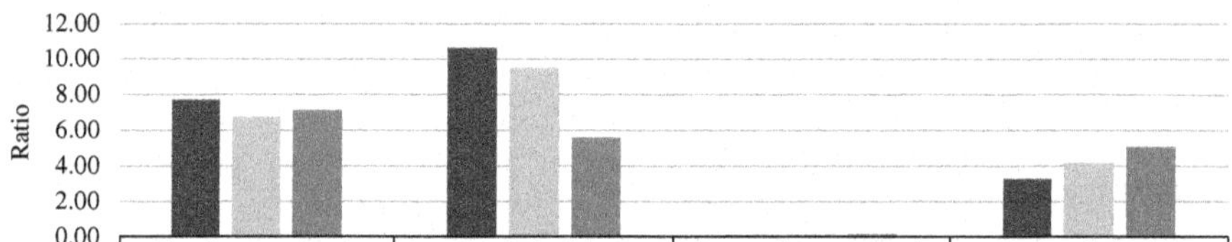

	Top 5 conventional firms	Top 5 *shariah*-compliant firms	Lowest 5 conventional firms	Lowest 5 *shariah*-compliant firms
2014	7.67	10.60	0.06	3.25
2015	6.75	9.51	0.13	4.16
2016	7.12	5.57	0.18	5.07

FIGURE 1.9 Conventional vs *shariah*-compliant firms, 2014–2016: Receivables turnover ratio
Source: Authors' own.

is operating on a cash basis. Receivables turnover is measured by dividing sales by average receivables. Figure 1.9 shows that the receivables turnover ratios of the top five *shariah*-compliant firms exceeded those of the top five conventional firms, while the lowest five *shariah*-compliant firms outperformed the lowest five conventional firms.

Total asset turnover ratio

The asset turnover ratio measures how efficiently a company deploys its assets to generate sales. Asset turnover ratio is measured by dividing sales by total assets. As can be seen from Figure 1.10, the total asset turnover ratio of both the top

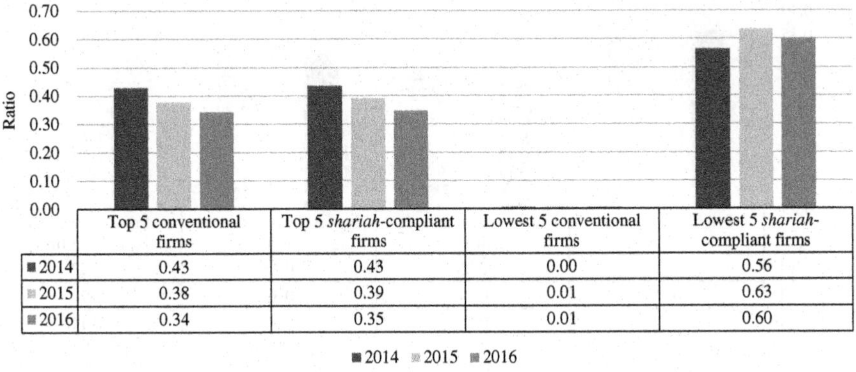

	Top 5 conventional firms	Top 5 *shariah*-compliant firms	Lowest 5 conventional firms	Lowest 5 *shariah*-compliant firms
2014	0.43	0.43	0.00	0.56
2015	0.38	0.39	0.01	0.63
2016	0.34	0.35	0.01	0.60

FIGURE 1.10 Conventional vs *shariah*-compliant firms, 2014–2016: Total asset turnover ratio
Source: Authors' own.

five conventional and the top five *shariah*-compliant companies were similar throughout the three years. Besides this, Figure 1.10 also shows that the lowest five *shariah*-compliant companies outperformed the lowest five conventional firms; the latter performed poorly, with lower reported values for their asset turnover ratios.

Overall, Figure 1.10 shows Islamic firms to be more efficient than their conventional counterparts in inventory, receivables, and total asset management.

Debt management ratio

Debt management ratios are an important indication of how efficiently a company manages its debts, and include the total debt ratio and the long-term debt ratio.

Debt-to-asset ratio

The debt-to-asset ratio measures the amount of assets a company holds against its debt and serves as an indicator of financial risk in a firm; a higher debt-to-asset ratio indicates a higher financial risk. From Figure 1.11, conventional firms seem to have higher debt-to-asset ratios compared with *shariah*-compliant firms, illustrating this higher financial risk. As a consequence of the obligatory screening processes to which *shariah*-compliant companies in Malaysia are subjected (the debt-to-asset ratio of these firms must be below 33%), the debt-to-asset ratios of *shariah*-compliant firms are reported to be lower than those of conventional firms.

Long-term debt ratio

The long-term debt ratio measures the amount of assets held by a company that are being financed with long-term debt; as before, a higher long-term debt ratio indicates greater financial risk. As shown by Figure 1.12, conventional firms have

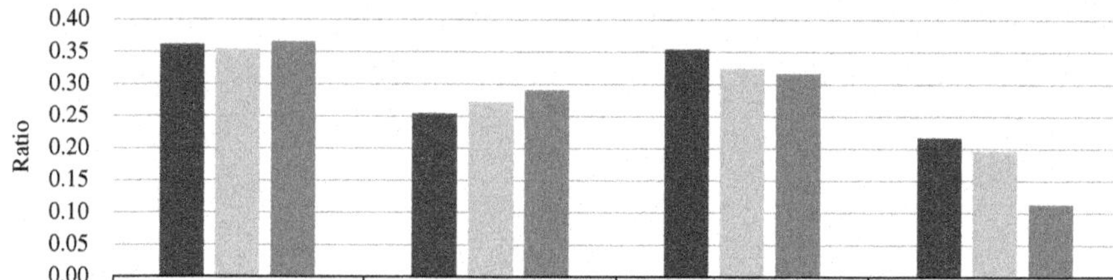

	Top 5 conventional firms	Top 5 *shariah*-compliant firms	Lowest 5 conventional firms	Lowest 5 *shariah*-compliant firms
2014	0.36	0.25	0.35	0.22
2015	0.35	0.27	0.32	0.20
2016	0.37	0.29	0.32	0.11

■2014 ■2015 ■2016

FIGURE 1.11 Conventional vs *shariah*-compliant firms, 2014–2016: Debt-to-asset ratio
Source: Authors' own.

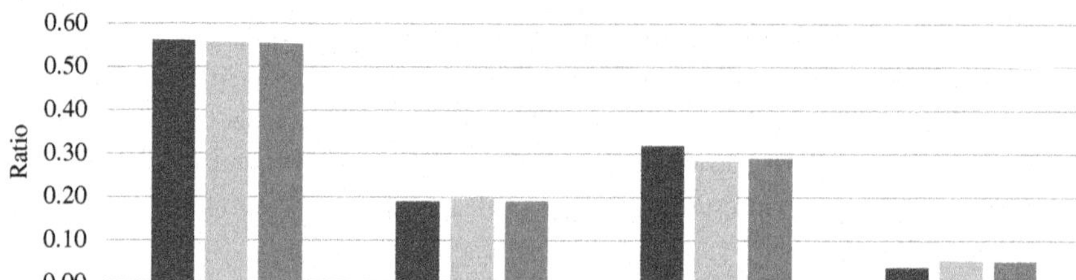

	Top 5 conventional firms	Top 5 *shariah*-compliant firms	Lowest 5 conventional firms	Lowest 5 *shariah*-compliant firms
2014	0.56	0.19	0.32	0.04
2015	0.56	0.20	0.28	0.05
2016	0.55	0.19	0.29	0.05

■2014 ■2015 ■2016

FIGURE 1.12 Conventional vs *shariah*-compliant firms, 2014–2016: Long-term debt ratio
Source: Authors' own.

higher long-term debt ratios than *shariah*-compliant firms, indicating the higher financial risks of conventional firms. The long-term debt ratios for the top five *shariah*-compliant firms are reported to be around 20%, indicating 10% of short-term debt for these firms (assuming a maximum of 30% total debt).

Profitability ratios

Profitability ratios are a measure of a company's ability to generate earnings to pay for their running expenses within a specific time-frame. Profitability ratios include the profit margin ratio, the return on assets, and the return on equity.

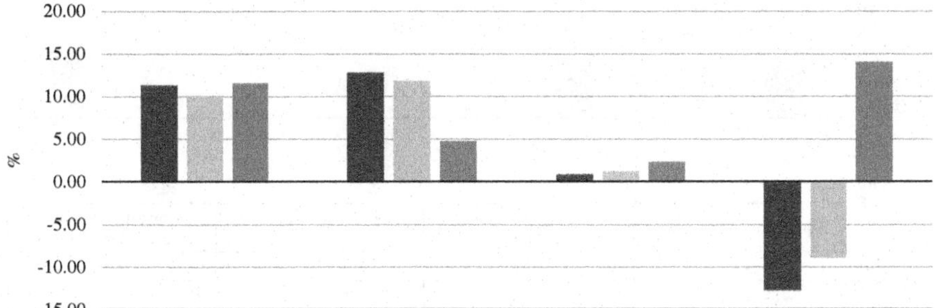

	Top 5 conventional firms	Top 5 *shariah*-compliant firms	Lowest 5 conventional firms	Lowest 5 *shariah*-compliant firms
2014	11.29	12.77	0.84	-12.73
2015	10.14	11.87	1.22	-8.90
2016	11.59	4.76	2.37	14.07

2014 2015 2016

FIGURE 1.13 Conventional vs *shariah*-compliant firms, 2014–2016: Profit margin
Source: Authors' own.

Profit margin

The profit margin measures the income earned by a company as a percentage of its sales figures; a higher profit margin indicates a higher income per unit of sale. It is calculated by dividing net profit over sales. Figure 1.13 shows the profit margin of the top five conventional firms remaining steady over the period, with each year achieving profit margin figures above 10%. While the profit margin of the top five *shariah*-compliant firms were reported to be higher than the top five conventional firms for 2014 and 2015, their profit margin fell considerably from 12% in 2015 to 5% in 2016. The lowest five *shariah*-compliant firms underperformed compared to the lowest five conventional firms, with negative profit margins for both 2014 and 2015, meaning that costs incurred exceeded revenue earned.

Return on assets

The return on assets measures income earned as a percentage of what a company holds in assets; a higher return on assets indicates a higher income per asset used in the running of a company. The return on assets is calculated by dividing net income by average total assets (Singh & Schmidgall, 2002). As Figure 1.14 shows, the return on assets of the top five conventional firms remained steady over the period between 2014 to 2016. While the return on assets of the top five *shariah*-compliant firms outperformed that of the top five conventional firms for both 2014 and 2015, the top five conventional firms outperformed the top five *shariah*-compliant firms in 2016. The lowest five conventional firms' value of return on assets for the three years stood at zero, while the lowest five *shariah*-compliant firms achieved negative values during for both 2014 and 2015, before subsequently achieving 8% of return on assets during the year 2016.

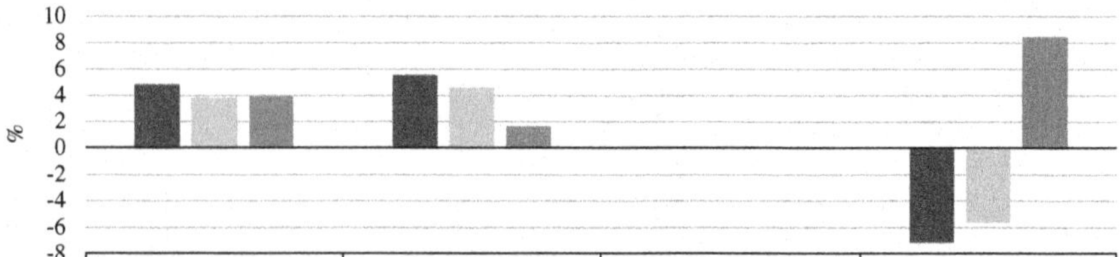

	Top 5 conventional firms	Top 5 *shariah*-compliant firms	Lowest 5 conventional firms	Lowest 5 *shariah*-compliant firms
2014	4.82	5.53	0.00	-7.15
2015	3.82	4.62	0.00	-5.63
2016	3.95	1.64	0.01	8.45

■2014 ■2015 ■2016

FIGURE 1.14 Conventional vs *shariah*-compliant firms, 2014–2016: Return on assets
Source: Authors' own.

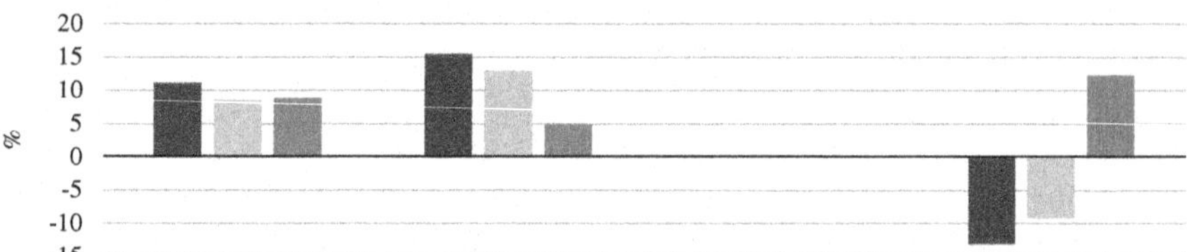

	Top 5 conventional firms	Top 5 *shariah*-compliant firms	Lowest 5 conventional firms	Lowest 5 *shariah*-compliant firms
2014	10.98	15.34	0.00	-13.09
2015	8.61	12.92	0.014	-9.18
2016	8.89	4.89	0.02	12.27

■2014 ■2015 ■2016

FIGURE 1.15 Conventional vs *shariah*-compliant firms, 2014–2016: Return on equity
Source: Authors' own.

Return on equity

Return on equity measures the percentage of income derived from equity, with a higher return on equity indicating higher income per equity; it is calculated by dividing the net income of a company over its equity. The return on equity of the top five conventional firms remained steady over the three-year period from 2014 to 2016. While the return on equity of the top five *shariah*-compliant firms outperformed that of the top five conventional firms for both 2014 and 2015, the situation was reversed in 2016. The lowest five conventional firms achieved a value of return on equity of zero in all three years, while the lowest five *shariah*-compliant firms reported negative values for both 2014 and 2015 before reaching a 12% of return on equity in 2016.

Overall, Islamic firms are reported to be more profitable than their conventional counterparts. This is true for almost all the compared ratios.

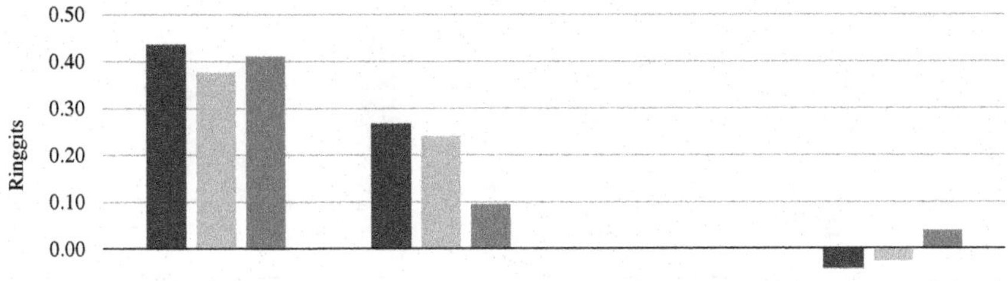

	Top 5 conventional firms	Top 5 *shariah*-compliant firms	Lowest 5 conventional firms	Lowest 5 *shariah*-compliant firms
2014	0.43	0.27	0.00	-0.04
2015	0.38	0.24	0.00	-0.03
2016	0.41	0.10	0.00	0.04

2014 2015 2016

FIGURE 1.16 Conventional vs *shariah*-compliant firms, 2014–2016: Earnings per share
Source: Authors' own.

Market value ratios

Market value ratios evaluate the value of a company's stock price and include the earnings per share, price–earnings ratio, and market-to-book ratio.

Earnings per share

Earnings per share measures the portion of firm's profit allocated to each common share held in a company and is measured by dividing net income by the number of common shares outstanding (Singh & Schmidgall, 2002). Earnings per share is an important indicator of a share's price. Since conventional firms dominate the Kuala Lumpur Stock Exchange (KLSE), the top five conventional firms had higher earnings per share throughout the three years compared to the top five *shariah*-compliant firms. Due to their reported negative earnings, the lowest five *shariah*-compliant firms similarly showed negative earnings per share for both 2014 and 2015 (Figure 1.16). This changed in 2016 when the lowest five *shariah*-compliant firms reported positive and higher earnings per share than the lowest five conventional firms. Although the *shariah*-compliant firms reported higher incomes for the period, their earnings per share may have been balanced out by their holding a higher level of shares outstanding.

Price–earnings ratio

The price–earnings ratio measures the share price relative to the earnings of a company. It indicates how much an investor is willing to pay in order to receive one ringgit (or dollar, or other currency) of a company's earnings and can be calculated by dividing the market price per share by the earnings per share (Singh & Schmidgall,

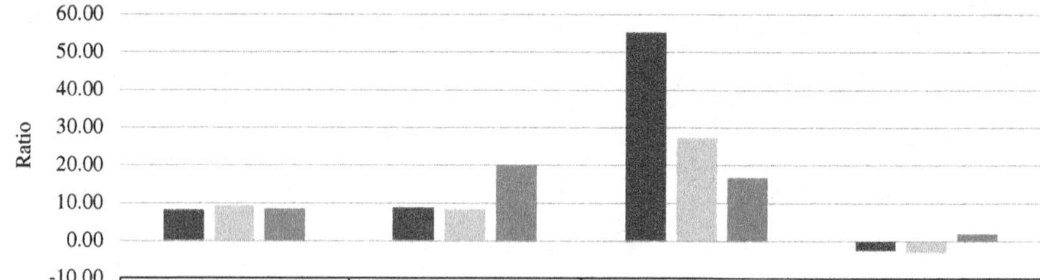

	Top 5 conventional cirms	Top 5 *shariah*-compliant firms	Lowest 5 conventional firms	Lowest 5 *shariah*-compliant firms
2014	8.07	8.62	55.06	-2.47
2015	9.31	8.33	27.18	-2.92
2016	8.51	19.99	16.72	1.91

■ 2014 ■ 2015 ■ 2016

FIGURE 1.17 Conventional vs *shariah*-compliant firms, 2014–2016: Price earnings ratio
Source: Authors' own.

2002). The price–earnings ratio of the top five conventional firms remained steady throughout the three years, at values from 8.07 to 9.30. The price–earnings ratios for the top five *shariah*-compliant firms remained steady for both 2014 and 2015, with an increase reported in 2016. Figure 1.17 shows that the lowest five conventional firms achieved significantly higher price–earnings ratios, while the lowest five *shariah*-compliant firms achieved negative price–earnings ratios in both 2014 and 2015 due to the negative average earnings reported during the period. However, the lowest five *shariah*-compliant firms achieved positive price–earnings ratios in the following year as their earnings improved compared to the previous two years.

Market-to-book ratio

The market-to-book value measures the value of a company as determined by the market relative to the values reported in the published accounts of the company ('book value'), and is calculated by dividing the market price of a share over the book value per share. When the market-to-book value is above 1, it indicates an overvalue in the company's shares and vice versa for when the market-to-book value falls below 1. From Figure 1.18 it will be seen that the market-to-book values for the top five conventional firms are slightly below 1, indicating that the conventional firms were slightly undervalued throughout all three years. By comparison, the market-to-book values for the top five *shariah*-compliant firms are closer to 1, with figures above 1 achieved for both 2014 and 2015, and falling below 1 in 2016. The lowest five conventional and *shariah*-compliant firms achieved poor market-to-book values in comparison, standing at figures that are far below 1, meaning that their shares are described as undervalued.

In conclusion, the comparison between market value ratios from conventional and *shariah*-compliant firms yielded mixed results, indicating no clear

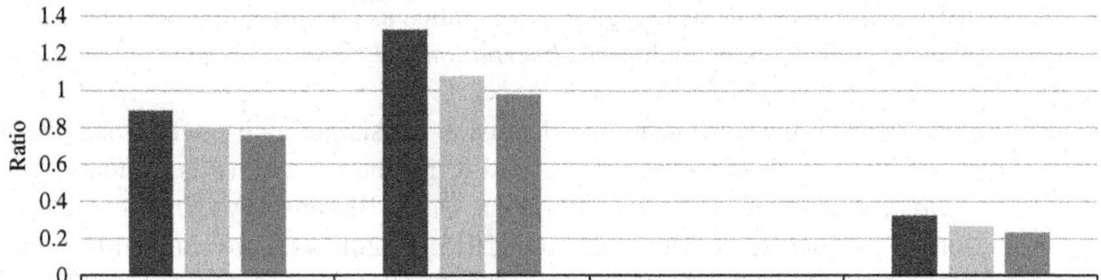

	Top 5 conventional firms	Top 5 *shariah*-compliant firms	Lowest 5 conventional firms	Lowest 5 *shariah*-compliant firms
■ 2014	0.88	1.32	0.00	0.32
■ 2015	0.80	1.07	0.00	0.26
■ 2016	0.75	0.97	0.00	0.23

■ 2014 ■ 2015 ■ 2016

FIGURE 1.18 Conventional vs *shariah*-compliant firms, 2014–2016: Market-to-book ratio
Source: Authors' own.

winner. Conventional firms fared better with higher earnings per share and price–earnings ratios than *shariah*-compliant firms. *Shariah*-compliant firms, however, performed relatively better in terms of market-to-book ratios, indicating a better shares market performance compared to conventional firms.

Summary

The performances of conventional and *shariah*-compliant firms vary in terms of measurements of liquidity, debt management, profitability, and market value. Owing to the more stringent screening criteria of *shariah*-compliant firms, the liquidity ratios and debt management ratios of these companies are also affected indirectly. An example of this exists in the requirement whereby *shariah*-compliant firms in Malaysia are prevented from holding more than 33% debt over total assets and cash over total assets. As the concerns of Muslim investors do not relate solely to the profitability of the companies that they may choose to invest in, they will continue to prefer investments in more *shariah*-compliant companies that will allow them the spiritual peace of mind that they are not indirectly engaging in business practices that contradict Islamic (*shariah*) law, but rather reflect its values.

References

Abdul Rahman, A., Yahya, M. A. & Mohd Nasir, M. H., 2010. Islamic norms for stock screening a comparison between the Kuala Lumpur Stock Exchange Islamic Index and the Dow Jones Islamic Market Index. *International Journal of Islamic and Middle Eastern Finance and Management*, 3(3), pp. 228–240.

Adedokun, B. O. & Rashid, M., 2019. Harmonization of Shari'ah screening in international markets: the case of Nigeria. In *Management of Shari'ah Compliant Businesses* (pp. 71–84). Springer, Cham.

Atieh, S., 2014. Liquidity analysis using cash flow ratios as compared to traditional ratios in the pharmaceutical sector in Jordan. *International Journal of Financial Research*, 5(3), pp. 146–158.

Barom, M. N., 2015. Social responsibility dimension in Islamic investment: a survey of investors' perspective in Malaysia. In H. A. El-Karanshawy et al. (Eds.), *Ethics, governance and regulation in Islamic finance*. Doha, Qatar: Bloomsbury Qatar Foundation.

Beck, T., Demirguc-Kunt, A. & Merrouche, O., 2013. Islamic vs. conventional banking: Business model, efficiency and stability. *Journal of Banking & Finance*, 37(2), pp. 433–447.

Bitar, M., Hassan, M. & Hippler, W., 2017. The determinants of Islamic bank capital decisions. *Emerging Markets Review*, 35(2018), pp. 48–68.

Derigs, U. & Marzban, S., 2008. Review and analysis of current Shariah-compliant equity screening practices. *International Journal of Islamic and Middle Eastern Finance and Management*, 1(4), pp. 285–303.

Dusuki, A., 2008. What does Islam say about corporate social responsibility? *Review of Islamic Economics*, 12(1), pp. 5–28.

Haniffa, R. & Hudaib, M., 2007. Exploring the ethical identity of Islamic banks via communication in annual reports. *Journal of Business Ethics*, 76(1), pp. 97–116.

Haron, R., Saringat, S. & Tahir, H., 2013. A study on timeliness of income recognition for *shariah* compliant companies: A Malaysian evidence. *International Journal of Social Science and Humanity*, 3(2), pp. 144–146.

Hashim, A., Habib, F., Isaacs, Z. & Gadhoum, M., 2017. Isra-Bloomberg sharī῾ah stock screening and income cleansing methodologies: A conceptual paper. *ISRA International Journal of Islamic Finance*, 9(1), pp. 27–42.

Hassan, M. K. Rashid, M., Wei, A. S. T., Adedokun, B. O. & Ramachandran, J., 2019. Islamic Business Scorecard and the screening of Islamic businesses in a cross-country setting, *Thunderbird International Business Review*, 1–13. https://doi.org/10.1002/tie.22038.

Hassan, M. K., Rashid, M., Imran, Y. & Shahid, A. I., 2010. Ethical gaps and market value in the Islamic banks of Bangladesh. *Review of Islamic Economics*, 14(1), pp. 49–75.

Htay, S., Abedeen, Z. & Salman, S., 2013. Towards standardization of shari'ah screening norms and practices. *International Journal of Humanities and Social Science Invention*, 2(1), pp. 23–30.

Ibrahim, M. & Ong, S. A. K., 2012. *Shariah* compliant real estate development financing and investment in the gulf cooperation council. *Journal of Property Investment & Finance*, 30(2), pp. 175–197.

Iqbal, M., Nisha, N. & Rashid, M., 2018. Bank selection criteria and satisfaction of retail customers of Islamic banks in Bangladesh. *International Journal of Bank Marketing*, 36(5), pp. 931–946.

Linares-Mustarós, S., Coenders, G. & Vives-Mestres, M., 2018. Financial performance and distress profiles. From classification according to financial ratios to compositional classification. *Advances in Accounting*, 40(2018), pp.1–10.

Lipka, M. & Hackett, C., 2017. *Why Muslims are the world's fastest-growing religious group*. Available at www.pewresearch.org/fact-tank/2017/04/06/why-muslims-are-the-worlds-fastest-growing-religious-group/, accessed 2018.

Meskovic, A., Hadzic, F. & Efendic, V., 2012. Capital market screening in Bosnia and Herzegovina – potentials for sharia-compliant investment. *International Islamic capital market conference*, Jakarta, Indonesia, pp. 1–14.

Natarajan, P. & Dharani, M., 2012. *Shariah* compliant stocks in India – a viable and ethical investment vehicle. *Arabian Journal of Business and Management Review*, 1(6), pp. 50–62.

Rashid, M., Abdeljawad, I., Ngalim, S. M. & Hassan, M. K., 2013. Customer centric corporate social responsibility: A framework for Islamic banks on ethical efficiency. *Management Research Review*, 36(4), pp. 359–378.

Rashid, M. & Hassan, M. K., 2014. Market value of Islamic banks and ethical identity. *American Journal of Islamic Social Sciences*, 31(2), pp. 43–79.

Rashid, M., Hassan, M. K., Amin, N. & Samina, Q. S., 2017. Shari'ah compliant companies in Bangladesh, *Journal of Islamic Economics Business and Finance*, 13(2), pp. 129–143.

Rashid, M., Hassan, M. K., Shi Min, H., & Ullah, G. M. W., 2017. Reporting of Zakat and charitable activities in Islamic banks: Theory and practice in a multi-cultural setting, In M. K. Hassan (Ed) *Handbook of empirical research on Islam and economic life* (pp. 163–192), United Kingdom: Edward Elgar Publishing.

S&P Global, 2017. S&P Global Annual Report. Available at https://www.spglobal.com/en/annual-reports/2017/, accessed July 2018.

Sanusi, Z., Ismail, R., Hudayati, A. & Harjito, D., 2015. Screening process of *shariah*-compliant companies: The relevance of financial risk management. *International Journal of Economics & Management*, 9(1), pp. 177–195.

Saw, A., 2017. *The Islamic Ethical Identity Scorecard for Islamic markets: a comparison.* Unpublished MSc Dissertation, Semenyih: University of Nottingham, Malaysia Campus.

Securities Commission Malaysia, 2017. List of *shariah*-compliant securities. Kuala Lumpur: Securities Commission Malaysia.

Singh, A. & Schmidgall, R., 2002. Analysis of financial ratios commonly used by US lodging financial executives. *Journal of Leisure Property*, 2(3), pp. 201–213.

Standard & Poor's, 2009. S&P Shariah Indices. Available at www.iefpedia.com/english/wp-content/uploads/2009/09/SP-SHARIAH-INDICES-INDEX-METHODOLOGY.pdf, accessed July 2017.

Thomson Reuters, 2015. Responsible Finance Report 2015. Available at https://ceif.iba.edu.pk/pdf/ThomsonReuters-ResponsibleFinanceReport2015TheEmergingConvergenceofSRIESGandIslamicFinance.pdf, accessed July 2018.

Ulrich, D. & Marzban, S., 2008. Review and analysis of current *shariah*-compliant equity screening practices. *International Journal of Islamic and Middle Eastern Finance and Management*, 1(4), pp. 285–303.

Ulrich, D. & Marzban, S., 2009. New strategies and a new paradigm for *shariah* compliant portfolio optimization. *Journal of Banking and Finance*, 33(6), pp. 1166–1176.

Zainudin, N., Miskam, S. & Sulaiman, M., 2014. Revised *shariah* screening methodology for *shariah*-compliant securities: New standard to meet global expectation. *Conference on Management and Muamalah*, 1, pp. 1–11.

2

IS THERE A COST FOR ADOPTING FAITH-BASED INVESTMENT STYLES?

Zaheer Anwer, Shamsher Mohamad Ramadili Mohamad and Mohamed Eskandar Shah Mohamed Rasid

Introduction

Investment is an activity that involves the commitment of resources for a certain holding period in anticipation of creating more resources (or wealth). The magnitude of the anticipated increase in resources varies positively with the length of time until maturity and the level of risk assumed. Risk is the chance of earning the expected increase in wealth from the initial commitment of resources. Given the size of the available resources, the commitment of resources usually involves many activities rather than just one particular one, to increase the chance of success if any of the activities fails to earn the anticipated increase in resources. A collection of investments in various types of activities forms a portfolio. Technically, portfolios are a collection of classes of assets that investors focus on; the classes can be equities, bonds, commodities, real estate, or even cash and/or money market instruments. Each class will itself have a variety of assets and the focus in portfolio management is more on the class rather than the individual assets in the class. The owners or sponsors of the portfolios usually hire a professional team of managers to manage the portfolio, but according to a guideline provided by the owners on the desired or expected returns, risks, level of diversification, investment horizon, choice of asset classes, economic sectors to focus on, level of tax liability, type of investment strategy, and other specific requirements.

Asset allocation decisions, i.e. decisions relating to investments in various asset classes, is an important component of the portfolio management process as it contributes significantly to the performance of the portfolio over the investment holding period. The common asset classes in investment management are equities, fixed-income securities, money market instruments, real estate, commodities, and even venture capital. To these have been added in the last decade also SRIs (socially responsible investments), ESG (environmental, social, and governance) investments, 'green' investments, and faith-based investments such as *shariah*-compliant portfolios. Each asset class varies in terms of marketability, liquidity, risk, costs of management, and length of maturity.

Portfolio managers usually target a specific combination of classes based on their expectations about the expected state of the economy in the short-term, medium-term, and long-term future. As real information and the actual economic situation unfold, managers will make the necessary adjustments (weight shifting) among the asset classes to either mitigate losses or maintain expected performance. The magnitude and frequency of the shifting of capital between asset classes depends on many factors, but the most common factors are persistency of the expected changes in market conditions, the investment strategy of the portfolio managers (passive, active, reactive, or a combination), and the cost effectiveness of making the changes.

This chapter focuses on the risk-adjusted performance of two specific classes of assets, namely, the socially responsible investment (SRI) class and the *shariah*-compliant classes of assets. The aim is to ascertain whether investors have to bear an extra cost for choosing these classes of assets in their portfolio. In managing the Islamic finance space, religiosity and/or ethical practices prompt investors to discard so-called 'sin stocks' and limit their investment horizons to permissible faith-based investment alternatives. Faith-based investing can be classified in two branches, namely Islamic finance and socially responsible investing (SRI). Islamic finance is governed by Islamic *shariah* rules and, for the *shariah*-screened portfolios, the selection of class of assets and the securities in each selected class is subjected to *shariah* requirements. Islamic law prohibits charging interest on loans, gambling, and trade of impermissible items like liquor, pork, pornography, etc. and also imposes restrictions on the capital structure of the business entity (Usmani, 2002). As for SRI, or ethical investing, it dates back to the start of the twentieth century (RBC Global Asset Management, 2012), and investors in this category are motivated by social, environmental, and ethical considerations in their investment decisions. They apply a set of investment screens to include or exclude assets based on ecological, social, corporate governance, or ethical criteria (Renneboog et al., 2008). The growing importance of faith-based investments can be judged by the mammoth increase in the overall size of the industry. The Islamic finance industry saw a double-digit compound annual growth rate (CAGR) –17% – between 2009 and 2013, and the industry is still expanding in terms of both numbers and geographical locations.[1] Similarly, the volume of assets acquired through socially responsible investing strategies stood at US$ 8.72 trillion in 2016 and is expected to increase further in the coming years.[2] There is potential for further growth for these faith-based investments, since religious or ethical values are becoming a serious concern to most investors even if the risk-adjusted returns they earn are lower than those for conventional investments (Renneboog et al., 2008).

Several factors explain the proliferation over the past decade of these investment styles that combine the financial goals of investors with their moral and social concerns (Haigh and Hazelton, 2004). The first is the presence of a multi-attribute utility for faith-based investors that is a function of a standard risk–reward optimization paradigm as well as a set of personal and societal values (Bollen, 2007). In addition, the frequent reports of accounting and environmental scandals in business practice has shifted investors' focus towards faith-based investments (Bauer et al., 2007). The third factor is the growing Muslim population and the increased awareness about investing and financing based on *shariah* requirements, together with the flow of oil money from the Middle East to these niche areas (Abu-Alkheil et al., 2017).

For these screened investments, investment managers and index providers need to employ qualitative and quantitative filters to screen the investment universe and discard stocks that do not meet the criteria set in the filters.

The ethical screening to formulate so-called socially responsible portfolios involves negative as well as positive screening. In the former, industries such as those involving tobacco, pornography, human rights violations, weapons, alcohol, gambling, abortion, workforce exploitation, activities not friendly to the environment, and genetic engineering are excluded. In the latter, investments in industries with better labour protection, human rights, environmental friendliness, biotechnology, corporate governance, and shareholder activism are given priority.[3] Islamic (or *shariah*-based) screening adopts a somewhat different methodology using 'line-of-business screens' and 'financial ratio screens'.[4] For the former, businesses such as those involving interest (*riba*), pork, activities involving extreme risk taking (*gharar*), gambling (*maysir*), weapons and defence, pornography, etc., are excluded. For the latter, companies meeting any of the following criteria are excluded:

1. Revenues in excess of 5% from impermissible business activities
2. Total debt and/or monetary assets accounting for 33% or more of market capitalization (based on a trailing 24-month average)
3. Accounts receivable of more than 33% of their total assets/market value of equity (based on a trailing 24-month average)
4. Cash to market value of equity higher than 33% (based on a trailing 24-month average)

This *shariah*-based screening is endorsed by a board of independent *shariah* scholars.

Screening and portfolio formation

The screening of assets in the construction of portfolios has implications for the risk–return profile as well as the dividend policy decisions of the investment firms.

First, the screening process restricts the investment universe to the screened portfolio of assets, which limits the fund managers' ability to exploit superior information as well as opportunities to invest in winning markets (Hoepner et al.,

2011), and consequently it also limits the opportunities for diversification, leading to the persistence of idiosyncratic risk in these portfolios.

To revisit the basic concepts of diversification and optimal portfolio selection, Markowitz (1952) asserts that most investors are risk averse and attempt to achieve a portfolio having an optimal risk–return trade-off. For any given two portfolios offering the same expected return, investors will prefer the portfolio with lower risk. Hence, an investor will be willing to assume increased risk only if compensated with higher expected return. In a similar manner, an investor who needs higher expected returns has to accept higher risk. Consequently, the exact risk–return trade-off will be the same for all investors, but due to individual risk aversion characteristics, different investors will evaluate this trade-off differently. Therefore, a rational investor will not invest in a given portfolio if another portfolio exists that has higher expected return for the same risk. In this model, portfolio return is equal to the weighted average of the constituent assets' returns, and portfolio variance is a function of the correlations of the component assets. Portfolio risk can be expressed as follows:

$$\sigma_p^2 = \sum_i w_i^2 \sigma_i^2 + \sum_i \sum_{j \neq i} w_i w_i \sigma_i \sigma_j \rho_{ij} \tag{2.1}$$

The portfolio risk can be reduced by holding combinations of assets that are not perfectly positively correlated. More formally, they can reduce their asset-specific risk exposure by holding multiple assets thereby creating a diversified portfolio of assets. The diversification can result in the same portfolio expected return with reduced risk. In Equation 2.1, if all the asset pairs '*i*, *j*' are uncorrelated (having zero correlations), the portfolio's return variance would be minimum, whereas if all the asset pairs '*i*, *j*' are perfectly positively correlated, having correlations equal to '1', the portfolio's variance would be maximum.

Moving ahead, possible under-diversification and the presence of idiosyncratic risk could affect the relative performance of these investments. There can be various possible theoretical arguments favouring this proposition.

Firstly, the universe of stocks available for selection by faith-based portfolios is restricted and there is a possibility that investors forgo attractive investment opportunities due to religious or ethical restrictions. In a capital asset pricing model (CAPM) world, these investors are at a disadvantage owing to the fact that they cannot optimally diversify their portfolios because of the restriction on certain business activities and the high correlation between the permissible stocks (Bodie et al., 2013). They also need to bear the costs of searching for and monitoring securities, which could negatively affect their returns (Bauer et al., 2006). The evidence of the performance of these portfolios is inconclusive, and studies such as those by Cortez et al. (2009), Saeed and Hassan (2013), and Lean et al. (2015) show that holders of faith-based portfolios are not at a disadvantage, whereas those by Al-Khazali et al. (2014), Kamil et al. (2014), Merdad et al. (2015), and Boo et al. (2017) document that these portfolios underperform the benchmark. An important reason for the underperformance is the lack of diversification opportunities for such investors (Kamil et al., 2012; Najeeb et al., 2015).

Secondly, in addition to the lack of diversification opportunity due to screening, the outcomes of financial screening may also influence the performance of *shariah*-compliant firms – as measured by key ratios – in the following ways:[5]

1. The first ratio, the *debt / market equity* ratio, has a significant impact on stock returns for any firm. This ratio represents a firm's financial structure, and a high debt-to-equity ratio implies that the firm uses debt financing assertively. Since debt is a cheaper source of capital as compared to equity, high-debt firms can start more value-enhancing projects than firms with low debt. However, a higher debt ratio increases the financial risk, and returns are more volatile for the highly leveraged firm. Therefore, the final impact of screening based upon the debt/equity ratio has implications for a portfolio's return volatility and performance.
2. The second ratio, the *receivables / market equity* ratio, shows a firm's receivables as a proportion of its market value. The receivables are instrumental in shaping a firm's capability to develop long-term relationships with its clients and build strong business networks. A high value of accounts receivable indicates that the firm has an effective and sustainable sales network and loyal customers. However, if not collected with a designated time, a high amount of receivables will affect the working capital and the financial performance of the firm.
3. The third financial ratio, the *cash / market equity* ratio, is related to the amount of cash and marketable securities available to the firm. An insufficient level of cash on a persistent basis will have adverse implications for the short-term financing and performance of the firm. However, firms having a high amount of cash have severe agency problems owing to the opportunistic behaviour of managers (Gul, 2001; Chung et al., 2005). Therefore, the firms with high cash may underperform in the long run.

Thirdly, there is a strand of literature suggesting that the suboptimal performance of Islamic investments is because they miss out on profitable opportunities due to their avoidance of high leverage (Saiti et al., 2014; Grira et al., 2016). Interestingly, Arouri et al. (2013) assert that Islamic indices bear high risk due to under-diversification and therefore offer high returns. It is important to note that existing evidence is not only inconclusive but also focused mostly on equity indices and investment funds alone.

Fourthly, the similar results for conventional and SRI portfolios can be explained by the mainstreaming argument put forward by Erragragui and Lagoarde-Segot (2016), who point to the double process of upstreaming 'ethical stocks' into conventional indices and portfolios, and 'downstreaming' conventional stocks into ethical indices and portfolios. It is expected that due to this double process the rates of return of both kinds of portfolios and indices should be similar.

Do investors bear a cost for investments in screened portfolios?

Our contention is that *shariah* and socially responsible investors bear the cost for their belief system in the form of under-diversification and additional monitoring costs. The contemporary literature argues that asset allocation explains more than 90% of returns over time (Ibbotson and Kaplan, 2000), and when portfolios are subject to specific screening, asset allocation decisions are not independent. As a result, investors are unable to achieve a higher efficient frontier and have to be content with suboptimal portfolios owing to the investment constraints imposed by the screening filters. They also have to incur costs on continuous screening of the stocks due to the possible changes in the line of business of some of the firms or changes in their capital structure that fail to comply with the screening requirements. Therefore, these investors face unique challenges compared to ordinary investors and their risk/return profile might differ from that of investors with conventional portfolios. It is, however, probable that even after screening there are adequate stocks to select from in the screened universe that offer diversification benefits. Also, the cost of monitoring may be minimal and may not significantly affect the returns. Thus, there is an important empirical issue regarding whether these special investment styles are in reality cost ineffective and disadvantaged compared to normal portfolios of similar risk.

It is obvious that many clichés are attached to faith-based investments without substantiating evidence. At present, there is no documented evidence on whether screened portfolios really are under-diversified and offer lesser investment opportunities. The existing studies (like Ashraf and Khawaja, 2016, and el Alaoui et al., 2016) discuss only the systematic risk of these portfolios. Although one argument suggests that screening results in shifting the mean–variance efficient frontier (MVEF) to the right as advanced by Johnson and Neave (1996), the counter argument posits that screened portfolios avoid risky firms (those having a higher probability of financial distress and bankruptcy) and therefore their total risk would be lower than that of the market, pulling the MVEF back to the left (Obaidullah, 2006). Similarly, one argument suggests that negative screening enhances portfolio risk and results in under-diversification (Humphrey and Lee, 2011), while the counter argument indicates that screening reduces systematic risk and hence the total risk for screened portfolios will be low (Lee et al., 2010). In line with these conflicting arguments, it is probable that there are still enough diversification opportunities available within the investment universe that can help investors choose the efficient frontier of their choice and not restrict their investment decisions. Their idiosyncratic risk can be higher than that of the market portfolio due to possible under-diversification on the basis of the 'shunned stock hypothesis',[6] but there is no evidence as to whether the risk-adjusted comparative performance (firm level) of these portfolios is better or worse than that of the market. Finally, better governance and the unique idiosyncratic risk of faith-based portfolios may or may not result in changing the relationship between governance and dividend policy for faith-based stocks. At present, these are research questions that require empirical validation to clear doubts regarding the performance of these investment styles. Answering these questions will require reflection on the practical implications for the screened investment industry.

Assessment of the effects of screening: some evidence

A comparative study of these faith-based stocks for the US market was conducted to validate the research questions mentioned above. The reason for selecting US data was for better empirical validity, as a reasonably large data set was available to test the objectives: vendors like Dow Jones have been screening stocks for *shariah* compliance and SRI criteria for the US market for a considerable period of time.

Three portfolios of stocks were considered for this research: first, a portfolio comprised of *shariah*-compliant stocks; second, a portfolio of socially responsible stocks; and, third, a market portfolio as a benchmark – i.e. a market proxy portfolio – composed of market-representative stocks. The objective was to compare the (possible) variance in idiosyncratic risk and performance of these investment classes. We were assuming here that the market (proxy) portfolio is the investment universe of a neutral investor, and setting the market portfolio as the benchmark would allow an assessment of whether value-driven investors are at a disadvantage compared to neutral investors. Moreover, this approach would allow the assessment of the relative performance of different portfolios without involving any transaction costs, consistent with the assumption of Ashraf et al. (2017) that investors follow passive strategies and track a certain index to formulate their portfolios. We chose 2006–2015 as the sample period as it allowed us to perform estimations for a reasonably long period of time. Owing to the probability of a structural break in the sample period during a crisis period, we made estimations for the subperiods to evaluate the risk–return trade-off for crisis and non-crisis period to address this issue.

The first objective was to estimate average idiosyncratic risk for the sample portfolios to ascertain if these screened portfolios had different levels of idiosyncratic risk compared to the market portfolio. Hence, the first research question was:

1. *Is there any difference in the magnitude of idiosyncratic risk for the screen-based portfolios (both* shariah *and SRI) and the market portfolio?*

The second objective was to assess the risk-adjusted performance of the screened portfolios vis-á-vis the market portfolio. The intention was to observe if these portfolios provided better returns than the market portfolio. This question is important as faith-based portfolios are not only followed by value-driven investors but also by profit seekers investing in these portfolios (Derwall et al., 2011).

The second research question was as follows:

2. *Do the* shariah *and SRI portfolios perform better (as measured by Jensen's alpha) than the market portfolio? Is there a significant difference between faith-based and market portfolios?*

Methodology, data, and sample period

The sample includes representative *shariah*, SRI and market proxy portfolios for the United States (US) market from 2006 to 2015. The *shariah* portfolio is comprised of constituent stocks of the Dow Jones Islamic Market Index – US (DJIM-US) and the market portfolio is represented by the Dow Jones United States Index (DJUSI).[7] The motivation for selecting Dow Jones S&P Indices is that both are among the oldest such indices and Dow Jones is a reliable vendor. Another advantage is the frequent rebalancing by the service provider as the DJIMI-US is rebalanced quarterly whereas the DJUSI is rebalanced once a year. Dow Jones finalizes the *shariah* screening by applying various qualitative and quantitative criteria,[8] and the screening done by Dow Jones is subsequently validated by an independent *shariah* supervisory board comprised of eminent scholars to ensure consistency with *shariah* law. The historical lists are vital for analysis because the firms selected in one period may not be present in the previous or subsequent periods. For a given calendar year, only those firms are included in *shariah* portfolio that passed the *shariah* screening for all the four quarters of the said year.

To create our SRI portfolio, we used constituents of Dow Jones Sustainability Index – US that are publicly available on the RobecoSam database (www.robecosam.com/csa/csa-resources/dow-jones-sustainability-indices-components.html).

For the estimation of idiosyncratic risk, Jensen's alpha, and factor sensitivities, daily observations were retrieved for holding period returns, market capitalization, and stock prices from the Center for Research in Security Prices (CRSP; www.crsp.com/) database. The factor loadings (daily frequency) on market risk, small-minus-big, high-minus-low, and momentum were sourced from Wharton Research Data Services (WRDS; https://wrds-web.wharton.upenn.edu/).

The issue of any possible structural break in data was addressed through sample tests by performing portfolio level estimations across three different time periods. The pre-crisis period was from 2006 to 2007, the crisis period was 2008–2009, and the post-crisis period was from 2010–2015. This classification was influenced by US Business Cycle Expansions and Contractions information provided by the National Bureau of Economic Research (NBER), which states December 2007 and June 2009 as turning point dates.[9] We extended the crisis period for our sample for a further six months for the reason that market sentiment usually takes more time to discount for changes in investment climate.

Model

The risk profile of the sample portfolios and the risk-adjusted performance of the portfolios were estimated using multifactor models. These models define the excess return of a portfolio as a function of multiple factors. The first is the capital asset pricing model (CAPM) developed by Sharpe (1964) and later Lintner (1965). It states that excess return for investor is a function of excess market return and the risk sensitivity represents the systematic risk for the portfolio as shown Equation 2.2.

$$R_t - R_{f,t} = \alpha_i + \beta_1 \left(R_{m,t} - R_{f,t} \right) + \varepsilon_t \tag{2.2}$$

Fama and French (1993) extend CAPM and argue that excess return cannot be explained only with market return. There is a probability that small-capitalization stocks offer higher return than large-capitalization stocks. Similarly, value stocks may outperform growth stocks. These authors added these two factors into their model as reflected by Equation 2.3.

$$R_t - R_{f,t} = \alpha_i + \beta_1 \left(R_{m,t} - R_{f,t} \right) + \beta_2\, SMB_t + \beta_3\, HML_t + \varepsilon_t \tag{2.3}$$

Finally, Carhart (1997) argues that there is a tendency for investors to hold long high-performing stocks (winners) and short low-performing stocks (losers), and he called this the momentum factor. Their model is represented by Equation 2.4.

$$R_t - R_{f,t} = \alpha_i + \beta_1 \left(R_{m,t} - R_{f,t} \right) + \beta_2\, SMB_t + \beta_3\, HML_t + \beta_4 WML_t + \varepsilon_t \tag{2.4}$$

The detailed definitions of the variables used in these three models are summarized in Table 2.1.

Our main results include estimations based on the Carhart (1997) model as this model explains excess returns by taking into consideration more factors than the CAPM or the Fama and French (1993) model. However, it is not necessary to add additional factors to improve the explanatory power of the model. Moreover, there is no evidence in the existing literature on the relative strength of these three models. Estimations were also made using the CAPM and the Fama and French model to observe whether there was any variation in the estimations owing to the different predictors.

To estimate idiosyncratic risk, daily excess stock returns for one calendar year for each firm in the portfolio are regressed on Carhart's (1997) four factors. The standard deviation of residuals from each regression represents the idiosyncratic risk for the respective firm for the said year. This firm-level estimation is made using only raw returns because the regressions of value-weighted firm-level returns on four factors yielded zero idiosyncratic risk up to five decimal points

TABLE 2.1 Definitions of variables for factor models

Variable	*Description*
R_t	Daily holding period returns
$R_{f,t}$	Risk-free rate (30 days T-bill rate)
$R_{m,t}$	Return offered by market portfolio
$R_t - R_{f,t}$	Excess return, i.e. holding period return for the investors in excess of risk-free rate
$R_{m,t} - R_{f,t}$	Market premium, i.e. the return on a market value-weighted equity index in excess of the one-month T-bill rate. This factor is included to account for the premium offered by the market portfolio in excess of the risk-free rate
SMB (small minus big)	Size premium, i.e. the average return on three small-market-capitalization portfolios minus three large-market-capitalization portfolios. This factor is included to account for the premium of being a small-capitalization stock
HML (high minus low)	Value vs. growth, i.e. the average return on two high-book-to-market portfolios minus the average return on two low-book-to-market portfolios. The high (low) book-to-market represents a value (growth) bias. This factor is added to account for a value return premium
Momentum	Prior year effect on current prices, i.e. the average return on the two high-prior-return portfolios minus the average return on the two low-prior-return portfolios. This factor reflects the premium earned by buying last year's winner stocks

The table reports the details of different components of factor models. The definitions are from Kenneth R. French's webpage: http://mba.tuck.dartmouth.edu/pages/faculty/ken.french/.

and it was redundant to report them. The averages of firm-level idiosyncratic risk are reported to indicate the risk at portfolio level as well as industry level. The industry classification is in line with the Standard Industrial Classification (SIC) codes used by US government agencies.[10] It was also ascertained whether the mean idiosyncratic risk was significantly different among portfolios at the consolidated as well as the industry level. Jensen's alpha was estimated by regressing the daily excess stock returns for the sample period (2006–2015) on Carhart's (1997) four factors.

The out-of-sample tests include estimations across three different time periods as mentioned earlier. The alphas are also estimated using the CAPM and Fama and French (1993) models using daily returns for robustness. The values of Jensen's alpha are annualized for better interpretation of results.

The slope coefficients estimated from these models were estimated to analyse the impact of factor sensitivities on the excess returns. The 'difference of coefficients' across factor models are tested using the Wald test.

Results and discussion

Idiosyncratic risk

Distribution of idiosyncratic risk across different periods

The first step is to observe the distribution of idiosyncratic risk during the sample period. Table 2.2 and Figure 2.1 show how idiosyncratic risk changes during the sample period. It is not surprising that the average idiosyncratic risk was highest during the years of the financial crisis. SRIs appear to be least risky, probably due to the fact that this class comprises seasoned companies with lower debt and comparatively higher liquidity. Additionally, the SRI portfolio comprises fewer companies in the portfolio as compared to the *shariah* and the market portfolios. The *shariah* portfolio also shows lower than market idiosyncratic risk, possibly due to lower debt in the capital structure.

Distribution of average idiosyncratic risk across different industries

The distribution of idiosyncratic risk by industry follows a similar pattern. The average unsystematic risk for the market and *shariah* portfolios is of similar magnitude, but the unsystematic risk of the SRI portfolio differs significantly from the other two. For most of the sectors (excluding transport and finance), idiosyncratic risk is lowest in the SRI portfolio, followed by the *shariah* portfolio. Furthermore, the mean idiosyncratic risk using capitalization-weighted returns approaches zero at portfolio level and also for the industry sectors.

TABLE 2.2 Variations in mean idiosyncratic risk across different years 2006–2015: comparison between sample portfolios

Year	*Market portfolio*	*SRI portfolio*	*Shariah portfolio*
2006	1.59%	1.22%	1.71%
2007	1.66%	1.23%	1.70%
2008	2.95%	2.37%	2.67%
2009	2.42%	1.88%	2.13%
2010	1.50%	1.15%	1.50%
2011	1.56%	1.25%	1.62%
2012	1.44%	1.11%	1.58%
2013	1.30%	1.11%	1.40%
2014	1.32%	1.11%	1.36%
2015	1.42%	1.21%	1.43%
Total	**1.72%**	**1.35%**	**1.72%**

The table shows the average idiosyncratic risk at stock level for portfolio level across different years. To calculate the idiosyncratic risk for each firm, the excess returns for each firm in one calendar year are regressed on Carhart four factors namely market risk premium, small-minus-big, high-minus-low and momentum. Idiosyncratic risk is the standard deviation of residuals from this regression.

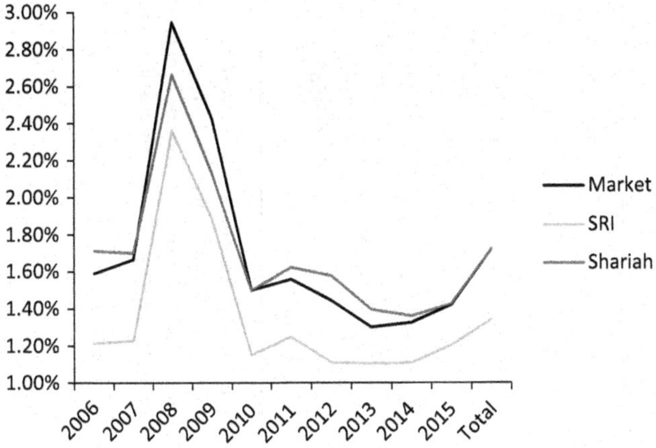

FIGURE 2.1 Average idiosyncratic risk (annual variations) in the three sample portfolios (market, SRI, and *shariah*) 2006–2015

It is worth mentioning here that the industry-specific risk is dependent upon the cyclicality of the industry (Bodie et al., 2014). Table 2.3 shows that the mining sector has the highest idiosyncratic risk. The obvious reason is that this business involves exploration and high investments with uncertain outcomes. In contrast, the transportation sector has the lowest risk. The retail trade is riskier than the wholesale trade, which may be a result of the difference in their respective volumes. The construction sector is riskiest after mining, owing to its significant size, and this sector is significantly the most volatile among the industrial sectors. This is understandable as our sample covers the period of subprime crisis when on the one hand housing prices sharply reduced and on the other hand construction activity virtually halted. It should be noted, however, that the average firm-specific risk for the *shariah* portfolio is lower for the construction sector, mainly due to the constraints on debt for these firms. Evidently, these *shariah*-compliant firms are less leveraged and therefore assume lower risk.

Figure 2.2 presents the distribution of mean idiosyncratic risk among the industry sectors. The industry classification was done using the Standard Industrial Classification (SIC) code list.

Risk-adjusted performance

Analysis of mean holding period return

To analyse the risk-adjusted performance, the mean returns at portfolio level as well as for various economic sectors were observed to identify the trends and differences in performance. Table 2.4 shows that the portfolio level returns were higher for the market and *shariah* portfolios than for the SRI portfolio, and there wes significant differences between means for the three different classes. Market

TABLE 2.3 Distribution of mean idiosyncratic risk (at stock level) across different industries

	Mean idiosyncratic risk			*Difference of means*		
	Market	*SRI*	*Shariah*	*Market–SRI*	*Market–shariah*	*SRI–shariah*
Portfolio level	0.0172	0.0136	0.0172	0.0036***	0.0000***	–0.0036***
Agriculture and forestry	0.0186	N/A	0.0154	N/A	0.0032***	N/A
Mining	0.0213	0.0160	0.0195	0.0026***	0.0018***	0.0006***
Construction	0.0203	0.0164	0.0190	0.0049	0.0014***	–0.0031***
Manufacturing	0.0178	0.0126	0.0170	0.0077***	0.0008***	–0.0064***
Transportation and utilities	0.0143	0.0112	0.0156	0.0066***	–0.0012***	–0.0058***
Wholesale trade	0.0158	0.0127	0.0134	0.0016***	0.0024***	–0.0029***
Retail trade	0.0186	0.0172	0.0179	-0.0014***	0.0006***	0.0038***
Finance and real estate	0.0158	0.0163	0.0204	0.0023***	–0.0047***	–0.0016***
Services	0.0183	0.0146	0.0174	0.0012***	0.0009***	–0.0058***
Others	0.0151	N/A	0.0092	N/A	0.0059***	N/A

The table shows the mean idiosyncratic risk at stock level for portfolio level and different industries. The difference of means test was performed using the *t*-statistic proposed by Dixon and Massey (1983). To calculate the idiosyncratic risk for each firm, the excess returns for each firm in one calendar year were regressed on Carhart's four factors, namely market risk premium, small-minus-big, high-minus-low, and momentum. Idiosyncratic risk is the standard deviation of residuals from this regression. The calculations were made using raw returns. ***, **, * denote statistical significance at the 1%, 5%, and 10% level, respectively. The industry classification was done using Standard Industrial Classification (SIC) codes.

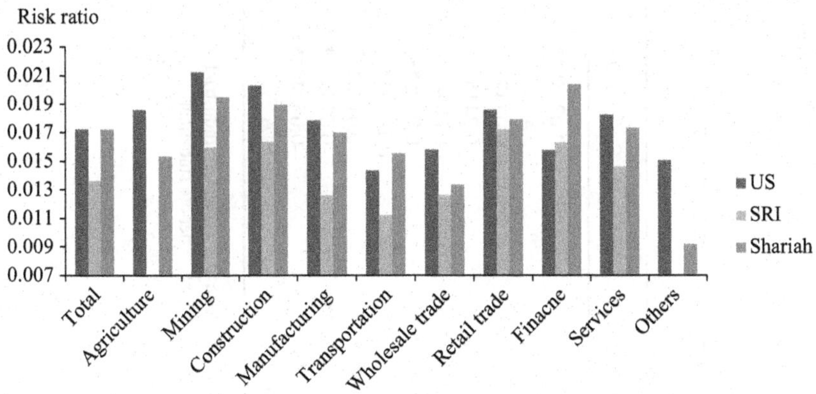

FIGURE 2.2 Mean idiosyncratic risk (raw returns) by industry (2006–2015)

and *shariah* returns were higher for all economic sectors except the wholesale trade segment. The most plausible explanation for this is that the market and *shariah* portfolios were much larger than the SRI portfolio.

Figure 2.3 presents the distribution of mean raw returns among the industry sectors. Again, the industry classification was done using the Standard Industrial Classification (SIC) code list.

Analysis of risk-adjusted performance using different models

To assess the risk-adjusted returns, Jensen's alpha and factor sensitivities were estimated for the portfolios (equally weighted and capitalization-weighted) to get the complete picture of the sample period and out-of-sample-periods performance.

The results using the Carhart (1997) model (Tables 2.5 and 2.6) show that the market portfolio was superior to the SRI and *shariah* portfolios, and there was marginal but significant difference in the alpha values among the three portfolios. The SRI portfolio performed slightly better than both the market and *shariah* portfolios. Out-of-sample tests show that although, before the crisis, the performance of the market and *shariah* portfolios significantly differed, the difference in magnitude was very small. In the crisis and post-crisis periods, a significant difference is found in the performance of the market proxy and the SRI portfolio, but no significant performance difference was recorded between the market proxy portfolio and the *shariah* portfolios. Similaly, there was no significant difference in performance for the SRI and *shariah* portfolios during most of the subperiods.

The risk-adjusted performance of the SRI portfolio was marginally but significantly better than that of the two other portfolios. We therefore argue that when a capitalization-weighted portfolio strategy is followed, there is no notable difference observed in the performance of market and faith-based portfolios.

The results for factor sensitivities as shown in Table 2.6 reveal that beta is positive and significant across the three portfolios exhibiting market risk for the

TABLE 2.4 Mean holding period returns (raw)

	Mean raw return			*Difference of means*		
	Market	*SRI*	*Shariah*	*Market—SRI*	*Market—shariah*	*SRI—shariah*
Portfolio	0.2120	0.1728	0.2006	0.0392***	0.0114***	–0.0278***
Agriculture and forestry	0.2435	N/A	0.2145	N/A	0.0291	N/A
Mining	0.1078	0.1485	0.2232	–0.0407	–0.11536	–0.0747
Construction	0.0790	–0.0197	0.2218	0.0987	–0.1428	–0.2415
Manufacturing	0.2261	0.1874	0.1920	0.0387***	0.00341	–0.0046
Transportation and utilities	0.1904	0.1571	0.1896	0.0333***	0.0008***	–0.0325***
Wholesale trade	0.2012	0.3402	0.2326	–0.1390***	–0.0315***	0.1076***
Retail trade	0.2365	0.1791	0.1914	0.0574***	0.0451***	–0.0123***
Finance and real estate	0.2024	0.1364	0.2120	0.0659***	–0.0096***	–0.0756***
Services	0.2365	0.1623	0.2147	0.0742***	0.0219***	–0.0524***
Others	0.3633	N/A	0.2522	N/A	0.1112***	N/A

The table shows the average raw returns for the sample at portfolio level and for different industries. The industry classification was done using Standard Industrial Classification (SIC) codes. The difference of means test was conducted using the t-statistic proposed by Dixon and Massey (1983). ***, **, * denote statistical significance at the 1%, 5%, and 10% level, respectively.

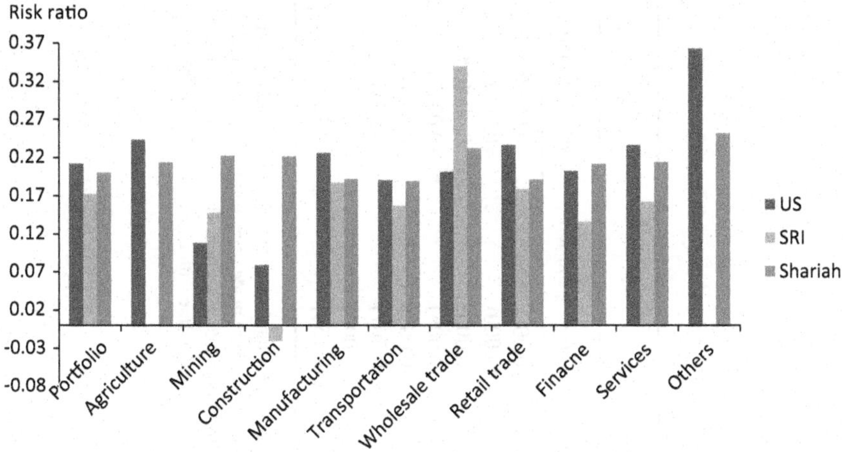

FIGURE 2.3 Mean holding period return (raw) by industry (2006–2015)

portfolios. The beta for the SRI portfolio is above 1 and significantly higher than those for the market (proxy) and *shariah* portfolios. This implies that the SRI portfolio exhibits higher than market risk for all the periods. The *shariah* portfolio also exhibits significantly higher than market risk, but lower than the SRI portfolio.

The results on the size effect is interesting as it shows that, for the sample period, the return of market portfolio is biased towards return from small stocks whereas return from SRI portfolio is driven by large firms' returns for the full sample and insignificant for *shariah* portfolio. However, the out-of-sample tests confirm that this effect exists for all the portfolios. Interestingly, during the crisis period, the returns for the sample portfolios predominantly come from large cap stocks.

The sample portfolios exhibit value bias, indicating that the returns are driven by investing in firms having a high book-to-market assets ratio.

The momentum effect is negative across the sample, showing that all three portfolios have not adopted the policy of choosing past year winners and shorting on past losers. However, the out-of-sample tests indicate positive momentum sensitivity for the market portfolio. It can be said that the momentum strategy generates returns for the market portfolio in shorter investment horizons.

The results of the CAPM model (Tables 2.7 and 2.8) and Fama French Model (Tables 2.9 and 2.10) are not qualitatively different from the Carhart model results, and we can conclude that risk-adjusted return for the sample portfolios is unaffected by the type of model used in estimating the performance.

Conclusion

Religious or social belief considerations in making investment decisions have now become a class of investments in their own right. The existing literature indicates the presence of a multi-attribute utility function for faith-based investors, which is

TABLE 2.5 Estimation of Jensen's alpha using the Carhart four-factor model

Period	*Annualized Jensen's alpha*			*Difference of alphas*		
	Market portfolio	*SRI portfolio*	Shariah *portfolio*	*Market–SRI*	*Market* – shariah	*SRI* – shariah
2006–2015	–0.0180***	–0.0138***	–0.0176***	–0.0042***	–0.0004***	0.0038***
	(0.000)	(0.000)	(0.000)	(0.000)	(0.000)	(0.000)
Pre-crisis	–0.0650***	–0.0646***	–0.0646***	0.0004**	–0.0003***	0.0000**
	(0.000)	(0.000)	(0.000)	(0.021)	(0.006)	(0.0247)
Crisis	–0.0123***	–0.0110***	–0.0117***	–0.0013***	–0.0006	0.0006
	(0.000)	(0.000)	(0.000)	(0.000)	(0.707)	(0.348)
Post-crisis	–0.0005***	–0.0004***	–0.0005***	0.0001***	0.0000	0.0001
	(0.000)	(0.000)	(0.000)	(0.001)	(0.258)	(0.524)

The table reports Jensen's alpha (annualized) at portfolio level. To calculate alpha, the daily excess returns were regressed on Carhart's four factors, namely market risk premium, small-minus-big, high-minus-low, and momentum. The alpha is the intercept term of this regression. The estimations were made using capitalization-weighted returns. *P*-values are reported in parentheses below each coefficient. A detailed description of the variables is given in the methodology section. The pre-crisis period is 2006–2007, the crisis period 2008–2009, and the post-crisis period 2010–2015. The difference of parameters tests are conducted in line with Clogg et al. (1995). ***, **, * denote statistical significance at the 1%, 5%, and 10% level, respectively.

TABLE 2.6 Factor coefficients using the Carhart four-factor model

Period	*Factor*	*Factor coefficient*			*Difference of coefficients*		
		Market portfolio	*SRI portfolio*	*Shariah portfolio*	*Market–SRI*	*Market – shariah*	*SRI – shariah*
2006–2015	Mkt-Rf	0.3316***	1.7447***	0.9921***	–1.4131***	–0.6605***	0.7526***
		(0.000)	(0.000)	(0.000)	(0.000)	(0.000)	(0.592)
	Smb	0.0402***	–0.1601***	–0.0031	0.2003***	0.0433***	–0.1570***
		(0.000)	(0.000)	(0.599)	(0.000)	(0.003)	(0.000)
	Hml	–0.1167***	–0.1415***	–0.2528***	0.0248	0.1360***	0.1113***
		(0.000)	(0.000)	(0.000)	(0.173)	(0.000)	(0.004)
	Mom	–0.0694***	–0.0922***	–0.0477***	0.0228**	–0.0217	–0.0445***
		(0.000)	(0.000)	(0.000)	(0.013)	(0.503)	(0.008)
Pre–crisis	Mkt-Rf	0.1997***	1.8568***	0.6908***	–1.6571***	–0.4911***	1.1659
		(0.000)	(0.000)	(0.000)	(0.000)	(0.000)	(0.592)
	Smb	0.0738***	–0.1340***	0.0702***	0.2077***	0.0035	–0.2042**
		(0.000)	(0.000)	(0.000)	(0.000)	(0.846)	(0.012)
	Hml	–0.1509***	–0.3037***	–0.2735***	0.1528***	0.1226***	–0.0302***
		(0.000)	(0.000)	(0.000)	(0.000)	(0.000)	(0.007)
	Mom	0.2094***	0.1235***	0.3360***	0.0859***	–0.1266***	–0.2126***
		(0.000)	(0.000)	(0.000)	(0.002)	(0.000)	(0.000)
Crisis	Mkt-Rf	0.2976***	1.9626***	0.9633***	–1.6650***	–0.6657***	0.9994
		(0.000)	(0.000)	(0.000)	(0.000)	(0.000)	(0.592)
	Smb	–0.0167***	–0.1888***	–0.0519***	0.1721	0.0352**	–0.1369***
		(0.000)	(0.000)	(0.000)	(0.152)	(0.013)	(0.000)
	Hml	–0.1678***	–0.2230***	–0.2978***	0.0552***	0.1300**	0.0748***
		(0.000)	(0.000)	(0.000)	(0.000)	(0.051)	(0.000)
	Mom	0.1375***	–0.0889***	–0.0799***	0.2264***	0.2174	–0.0090***

(continued)

TABLE 2.6 (Cont.)

Period	*Factor*	*Factor coefficient*			*Difference of coefficients*		
		Market portfolio	*SRI portfolio*	*Shariah portfolio*	*Market–SRI*	*Market – shariah*	*SRI – shariah*
		(0.000)	(0.000)	(0.000)	(0.001)	(0.589)	(0.000)
Post-crisis	Mkt-Rf	0.3191***	1.4075***	1.0140***	–1.0884***	–0.6949***	0.3935
		(0.000)	(0.000)	(0.000)	(0.000)	(0.000)	(0.592)
	Smb	–0.0287***	–0.1333***	–0.0889	0.1046***	0.0602***	–0.0445***
		(0.000)	(0.000)	(0.599)	(0.000)	(0.000)	(0.000)
	Hml	–0.0055***	0.0742	–0.1564***	–0.0796***	0.1510***	0.2306***
		(0.002)	(0.706)	(0.000)	(0.000)	(0.000)	(0.000)
	Mom	0.0000***	–0.0236***	–0.0226***	0.0236***	0.0226***	–0.0010***
		(0.000)	(0.000)	(0.000)	(0.000)	(0.000)	(0.000)

The table reports the factor coefficients at portfolio level for the regression of the daily excess returns on market risk premium, small-minus-big, high-minus-low, and momentum (Carhart model). The estimations are made using capitalization-weighted returns. *P*-values are reported in parentheses below each coefficient. A detailed description of the variables is given in the methodology section. The pre-crisis period is 2006–2007, the crisis period 2008–2009, and the post-crisis period 2010–2015. The difference of parameters tests were conducted in line with Clogg et al. (1995). ***, **, * denote statistical significance at the 1%, 5%, and 10% level, respectively. Mkt–Rf, market risk premium; Smb, small-minus-big; Hml, high-minus-low; Mom, momentum.

TABLE 2.7 Estimation of Jensen's alpha using the capital asset pricing model

Period	*Market portfolio*	*SRI portfolio*	*Shariah portfolio*	*Difference of alphas*		
				Market–SRI	*Market – shariah*	*SRI – shariah*
2006–2015	–0.0181***	–0.0138***	–0.0176***	–0.0042***	–0.0005***	0.0038***
	(0.000)	(0.000)	(0.000)	(0.000)	(0.000)	(0.000)
Pre-crisis	–0.0650***	–0.0646***	–0.0646***	–0.0004***	–0.0003***	0.0000***
	(0.000)	(0.000)	(0.000)	(0.007)	(0.000)	(0.000)
Crisis	–0.0122***	–0.0110***	–0.0117***	–0.0012***	–0.0005	0.0007**
	(0.000)	(0.000)	(0.000)	(0.000)	(0.381)	(0.018)
Post-crisis	–0.0005***	–0.0004***	–0.0005***	–0.0001***	–0.0001	0.0001
	(0.000)	(0.000)	(0.000)	(0.001)	(0.844)	(0.567)

The table reports Jensen's alpha (annualized) at portfolio level. To calculate alpha, the daily excess returns were regressed on market risk premium. The alpha is the intercept term of this regression. The estimations were made using capitalization-weighted returns. *P*-values are reported in parentheses below each coefficient. A detailed description of variables is given in the methodology section. The pre-crisis period is 2006–2007, the crisis period 2008–2009, and the post-crisis 2010–2015. The difference of parameters tests were conducted in line with Clogg et al. (1995). ***, **, * denote statistical significance at the 1%, 5%, and 10% level, respectively.

TABLE 2.8 Factor coefficients using the capital asset pricing model

Period	*Factor*	*Factor coefficient*			*Difference of coefficients*		
		Market portfolio	*SRI portfolio*	*Shariah portfolio*	*Market–SRI*	*Market – shariah*	*SRI – shariah*
2006–2015	Mkt-Rf	0.3287***	1.7049***	0.8931***	–1.3762***	–0.5643***	0.8120***
		(0.000)	(0.000)	(0.000)	(0.000)	(0.000)	(0.000)
Pre-crisis	Mkt-Rf	0.2584***	1.8360***	0.0605***	–1.5776***	0.1979***	1.776***
		(0.000)	(0.000)	(0.000)	(0.000)	(0.017)	(0.000)
Crisis	Mkt-Rf	0.3229***	1.8987***	0.8454***	–1.5757***	–0.5225***	1.0532
		(0.000)	(0.000)	(0.000)	(0.002)	(0.031)	(0.752)
Post-crisis	Mkt-Rf	0.3109***	1.3555***	0.9349***	–1.0445***	–0.6240***	0.4206***
		(0.000)	(0.000)	(0.000)	(0.000)	(0.001)	(0.000)

The table reports the factor coefficients at portfolio level for the regression of the daily excess returns on market risk premium (capital asset pricing model). The estimations were made using capitalization-weighted returns. *P*-values are reported in parentheses below each coefficient. A detailed description of the variables is given in the methodology section. The pre-crisis period is 2006–2007, the crisis period 2008–2009, and the post-crisis period 2010–2015. The difference of parameters tests were conducted in line with Clogg et al. (1995). ***, **, * denote statistical significance at the 1%, 5%, and 10% level, respectively. Mkt-Rf, market risk premium.

TABLE 2.9 Estimation of Jensen's alpha using capitalization-weighted returns (FF3)

				Difference of alphas tests		
	US	*SRI*	*Shariah*	*US–SRI*	*US – shariah*	*SRI – shariah*
2006–2015	–0.0181***	–0.0138***	–0.0176***	–0.0042***	–0.0004***	0.0038***
	(0.000)	(0.000)	(0.000)	(0.000)	(0.000)	(0.000)
Pre-crisis	–0.0650***	–0.0646***	–0.0646***	–0.0004**	–0.0003***	0.0000***
	(0.000)	(0.000)	(0.000)	(0.021)	(0.000)	(0.001)
Crisis	–0.0122***	–0.0110***	–0.0116***	–0.0012***	–0.0006	0.0006
	(0.000)	(0.000)	(0.000)	(0.000)	(0.879)	(0.121)
Post-crisis	–0.0005***	–0.0004***	–0.0005***	–0.0001***	0.0000	0.0001
	(0.000)	(0.000)	(0.000)	(0.005)	(0.174)	(0.430)

The table reports the Jensen's alpha (annualized) at portfolio level. To calculate alpha, the daily excess returns are regressed on three Fama and French factors (FF3), namely market risk premium, small-minus-big and high-minus-low. The alpha is the intercept term of this regression. The estimations were made using capitalization-weighted returns. *P*-values are reported in parentheses below each coefficient. A detailed description of the variables is given in the methodology section. The pre-crisis period is 2006–2007, the crisis period is 2008–2009, and the post-crisis period 2010–2015. The difference of parameters tests were conducted in line with Clogg et al. (1995). ***,**,*denote statistical significance at the 1%, 5%, and 10% level, respectively.

TABLE 2.10 Factor coefficients – capitalization-weighted portfolio (FF3)

Period	*Factor*	*Factor coefficient*			*Difference of coefficients*		
		Market portfolio	*SRI portfolio*	*Shariah portfolio*	*Market–SRI*	*Market – shariah*	*SRI – shariah*
2006–2015	Mkt-Rf	0.3448***	1.7748***	1.0067***	–1.4300***	–0.6619***	0.7681***
		(0.000)	(0.000)	(0.000)	(0.000)	(0.015)	(0.014)
	Smb	0.0343***	–0.1659***	–0.0072	0.2002***	0.0415**	–0.1587***
		(0.000)	(0.000)	(0.226)	(0.000)	(0.045)	(0.000)
	Hml	–0.0646***	–0.0724***	–0.2230***	0.0078***	0.1584***	0.1506***
		(0.000)	(0.000)	(0.000)	(0.000)	(0.000)	(0.000)
Pre-crisis	Mkt-Rf	0.2312***	1.8987***	0.7600***	–1.6675***	–0.5288***	1.1387**
		(0.000)	(0.000)	(0.000)	(0.000)	(0.691)	(0.014)
	Smb	0.0816***	–0.1324***	0.0785***	0.2140***	0.0032	–0.2109***
		(0.000)	(0.000)	(0.000)	(0.000)	(0.892)	(0.000)
	Hml	–0.2014***	–0.3308***	–0.3405***	0.1294***	0.1391***	0.0097***
		(0.000)	(0.000)	(0.000)	(0.000)	(0.000)	(0.000)
Crisis	Mkt-Rf	0.3567***	2.0613***	1.0214***	–1.7046***	–0.6647***	1.0399**
		(0.000)	(0.000)	(0.000)	(0.000)	(0.000)	(0.014)
	Smb	–0.0047***	–0.1828	–0.0450***	0.1781***	0.0402***	–0.1378***
		(0.000)	(0.369)	(0.000)	(0.000)	(0.000)	(0.000)
	Hml	–0.0768***	–0.1629***	–0.2492***	0.0861***	0.1724***	0.0863***
		(0.000)	(0.000)	(0.000)	(0.000)	(0.000)	(0.000)
Post-crisis	Mkt-Rf	0.3191***	1.3988***	1.0140***	–1.0797***	–0.6949***	0.3848***
		(0.000)	(0.000)	(0.000)	(0.000)	(0.000)	(0.014)
	Smb	–0.0287***	–0.1330***	–0.0889***	0.1043***	0.0602***	–0.0441***
		(0.000)	(0.000)	(0.000)	(0.000)	(0.000)	(0.000)
	Hml	–0.0054***	0.0868	–0.1478***	–0.0922***	0.1424***	0.2345***
		(0.001)	(0.104)	(0.000)	(0.000)	(0.000)	(0.000)

The table reports the factor coefficients at portfolio level for the regression of the daily excess returns on three Fama and French factors (FF3), namely market risk premium, small-minus-big and high-minus-low. The estimations are made using capitalization returns. *P*-values are reported in parentheses below each coefficient. A detailed description of the variables is given in the methodology section. The pre-crisis period is 2006–2007, the crisis period 2008–2009, and the post-crisis period 2010–2015. The difference of parameters tests were conducted in line with Clogg et al. (1995). ***, **, * denote statistical significance at the 1%, 5%, and 10% level, respectively. Mkt–Rf, market risk premium; Smb, small-minus-big; Hml, high-minus-low; Mom, momentum.

not only dependent on the standard risk-reward optimization but also screened for a set of personal and societal values. This chapter has addressed the issue concerning the possibility of extra costs for investors in these niche classes of screened assets. The first objective was to assess whether there is idiosyncratic risk in these portfolios, and if yes, whether these portfolios are capable of diversifying their unsystematic risk. The second objective was to evaluate the risk-adjusted performance of screened portfolios. The sample included three type of portfolios, namely *shariah*-compliant, 'socially responsible' (SRI) and market (proxy) portfolios in the United States. The portfolios were formulated based upon the constituent lists of different Dow Jones Indices to add credibility to the stock selection.

The SRI portfolio recorded the lowest average unsystematic risk, followed by the *shariah* portfolio. The analysis of risk-adjusted return revealed that the SRI portfolio had superior performance compared to the other two portfolios during the sample period. However, there was not much difference in performance among the sample portfolios during the subperiods. It was found that SRI portfolio had highest systematic risk followed by *shariah* portfolio. The returns for SRI portfolio were predominantly generated by small stock premium. All the portfolios manifested value bias and no momentum effect.

The results indicate that both negative and positive screenings result in increase of systematic risk. As SRIs exercise both type screenings, they record the highest level of systematic risk.

Intuitively, it was expected that *shariah* portfolios would have lowest betas owing to their low financial leverage. However, the findings show that the beta for *shariah* stocks is higher, implying that these companies have higher systematic risk. This may be due to the fact that, since beta is the sum of both operating and financial leverage, the operating leverage may possibly be higher for *shariah* stocks, resulting in a high beta for these companies.[11] This finding is consistent with the literature which argues that financial leverage and systematic risk are not necessarily positively correlated (Omet and Di'bie, 2000; Rowe and Kim, 2010; Tan et al., 2015). It is also possible that, by having high betas compared to the market, *shariah* firms are not fully utilizing their allowable debt ratio and their suboptimal capital structure lowers their performance (Goetzmann et al., 2001).

The findings make important contributions to the existing literature in different ways. Firstly, they formally document valuable information on the idiosyncratic risk for faith-based portfolios and their risk-adjusted performance for the US market. There is a dearth of firm-level studies in the existing Islamic finance literature in these areas. Secondly, the findings show that there is no cost when social values are considered in making investment decisions. We have shown that the risk-adjusted performance of faith-based portfolios is superior to the market, though it is possible that this performance was due to the higher-than-market systematic risk reported in the screened portfolios.

The findings add various new insights to existing corporate finance studies. This is the first study that has used Dow Jones proprietary firm-level data to assess the presence of idiosyncratic risk in SRI and *shariah* portfolios vis-à-vis a market proxy portfolio. This new evidence may help initiate further exploration in similar areas in other countries. Furthermore, we estimated Jensen's alpha for the sample portfolios using three different factor models. This approach may not only help an understanding of comparative performance, but also reveals the explanatory power of these multifactor models which may be useful for other researchers.

For investors who want to design their respective portfolios to achieve diversification and earn risk-adjusted returns at par with market should be prepared to assume higher market risk when investing in faith-based portfolios.

Notes

1 IFSB (2015) *Islamic financial services industry stability report 2015*: Islamic Financial Services Board. Available at: www.ifsb.org/docs/IFSB%20Islamic%20Financial%20Services%20Industry%20Stability%20Report%202015_final.pdf.
2 USSIF (2016) *Report on US sustainable, responsible and impact investing trends*, Washington: US SIF Foundation. Available at: www.ussif.org/content.asp?contentid=40.
3 The details of SRI screening methodology can be viewed at http://us.spindices.com/documents/methodologies/methodology-dj-sustainability-indices.pdf
4 The details of *shariah* screening methodology can be viewed at http://us.spindices.com/documents/methodologies/methodology-dj-islamic-market-indices.pdf
5 Ahmed, N. and Farooq, O. (2017) 'Does the degree of Shari'ah compliance affect the volatility? Evidence from the MENA region', *Research in International Business and Finance*.
6 This hypothesis states that people shy away from investing in socially controversial stocks that have a negative image attached to them, and as a result these stock carry higher risk due to lesser liquidity.
7 In order to design the *shariah* and market proxy portfolios, we utilized the constituent lists of the Dow Jones US Index and Dow Jones Islamic Markets Index – US. This data is not publicly available and we purchased it directly from Dow Jones through a research grant extended by BNP Paribas – INCEIF Centre for Islamic Asset and Wealth Management, Malaysia. We are thankful to them for this gesture..
8 The details of these *shariah* compliance screens are provided in the appendix to this chapter. The complete screening methodology can be viewed at https://us.spindices.com/index-family/Shariah/all.
9 www.nber.org/cycles.html
10 The complete list may be viewed at www.census.gov/eos/www/naics/ (retrieved on 15 May 2017)
11 We are indebted to el Alaoui, A. O., Bacha, O. I., Masih, M. and Asutay, M. (2016) 'Shari'ah screening, market risk and contagion: A multi-country analysis', *Journal of Economic Behavior & Organization*, 132, pp. 93–112, for suggesting this argument.

References

Abu-Alkheil, A., Khan, W. A., Parikh, B. and Mohanty, S. K. (2017) 'Dynamic co-integration and portfolio diversification of Islamic and conventional indices: Global evidence', *The Quarterly Review of Economics and Finance*, 66, pp. 212–224.

Ahmed, N. and Farooq, O. (2017) 'Does the degree of Shari'ah compliance affect the volatility? Evidence from the MENA region', *Research in International Business and Finance*, 45, pp. 150–157.

Al-Khazali, O., Lean, H. H. and Samet, A. (2014) 'Do Islamic stock indexes outperform conventional stock indexes? A stochastic dominance approach', *Pacific-Basin Finance Journal*, 28, pp. 29–46.

Arouri, M., Ben Ameur, H., Jawadi, N., Jawadi, F. and Louhichi, W. (2013) 'Are Islamic finance innovations enough for investors to escape from a financial downturn? Further evidence from portfolio simulations', *Applied Economics*, 45(24), pp. 3412–3420.

Ashraf, D., Felixson, K., Khawaja, M. and Hussain, S. M. (2017) 'Do constraints on financial and operating leverage affect the performance of Islamic equity portfolios?', *Pacific-Basin Finance Journal*, 42, pp. 171–182.

Ashraf, D. and Khawaja, M. (2016) 'Does the *Shariah* screening process matter? Evidence from *Shariah* compliant portfolios', *Journal of Economic Behavior & Organization*, 132, pp. 77–92.

Bauer, R., Derwall, J. and Otten, R. (2007) 'The ethical mutual fund performance debate: New evidence from Canada', *Journal of Business Ethics*, 70(2), pp. 111–124.

Bauer, R., Otten, R. and Rad, A. T. (2006) 'Ethical investing in Australia: Is there a financial penalty?', *Pacific-Basin Finance Journal*, 14(1), pp. 33–48.

Bodie, Z., Kane, A. and Marcus., A. J. (2013) *Investments*. 9th edn. New York: McGraw-Hill Education, p. 214.

Bodie, Z., Kane, A. and Marcus, A. J. (2014) *Investments*. 10th edn. New York: McGraw-Hill Education.

Bollen, N. P. (2007) 'Mutual fund attributes and investor behavior', *Journal of Financial and Quantitative Analysis*, 42(03), pp. 683–708.

Boo, Y. L., Ee, M. S., Li, B. and Rashid, M. (2017) 'Islamic or conventional mutual funds: Who has the upper hand? Evidence from Malaysia', *Pacific-Basin Finance Journal*, 42, pp. 183–192.

Carhart, M. M. (1997) 'On persistence in mutual fund performance', *The Journal of Finance*, 52(1), pp. 57–82.

Chung, R., Firth, M. and Kim, J.-B. (2005) 'Earnings management, surplus free cash flow, and external monitoring', *Journal of Business Research*, 58(6), pp. 766–776.

Clogg, C. C., Petkova, E. and Haritou, A. (1995) 'Statistical methods for comparing regression coefficients between models', *American Journal of Sociology*, 100(5), pp. 1261–1293.

Cortez, M. C., Silva, F. and Areal, N. (2009) 'The performance of European socially responsible funds', *Journal of Business Ethics*, 87(4), pp. 573–588.

Derwall, J., Koedijk, K. and Ter Horst, J. (2011) 'A tale of values-driven and profit-seeking social investors', *Journal of Banking & Finance*, 35(8), pp. 2137–2147.

Dixon, W. J. and Massey, F. J. (1983) *Introduction to Statistical Analysis*. 4th edn. New York: McGraw-Hill.

el Alaoui, A. O., Bacha, O. I., Masih, M. and Asutay, M. (2016) 'Shari'ah screening, market risk and contagion: A multi-country analysis', *Journal of Economic Behavior & Organization*, 132, pp. 93–112.

Erragragui, E. and Lagoarde-Segot, T. (2016) 'Solving the SRI puzzle? A note on the mainstreaming of ethical investment', *Finance Research Letters*, 18, pp. 32–42.

Fama, E. F., & French, K. R. (1993). Common risk factors in the returns on stocks and bonds. *Journal of Financial Economics*, 33(1), pp. 3–56.

Goetzmann, W. N., Li, L. and Rouwenhorst, K. G. (2005) 'Long-term global market correlations', *Journal of Business*, 78(1), pp. 1–38.

Grira, J., Hassan, M. K. and Soumaré, I. (2016) 'Pricing beliefs: Empirical evidence from the implied cost of deposit insurance for Islamic banks', *Economic Modelling*, 55, pp. 152–168.

Gul, F. A. (2001) 'Free cash flow, debt-monitoring and managers' LIFO/FIFO policy choice', *Journal of Corporate Finance*, 7(4), pp. 475–492.

Haigh, M. and Hazelton, J. (2004) 'Financial markets: A tool for social responsibility?', *Journal of Business Ethics*, 52(1), pp. 59–71.

Hoepner, A. G., Rammal, H. G. and Rezec, M. (2011) 'Islamic mutual funds' financial performance and international investment style: Evidence from 20 countries', *The European Journal of Finance*, 17(9–10), pp. 829–850.

Humphrey, J. E. and Lee, D. D. (2011) 'Australian socially responsible funds: Performance, risk and screening intensity', *Journal of Business Ethics*, 102(4), pp. 519–535.

Ibbotson, R. G. and Kaplan, P. D. (2000) 'Does asset allocation policy explain 40, 90, or 100 percent of performance?', *Financial Analysts Journal*, 56(1), pp. 26–33.

IFSB (2015) *Islamic financial services industry stability report 2015*: Islamic Financial Services Board. Available at: www.ifsb.org/docs/IFSB%20Islamic%20Financial%20Services%20Industry%20Stability%20Report%202015_final.pdf.

Johnson, L. and Neave, E. (1996) *Efficiency and effectiveness of Islamic financing: the cost of orthodoxy*: Working Paper No. 96.

Kamil, N., Bacha, O. and Masih, M. (2012) 'Do "sin stocks" deprive Islamic stock portfolios of diversification? Some insights from the use of MGARCH-DCC', *Capital Markets Review*, 20(1), pp. 1–20.

Kamil, N. K. M., Alhabshi, S. O., Bacha, O. I. and Masih, M. (2014) 'Heads we win, tails you lose: Is there equity in Islamic equity funds?', *Pacific-Basin Finance Journal*, 28, pp. 7–28.

Lean, H. H., Ang, W. R. and Smyth, R. (2015) 'Performance and performance persistence of socially responsible investment funds in Europe and North America', *The North American Journal of Economics and Finance*, 34, pp. 254–266.

Lee, D. D., Humphrey, J. E., Benson, K. L. and Ahn, J. Y. (2010) 'Socially responsible investment fund performance: The impact of screening intensity', *Accounting & Finance*, 50(2), pp. 351–370.

Lintner, J. (1965) 'The valuation of risk assets and the selection of risky investments in stock portfolios and capital budgets', *The Review of Economics and Statistics*, pp. 13–37.

Markowitz, H. (1952) Portfolio selection. *The Journal of Finance*, 7(1), 77–91.

Merdad, H. J., Kabir Hassan, M. and Hippler III, W. J. (2015) 'The Islamic risk factor in expected stock returns: An empirical study in Saudi Arabia', *Pacific-Basin Finance Journal*, 34, pp. 293–314.

Najeeb, S. F., Bacha, O. and Masih, M. (2015) 'Does heterogeneity in investment horizons affect portfolio diversification? Some insights using M-GARCH-DCC and wavelet correlation analysis', *Emerging Markets Finance and Trade*, 51(1), pp. 188–208.

Obaidullah, M. (2006) *Teaching Corporate Finance: From an Islamic Perspective*. Islamic Economics Research Centre, King Abdul Aziz University.

Omet, G. and Di'bie, M. (2000) *The Association between Systematic Risk and Debt-to-Equity Ratio in Amman Financial Market*. Dirasat, The University of Jordan.

RBC Global Asset Management. (2012) *Does socially responsible investing hurt investment returns?* Available at: http://funds.rbcgam.com/_assets-custom/pdf/RBC-GAM-does-SRI-hurt-investment-returns.pdf.

Renneboog, L., Ter Horst, J. and Zhang, C. (2008) 'Socially responsible investments: Institutional aspects, performance, and investor behavior', *Journal of Banking & Finance*, 32(9), pp. 1723–1742.

Rowe, T. and Kim, J. S. (2010) 'Analyzing the relationship between systematic risk and financial variables in the casino industry', *UNLV Gaming Research & Review Journal*, 14(2), p. 47.

Saeed, B. and Hassan, M. K. (2013) 'Sustainable and socially responsible investing: Does Islamic investing make a difference?', *Humanomics*, 29(3), pp. 164–186.

Saiti, B., Bacha, O. I. and Masih, M. (2014) 'The diversification benefits from Islamic investment during the financial turmoil: The case for the US-based equity investors', *Borsa Istanbul Review*, 14(4), pp. 196–211.

Sharpe, W. F. (1964) 'Capital asset prices: A theory of market equilibrium under conditions of risk', *The Journal of Finance*, 19(3), pp. 425–442.

Tan, N., Chua, J. and Salamanca, P. (2015) 'Study of the overall impact of financial levearge and other determinants of systematic risk'. DLSU Research Congress, De La Salle University, Manila, Philippines.

Usmani, M. T. (2002) *An Introduction to Islamic Finance*. 1st edn. Karachi: Brill.

USSIF (2016) *Report on US Sustainable, Responsible and Impact Investing Trends*. Washington: US SIF Foundation. Available at: www.ussif.org/content.asp?contentid=40.

3

ISLAMIC CORPORATE FINANCE

Capital structure

Mohamed Eskandar Shah Mohd Rasid, Ajim Uddin and Mohammad Ashraful Ferdous Chowdhury

Introduction

As you read this chapter, you will understand that apart from the investment decision, the financing strategy, i.e. finding an optimal combination between equity and debt to finance operation and growth, is crucial for firms' long-term survival. When we say 'optimal', we mean a combination that strikes a balance between the nature of business and the risk of bankruptcy. By reading this chapter, you will appreciate the fact that the financing decision is very critical, and not getting it right is not an option for any firms. Often, firms have to wind up or enter liquidation due to wrong financing choices.

As discussed previously, firms have two main sources of financing: debt and equity. Equity consists of common stock, preferred stock, and retained earnings. Equity is perpetual, i.e. these securities have no underlying maturity and the owners can hold them as long as they want. On the other hand, debt by default has a fixed maturity, except for perpetual bonds. Based on the maturity period, debt can be short-term, such as commercial paper, or long-term, such as bonds and notes payable. The combination of short-term debt, long-term debt, common equity, preferred equity, and retained earnings, as sources of financing, determines the firm's capital structure. In general, firms have three options when it comes to financing their investment: either 100% debt, or 100% equity, or a combination of debt and equity. Firms will start with 100% equity and then decide how much debt they want to raise, thence altering their balance sheet and capital structure.

The capital structure decision involves choosing the appropriate combination of these financing sources so as to maximize shareholders' wealth. However, deciding the best mix is not easy. Each of these financing sources has its own costs, both direct costs and indirect costs. Direct cost is the cost associated with issuing each security, such as interest paid to the bondholders or the required rate of return expected by shareholders; whereas indirect cost arises from the associated risk of issuing debt and bankruptcy cost. A successful financial manager has to weigh each of these sources' feasibility and associated costs and then decide the optimal capital structure for the firm. Due to the risk and cost constraint, capital structure choices remain a pertinent issue in modern finance. Notwithstanding the progress that we have witnessed since the seminal work of Modigliani and Miller (1958), the debate on what is optimal remains an intriguing issue among academics. In the conventional space, the trade-off hypothesis, pecking order theory, and free cash flow hypothesis continue to be the building blocks for empirical works, in which the findings enlighten our understanding of the behavior of firms, particularly the insight behind their financing choices. Nevertheless, the same theories may or may not apply to *shariah*-compliant firms due to the constraints or limitations imposed on them. The quest to understand the financing behavior of *shariah*-compliant firms, specifically the issue of optimality and the impact of the constraints imposed on them, is a recent phenomenon in academia.

We will begin the chapter with a review of conventional theories of capital structure and the empirical findings of these theories. Our narrative continues with a critical evaluation of the relevance of conventional theories on capital structure decisions of *shariah*-compliant firms and their debt restrictions. Finally, we conclude with exploring the possibility of an alternative explanation for firms with religious constraints.

Theories of capital structure

The modern theory of capital structure was formally laid out in the seminal paper by Modigliani and Miller, 'The cost of capital, corporation finance and the theory of investment' (Modigliani and Miller, 1958). In their capital structure irrelevance theorem, Modigliani and Miller suggested that in an efficient market, and in the absence of taxes and bankruptcy cost, the market value of a firm is not affected by its choice of capital structure composition. According to them, the market value of a firm is determined by its earning power and the risk of its underlying assets, and not by its capital structure or dividend decisions. Briefly, Modigliani and Miller's initial argument concludes that capital structure is irrelevant and has no impact on the firm's value – implying that firms should be concentrating on choosing projects which add value to them, instead of focusing on their financing strategy.

The underlying assumption of the initial Modigliani and Miller proposition is a 'tax-free world'. However, in reality, most countries in the world impose corporate and personal taxes. Thus, to account for the tax effect, Modigliani and Miller modified their initial model in their subsequent study published in 1963. They suggest that in a world with corporate taxes and tax-deductible interest expenses, a firm's value can increase proportionately to its use of debt capital. This effect of debt on a firm's value is known as the leverage effect, and is generated from tax savings, as interest payments are tax deductible. For instance, consider two hypothetical firms, Firm E and Firm D. Both firms are identical in every sense except

TABLE 3.1 Explanation of leverage advantage

	Firm E ($)	*Firm D ($)*
Revenue	1000	1000
Expenses	500	500
EBIT (revenue – expenses)	**500**	**500**
Interest expenses (8% of debt capital)		120
EBT	500	380
Taxes (35%)	175	133
Net income	325	247
Return on equity (net income/equity)	**10.83%**	**16.47%**

Note: EBIT, earnings before interest and taxes; EBT, earnings before tax.

that Firm E uses 100% equity capital whereas Firm D uses 50% equity capital and 50% debt capital. Both firms start with a capital of $3000. As seen in Table 3.1, Firm D is able to increase its return on equity (ROE) by having 50% debt in its capital structure. Furthermore, Firm D's cost of capital will also be lower as the nominal cost of debt is always less than the cost of equity.

Modigliani and Miller's capital structure irrelevance theory laid the foundation stone for the capital structure literature. However, mixed empirical findings and inconclusiveness of the theory led to the introduction of alternative theories such as the pecking order theory and the free cash flow hypothesis. The former was introduced by Myers (1984), and the latter was proposed by Jensen and Meckling (1976). Unlike Modigliani and Miller's theory, which builds on tax and bankruptcy, both the pecking order theory and the free cash flow hypothesis were built on the presence of adverse selection and agency cost. What is the significance of these theories in the context of *shariah*-compliant firms? Before discussing the capital structure of *shariah*-compliant firms it would be a good idea to develop an understanding of these theories first.

The trade-off theory

The main idea behind the trade-off theory is that firms evaluate various costs and benefits of debt financing and try to balance costs with benefits. The original version of the trade-off theory was first proposed by Kraus and Litzenberger (1973) in order to reconcile the debate over Modigliani and Miller's capital irrelevance theorem. The latter had proposed that in the presence of corporate tax a firm can increase its value by increasing the level of its debt. In such a situation, without any other cost associated with raising debt, a profit-maximizing firm will end up with 100% debt. To avoid this extreme scenario, Kraus and Litzenberger (1973) introduced the concept of an indirect cost of debt: the cost of bankruptcy. Bankruptcy cost has two components: deadweight cost and indirect cost. Deadweight cost is the actual or direct cost of going bankrupt, i.e. legal and liquidation costs. Indirect cost is the cost that arises because of related parties' perceptions of a firm going bankrupt, e.g. loss of sales or increasing supplier bargaining power. Both deadweight cost and indirect cost of bankruptcy rise with increasing debt. Thus, optimal leverage is a trade-off between the tax benefits of debt and the cost of bankruptcy.

Myers (1984) refines Kraus and Litzenberger's (1973) original idea and suggests that firms adopting the trade-off theory set a target debt ratio and try to move towards this target. According to Myers, firms try to balance the benefits of a tax shield against the various costs of bankruptcy and other financial predicaments. Notwithstanding the criticism of the actual benefits of a tax shield and the cost of bankruptcy, he gives a generalized idea about a firm's value-maximizing effort of substituting debt for equity or equity for debt. Figure 3.1 illustrates Myers' original idea of the static trade-off theory. The horizontal axis represents debt and the vertical axis represents the market value of a firm. In a no-debt scenario, a firm's market value is constant (represented by the horizontal line). The upper curve represents the benefits of using tax shields, while the lower curve represents the cost of financial distress. The optimal capital structure is found at the maximum point on the present value of financial distress curve (dotted line). At any point beyond this, the cost of financial distress outweighs the benefits of the debt tax shield.

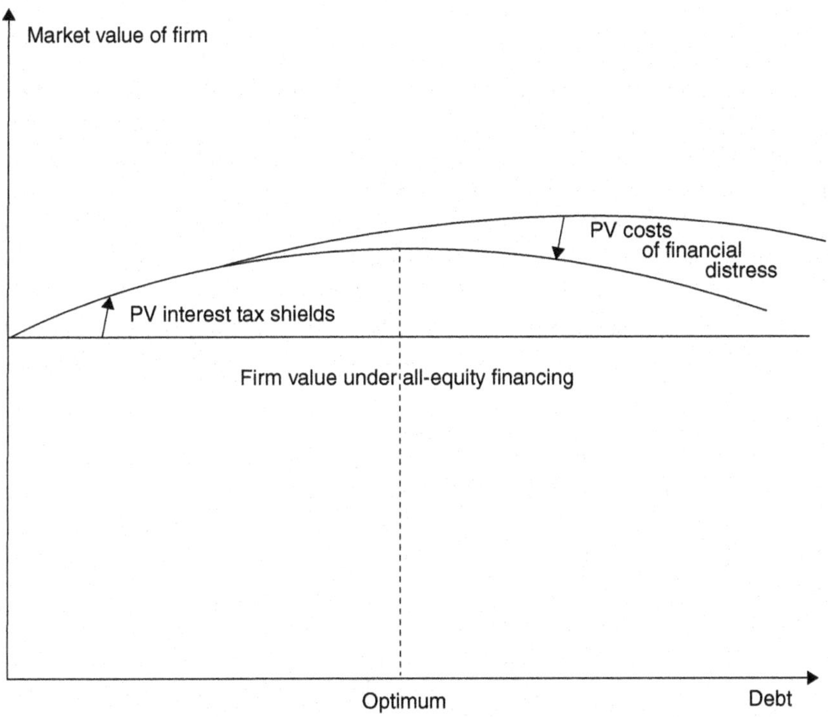

FIGURE 3.1 The static trade-off theory (Myers, 1984). PV, present value

However, as the optimal point is dynamic in nature, firms normally set a target debt level and gradually move towards it. In reality, this adjustment involves costs and lags which prevents two firms from having the exact same debt ratio. The other reasons why firms may have different optimum debt ratios include:

- *The rate of adjustment:* In the real world, the rate of adjustment varies across firms. In addition, the cost of adjustment and the associated lag also varies between firms, especially if they are operating in different industries.
- *Firm-specific factors:* For some firms, firm-specific events may hinder their ability to move towards their target leverage ratio.
- *Tax law:* The complex tax code in the real world also causes variations in the target level. Diversified features of tax codes and varying tax rates across countries, or across industries within the same country produce different conclusions regarding the target and how this target can be reached.
- *Bankruptcy cost:* The bankruptcy cost can be explained as the cost of financial distress. For liquidation, it includes legal and administrative costs of bankruptcy. For a surviving firm, it includes moral hazard, monitoring costs, and the loss of the firm's goodwill. Firms also differ in their level of bankruptcy exposure and associated bankruptcy costs, based on which their optimum debt ratios may also differ.

Pecking order theory

The pecking order theory was popularized by Myers in 1984 in his paper 'The capital structure puzzle'. According to Myers, 'A firm is said to follow a pecking order if it prefers internal to external financing and debt to new equity if external financing is used' (Myers, 1984). Pecking order theory advocates that firms should follow a hierarchical order when issuing securities. The order arises because of the costs associated with issuing securities, such as transaction cost and the cost of having asymmetric information. The pecking order theory prevails in situations where the cost of issuing risky securities is higher than the costs and benefits proposed by the trade-off model (Fama and French, 2005).

Myers and Majluf (1984) did not formally include debt in their analysis. If debts are available and risk-free, this works similar to internal financing. If debts are riskier, then a pecking order exists and debt falls somewhere between retained earnings and new equity. However, identifying the equilibrium point for debt in the pecking order is not easy. When both equity and debt financing are feasible, there could be multiple equilibria.

The sequence of financing according to the pecking order theory is as follows: firms should use retained earnings first, because this does not create any asymmetric information problem; then they should use low-risk debt, and then risky debt (Figure 3.2). Finally, new equity should be issued only under duress, or when investment exceeds earnings such that financing with debt would produce

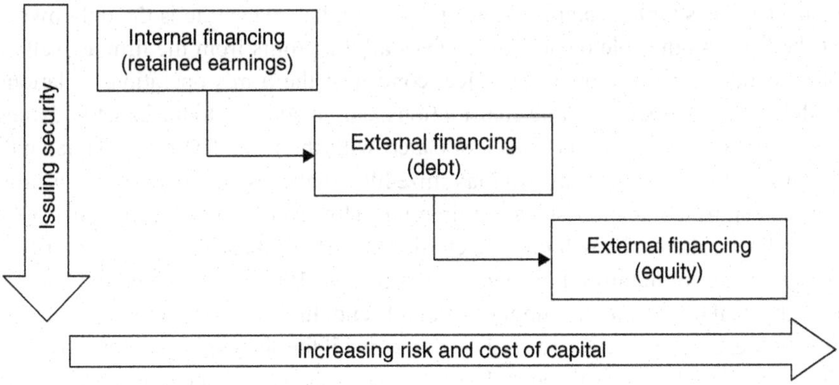

FIGURE 3.2 The pecking order hierarchy of financing

excessive leverage (Myers, 1984). Similarly, for retiring securities, firms should retire debt first. In subsequent studies, Shyam-Sunder and Myers (1999) argued that the problem of asymmetric information of new common stock also applies to repurchase, and should be treated similarly. Therefore, firms should only retire equity when leverage is low or when poor investment opportunities lower the value of debt capacity.

The two most cited reasons for the existence of the pecking order theory of financing are adverse selection and agency problems.

Adverse selection: Adverse selection is the result of asymmetric information; it arises in a situation when one party has more information than others. In any firm, owners and managers tend to possess more knowledge about the firm, and know its true value and growth opportunities. Outside investors normally possess less information and often become skeptical about management's choice of issuing new securities or buyback of securities. When a firm declares the issuance of new equity, outside investors start to think that the firm 'is overvalued, that's why the management is issuing equity'. As a reflex of their perception, they adjust the valuation of the firm downwards, and as a result, the market price of the firm's share declines. On the other hand, when the management announces its decision to buy back securities, investors tend to believe that the shares of the company 'is undervalued, that's why the management is repurchasing their stocks'. Consequently, they adjust their valuation about the firm upwards, and as a result, the market price of that firm's share increases. This unwarranted movement of a firm's share price can have an adverse impact on its survival. Internal financing, on the other hand, poses no such problems, and as such, whenever feasible, should be the preferred option.

Agency problem: The agency problem is the conflict of interest between the managers (agents) and the shareholders (principals). In modern diffused-ownership corporations, the owners are normally separate from the management, which creates agency problems, and therefore, agency costs. The problem arises when management prioritizes its own preferences and benefits over shareholders' goals.

Consider this simple example: James manages a firm where he is the only owner of the firm. As the sole owner, he receives all the profits from the firm as well as other benefits, e.g. the physical office, control of the firm's operations, relations with his employees, charitable contributions, etc. In addition to the benefits, James also bears all the costs and risks associated with the firm. Therefore, James will always try to make decisions that maximize his benefits as well as his firm's wealth while keeping costs and risks at a minimum. However, if James owns only 50% of the firm's shares, he will only be entitled to 50% of its profits, costs, and risks. As a manager of the firm, however, he can receive 100% of all the other benefits, e.g. physical office, buying supplies from a friend, luxury business tours, while the cost of these non-monetary rewards is borne by all the shareholders. Now consider the case where James owns only 5% of the firm's shares. In such a scenario, James as a manager will be more concerned about increasing his personal benefits by improving non-monetary rewards, because he knows he is only incurring a fraction of the cost while receiving the full benefits. To maximize his benefits, he is also more likely to take decisions that no longer maximize shareholders' wealth.

This tendency to put managers' own benefits above shareholders' wealth can also be seen in the choices managers make when it comes to choosing financing sources and selecting investment options. Consider the example of two investment opportunities (A and B) with the same initial investment shown in Table 3.2. With an equal probability of each set of return, both options have the same expected rate of return, option A,

$$\frac{15+15+15}{3}=15\%,$$

and option B,

$$\frac{25+15+5}{3}=15\%.$$

However, the standard deviation of the return for option B,

$$\sqrt{\frac{(25-15)^2+(15-15)^2+(5-15)^2}{3}}=8.16,$$

TABLE 3.2 Financing options

Option A	*Option B*
15%	25%
15%	15%
15%	5%

is much higher than that for option A,

$$\sqrt{\frac{(15-15)^2+(15-15)^2+(15-15)^2}{3}}=0.00,$$

signifying more risk for option B. James, when he is the sole owner, will choose option A, with an equal return and lower risk. However, when he is the owner of only a fraction of the firm, he will be indifferent between the two options. There is a higher probability that he will choose option B if the firm is in distress or his remuneration is tied to his performance, because in option B there is a chance of getting 25% return while increasing shareholders' risk.

To reduce the magnitude of this problem, other shareholders can increase their monitoring of James' activities or tie James' remuneration to his performance. Both monitoring and issuing performance bonuses involve cost, referred to as agency cost. Excessive monitoring activities to control managers' behaviour also creates another type of agency problem. Typically, managers are reluctant to explain details of their projects to outside investors and expose themselves to investors' monitoring. Therefore, they prefer retained earnings to external financing (Frank and Goyal, 2008). Management's reluctance to explain details of their projects to outsiders is one of the main arguments behind agency theory.

According to Myers (2003) and Jensen and Meckling (1976), some version of agency theory, especially the agency cost of equity, implies the existence of a financing hierarchy, i.e. a pecking order. They argue that using internal financing or even risk-free external debt is acceptable, but the introduction of equity results in underinvestment. A simple example can help illustrate this problem. James is the only shareholder of his firm and he has two investment opportunities – building a factory for producing a new product, or building a new office for himself. Both require the same amount of investment. If he has the funds for only one project, it is more likely that he will build the factory as it will increase his future earnings. If internal funding is not available, then James has two options – use debt or issue new equity. If he uses debt, he needs to pay a fixed amount as interest to his creditors. Therefore, in order to ensure his firm generates the additional amount of cash flow to cover the interest, he will opt to build the factory. However, if he uses equity, he is not committed to pay any fixed amount to the shareholders. In this situation, building an office is more attractive to James, since he gets the benefits from the office exclusively, whereas he would have to share the profits from the factory with other owners. This tendency of managers to maximize their own benefits by opting to issue external equity leads to underinvestment in the firm.

Transaction cost: In addition to adverse selection and the agency problem, transaction cost is also a major determinant of the existence of a pecking order. According to Myers (1984), transaction cost alone can produce pecking order behaviour if it is higher for equity than for debt, and higher for debt than for retained earnings. For example, issuing equity involves many complex and time-consuming activities. It also incurs investment banking cost, legal and regulatory fees, taxes, and marketing and promotional cost. Issuing debt also incurs such costs, but investment bankers normally charge less for debt than for equity. In addition, taxes and legal requirements are also less restrictive for debt than for equity. Therefore, in situations where the transaction cost is higher for equity than for debt, and higher for debt than for retained earnings, even without any information asymmetry, a pecking order can exist.

Real-world evidence of traditional models

The two traditional theories of capital structure, the trade-off model and the pecking order theory, have experienced a broad spectrum of success. Both models are able to explain general patterns in capital structure choices in the real world. The effect and influence of leverage on capital structure and the impact of firms' characteristics on firms' financing decisions are well documented. Empirical studies have found that firms with high leverage ratios differ fundamentally from firms with low leverage ratios, and there is a positive relationship between the level of leverage and debt maturity. Large, mature, slow-growth, and profitable firms, with more tangible assets, have longer debt maturity periods than smaller, younger, high-growth, less profitable firms, with fewer tangible assets. Firms in the latter group also use more lease financing than debt (Graham and Leary, 2011). In addition to that, Lemmon, Roberts, and Zender (2008) and Graham and Leary (2011) find that the variation in leverage is more cross-sectional than within a firm. Furthermore, most of this cross-sectional variation is within an industry rather than across industries. However, neither models can comprehensively explain the observed heterogeneity in capital structures.

Existence of a pecking order

The main proponent of the pecking order hypothesis was Myers himself. In his paper 'The capital structure puzzles', he empirically proved that the static trade-off theory fails to explain firms' financing behaviour. In support of his pecking order hypothesis, he showed that aggregate investment is mainly financed by internally generated funds. New issue of equity is relatively very small. According to him, companies avoid common stock and other risky securities to avoid the dilemma between rejecting positive net present value projects and issuing stock at a very low rate. They also maintain a low level of dividend to avoid the need for issuing stock. Firms do borrow debt, but at a restricted level to ensure it is safe. He also suggests that the pecking order theory depends on 'sticky dividends', i.e. a company sets a target dividend, prefers to stick to it, and, if possible, constantly increases the dividend so as to not offer an amount lower than past dividends.

Some companies even follow this positively sticky dividend so strongly that they increase dividends even in bad times, and in the worst case they do not issue any dividend at all, but they never issue a dividend lower than any amounts they issued in the past periods.

The proponents of pecking order theory mainly used stationary aggregate leverage to validate their theory. In his study, Wright (2004) showed that, despite some fluctuations between 1900–2002, the leverage stayed within a very narrow band. A similar trend was also observed in the ratio of leverage. Over the past half century, the aggregate market-based leverage ratio has been about 32% (Frank and Goyal, 2008). Researchers also focused on the changes in debt in order to assess the pecking order theory. Shyam-Sunder and Myers (1999) examined how short-term variations in investment and earnings influenced the level of debt. The theory predicts that with short-term sticky dividends, debt increases when investments exceed earnings, and debt falls when earnings exceed investments. According to their theory, in the case of financing deficit, the estimated slope coefficient of net debt issue should be 1. In an analysis of 157 large firms with an estimated coefficient of 0.75, they found strong support for the pecking order hypothesis (Shyam-Sunder and Myers, 1999). Korajczyk, Lucas, and McDonald (1990) found evidence that stock issues are typically followed by debt issues, and therefore leverage changes caused by equity issuances are only temporary (Eckbo and Masulis, 1995; Alti, 2006). Other empirical studies on small and medium-sized firms also found evidence consistent with the pecking order argument (Chittenden, Hall, and Hutchinson, 1996; Michaelas, Chittenden, and Poutziouris, 1999).

Deviation from the pecking order

Whereas earlier literature strongly supports the pecking order theory, more recent studies provide evidence that rejects the pecking order hypothesis in firms' capital structure choices. Empirical studies have proved that firms adjust their debt frequently. The financing deficit plays a role in these decisions. In a study on a large cross-section of publicly traded US firms, Frank and Goyal (2003) found that firms use external financing heavily. Net issue of equity is a better predictor of financing deficit than the net issue of debt. Apart from the aforementioned study, Eugene Fama and Kenneth French reject the pecking order hypothesis on several occasions (Fama and French, 2002; Fama and French, 2005). In their study 'Financing decisions: who issues stock?', they conducted a comprehensive analysis on about 5000 firms and divided them into two groups, small and big. They found that during 1973–1982, on average, 67 per cent of the firms issued some equity each year, and the proportion rose to 74 per cent for 1983–1992, and to 86 per cent for 1993–2002. The trend is more conclusive for S&P 100 firms. Most of the firms in the S&P 500 index made net issues rather than net repurchases, and every firm issued shares every year. In conclusion, they rejected the pecking order hypothesis because, while the theory suggests that firms issue equity only under duress, in reality almost every firm issues equity in every year (Fama and French, 2005).

Reconciliation

Some researchers tried to reconcile the findings presented by Fama and French (2002) and Frank and Goyal (2003) with the findings of Shyam-Sunder and Myers (1999). Lemmon and Zender (2010) argued that the idea of debt capacity is important in understanding the rejection of the pecking order theory. According to them, firms issue debt when there is no debt restriction, but when there is a debt constraint they issue equity. To test their hypothesis, they used debt rating as a measure of debt constraint, and firms with debt rating were considered unconstrained. The empirical analysis proved that firms with no debt rating are small, high-growth firms that use equity extensively. This result is consistent with both Fama and French (2002) and Frank and Goyal (2003).

Some researchers have highlighted firm-specific factors as the main reasons for the existence of a pecking order. Petersen and Rajan (1994) argued that firms follow a pecking order of borrowing over time, starting with the closest sources and then progressing to more external sources. Leverage decreases with maturity, and firms only use retained earnings and equity at a mature stage (Petersen and Rajan, 1994). La Rocca et al. (2009), in an analysis of small European firms, found that firms' life cycle plays a major role in their capital structure. In the early stage, firms use debt as a first choice, but tend to replace debt by internal capital during the maturity stage. The study also showed that the life cycle theory is homogenous across industries and over time (La Rocca et al., 2009). Anderson and Carverhill (2011) suggested that general business conditions play an important role in firms' financing hierarchy. In times of good business conditions, the hierarchy of financing is first internal funds, then short-term debt, and then finally equity. However, in poorer business conditions, firms tend to avoid short-term debt; instead, they use equity if internal funds are not available (Anderson and Carverhill, 2011).

In a study of US firms, De Jong, Verbeek, and Verwijmeren (2011) revealed that pecking order theory is a better predictor of firms' security issue decisions, whereas trade-off theory is a stronger predictor of repurchase decisions. Using the state-dependent nature of financing policy, Leary and Roberts (2008) found that while firms follow a financing hierarchy, there are three different forms of hierarchy. The first is the pecking order hierarchy (internal funds first, then debt, then equity); the second is the debt capacity constraint hierarchy (cash first, then equity); and the final one is the cash constraint hierarchy (debt first, then equity). In a recent study using the quantile regression method, Chay et al. (2015) supported the first (internal–external) rung of the pecking order. They found that investment is more responsive to internal funds than to external funds, except for top-level investment. However, they found little evidence to support the second (debt-equity) rung of the pecking order, as investments are more responsive to equity than debt (Chay et al., 2015).

Determinants of capital structure for traditional firms

The discussion of trade-off theory and pecking order theory, and the associated literature, helps us to identify the factors that affect the capital structure choices of firms.

- *Firm's characteristics:* Firm-specific characteristics, like size, profitability, liquidity, and growth opportunity, explain firms' capital structure behaviour. The trade-off theory and the pecking order theory have different views of the impact of size on firms' capital structures. The trade-off theory suggests that larger firms have greater leverage ratios because they have better access to credit. In addition, diversification reduces large firms' probability of bankruptcy and increases their ability to incorporate more debt into their capital structure. In contrast, the pecking order theory suggests that larger firms should have less debt because there is less information asymmetry. As using debt involves fixed interest payments, highly profitable firms tend to use more debt than do struggling firms. In the context of liquidity, firms with sufficient liquid assets will use the excess cash to fund their investment, and thus they tend to possess less debt. This proposition is also supported by agency theory, which suggests that firms with excessive liquid assets are more attractive for a takeover, and in order to minimize this risk, managers of these firms are inclined to invest these funds more aggressively, even in unprofitable projects. Lastly, high-growth firms normally use more debt financing than low-growth firms.
- *Stage of a firm's life cycle:* Modern firms are initially funded mostly by debt capital. Furthermore, firms utilize debt more extensively in earlier stages of their business life cycle. As the firm approaches maturity, however, it gradually replaces debt with internal capital.
- *Earnings variability:* Both the pecking order and trade-off models predict that riskier firms have a lower leverage ratio, but for different reasons. According to the trade-off theory, earnings variability reduces forecasted future earnings, increasing the cost of debt and making debt less attractive. As per the pecking order theory, volatile earnings increase the probability of default, resulting in lower leverage.
- *Asset tangibility:* Tangible assets can be used as collateral for the issuance of debt. The existence of tangible assets reduces agency cost and information asymmetry. Therefore, firms with more tangible assets hold more debt in their capital structure composition. Debt maturity is also longer for these type of firms.

- *Agency problem and asymmetric information:* Managers tend to possess more information about the firm than ordinary shareholders do. This information asymmetry gives managers an advantage when deciding the best sources of funds for the firms. Sometimes, however, managers may use this information to maximize their own benefits instead of those of the shareholders, giving rise to the agency problem. Issuing of debt requires contractual obligations and monitoring of the firm's operations by the debt providers. As such, managers prefer to use equity instead of debt to retain control themselves.
- *Tax implications:* The main motivation for using debt, and all the related theories of capital structure, is the existence of tax. Without taxes, firms would be indifferent between using equity and debt. Tax-deductible interest expenses incentivize firms to use debt and maximize earnings per share for their shareholders. Before issuing debt, every firm weighs the tax–bankruptcy benefits and costs, and chooses the mix of debt and equity that maximizes tax benefits while minimizing bankruptcy costs.

Islamic finance and prohibition of debt

Unlike the case for conventional finance, theories describing optimal capital structure choices for *shariah*-compliant firms are still at the infancy stage. In the conventional space, the option of choosing different capital structure compositions arises from the ability of a firm to use debt capital and receive tax benefits from interest expenses. However, one of the key principles of Islamic finance is the prohibition of *riba* – 'any predetermined or expected return on financial transactions' (Aggarwal and Yousef, 2000). In the Holy *Quran*, it is stated that Muslims should not involve themselves in interest-related transactions. In Islamic finance, the strict Quranic prohibition of *riba* is interpreted as a prohibition of any form of interest, which has the result of restricting the use of debt. Rather than engaging in a business as a creditor (debt financing), the Islamic religion promotes the concept of partnership (equity-based financing). Islamic scholars, as an alternative to debt, proposed using financial instruments that involve profit and loss sharing, such as *mudarabah* (joint venture) or *musharakah* (equity participation). These equity-based financing instruments offer profit and loss sharing and risk transformation between the borrower and lender.

While Islam strongly discourages the use of interest-bearing instruments like debts, there are some debt-like instruments issued by Islamic banks that can be used by firms as a substitute for debt. Both *murabaha* (cost plus mark-up) and *ijarah* (lease-based funding) offer a number of debt-like features. Through these instruments, the bank purchases an asset and then resells the asset to the firm at a fixed markup price over a certain period of time. Although these assets are widely used by Islamic banks and *shariah*-compliant firms, Islamic scholars have proposed restricting the use of such instruments as these could be used as a back door for charging interest.

From the macro perspective, many Islamic scholars believe that interest-based debt financing, a major component of capital structure, is the root cause of all financial crises. Therefore, Islamic regulatory bodies have issued regulations that restrict the use of debt financing. The objective of this restriction is to protect the *shariah* compatibility status of the firms listed in the capital market. For example, Accounting and Audit Organization for Islamic Financial Institutions (AAOIFI) *shariah* standard no. 21 approved debt financing of up to 30 per cent of total capital (AAOIFI 2010). Similarly, the Dow Jones Islamic Market and Financial Times Stock Exchange require that the debt to equity ratio must be equal to or less than 33 per cent, and income generated from interest must not exceed 9 per cent of a firm's total income (Rahman, 2010). Likewise, the Bursa Malaysia requires *shariah*-compliant firms to have proper debt ratios, implying that firms with high debt ratios compared to their assets cannot be listed in the exchange as a *shariah*-compliant firm. It also requires that interest-related income shall not exceed 10 per cent of a firm's total income.

To better illustrate the restriction of debt in Islamic finance, Ahmed (2007) put forward a refined equation from the basic balance sheet model. We know that assets equal liabilities plus owners' equity:

$$A = L + E$$

Separating the current portion of assets and liabilities from the fixed portion, we get

$$A_c + A_{ft} + A_{fi} = L_c + L_d + E_c + E_a + \mathrm{RE},$$

where assets are classified as current assets (A_c), tangible fixed assets (A_{ft}), and intangible fixed assets (A_{fi}). Similarly, liabilities are classified as current liabilities (L_c) and long-term debt (L_d). Finally, equity is classified as common stock (E_c), paid in capital (E_a), and retained earnings (RE). As the capital structure decision of a firm involves long-term debt and equity, and since Islamic finance requires that debt must be asset-backed and must not exceed the tangible assets, we propose the constraint of debt restriction to be:

$$L_d \leq A_{ft}.$$

We can denote the debt constraints in terms of ratios by dividing both sides by total assets:

$$l_d \leq a_{ft},$$

where l_d is the debt to total assets ratio and a_{ft} is the tangible fixed assets to total assets ratio. Therefore, the leverage ratio of an Islamic firm must be equal to or lower than the tangible assets ratio of that firm (Ahmed, 2007).

Capital structure of Islamic firms: additional factors to consider

The concept and utilization of debt is one of the most controversial issues in Islamic finance. Debt is a major building block of the modern financial system. Conventional finance promotes debt financing by improving firms' value with an increasing debt ratio. However, the debt-to-equity combination decision is not straightforward for Islamic firms due to the unfair return associated with debt financing. Debt allows its providers to receive money (interest) without exerting any effort. Thus, a financial system that consists of debt will not ensure justice to its beneficiaries. To ensure justice in society, Islamic finance prohibits the use of debt as a source of funds. This restriction makes the application of most of the traditional capital structure models irrelevant for *shariah*-compliant firms. Recalling both the trade-off theory and the pecking order theory from the earlier discussion, the idea of an optimum capital structure comes from the use of debt as a source of funds. Trade-off theory suggests firms evaluate both benefits and costs of debt, and use debt until costs outweigh benefits; while pecking order theory suggests using debt before using additional equity. Both these traditional models prefer debt before equity in some form.

However, debt is restricted in Islamic finance. Although some contemporary scholars and institutions have agreed to allow the use of some limited amount of debt, they still prefer equity to debt. It is yet to settle whether *shariah*-compliant firms should be allowed to use debt at all, and if not, what other instruments could be used to effectively compete with traditional firms. Due to the aforementioned reasons, we cannot directly apply the traditional models to calculate the optimum capital structure for *shariah*-compliant firms. As Islamic finance is a relatively new phenomenon, researchers have yet to reach a consensus about what constitutes an optimum capital structure for *shariah*-compliant firms. Ongoing research seeks to identify the factors that affect *shariah*-compliant firms' capital structures and develop models that will effectively capture both the debt restriction and the profit-maximizing aspect of *shariah*-compliant firms. This part of the chapter will provide an idea of current developments in the Islamic capital structure literature, and of the extent to which the traditional models can help explain the capital structure choices of *shariah*-compliant firms.

Although traditional models cannot be applied directly to *shariah*-compliant firms, various aspects of traditional models can help us understand capital structure choices of these firms. Similar to conventional firms, many traditional determining factors are found to be influential on the capital structure of *shariah*-compliant firms as well. The impact of size, profitability, liquidity, and growth on Islamic firms' capital structure is similar to that of conventional firms. In line with the agency theory of capital structure, empirical studies have found that profitability has a negative impact on a firm's leverage ratio (Al-Ajmi, Hussain, and Al-Saleh, 2009; Omet, 2006). Also, larger Islamic firms have less information asymmetry, less risk of bankruptcy, and greater power to issue more debt. The pecking order theory is also valid when it comes to the impact of growth on Islamic firms. Due to higher demand for funds, growth firms use more short-term debt than mature, slow-growth firms. Adopting both trade-off theory and pecking order theory, the empirical studies found that the effect of liquidity on leverage is negative for most *shariah*-compliant firms (Al-Ajmi, Hussain, and Al-Saleh, 2009; Omet, 2006; De Jong, Verbeek, and Verwijmeren, 2011). However, asset tangibility has a contradictory effect on Islamic firms' capital structure, unlike in the case of conventional firms. Due to the *zakat* effect (see p. 70) and low access to long-term debt, unlike conventional firms, *shariah*-compliant firms use equity to fund their long-term assets (Omet, 2006). In addition to the traditional factors, there are a few other factors that significantly influence the capital structure decisions of Islamic firms.

Debt threshold

Given tax shield benefits, it is very difficult for an all-equity firm to compete with a leveraged firm. Furthermore, initially raising sufficient capital for a start-up is also very difficult without debt. Considering these factors, some scholars agreed to allow Islamic firms to have a certain level of debt in their capital structure. This acceptable threshold permits a debt to equity ratio of 30–33 per cent. In Saudi Arabia, the maximum debt ratio allowed for a *shariah*-compliant firm is 33 per cent. If the debt ratio exceeds this threshold, the company is excluded from the Islamic *shariah*-compliant index (Al-Ajmi, Hussain, and Al-Saleh, 2009). The same maximum debt ratio (33 per cent) is also required by the Dow Jones Islamic Market and Financial Times Stock Exchange, while the AAOIFI only allows debt financing up to 30 per cent. Islamic firms' tendency to maintain a *shariah*-acceptable debt-equity ratio varies across countries. In a study on Malaysian firms, Hassan, Shafi, and Mohamed (2012) found a significant difference in the debt ratio between conventional and *shariah*-compliant firms. In Saudi Arabia, where religious belief influences the capital structure of domestically owned banks, a study found that the debt ratio is significantly lower in domestically owned banks than in foreign-owned banks (Abraham, 2013). As domestic banks are mainly Islamic banks, they tend to maintain *shariah*-approved levels of low debt in their capital structure. Firms in Kuwait, Jordan, Oman, and Saudi Arabia in general have a low leverage ratio (Omet, 2006). However, as the latter study does not compare the firms from these Islamic countries to those in non-Islamic countries, conclusive evidence cannot be drawn about whether this low leverage ratio is the result of the influence of Islam or if it is a general phenomenon for all firms in this region.

Dual banking system

Most Muslim countries do not have a well-developed secondary market for debt, and therefore the only source of debt is bank loans. This restricts the ability of firms to use high leverage. In most Muslim countries, Islamic banks and conventional banks operate side by side. Islamic banks, however, do not offer traditional interest-based credit facilities. Conforming to Islamic law, they offer sale-based, lease-based, and equity-based credit facilities such as *murabaha* (cost plus mark-up), *ijarah* (lease-based), *mudarabah* (joint-venture), and *musharakah* (equity participation). The existence of an Islamic banking system allows *shariah*-compliant firms in Muslim countries to use *shariah*-compliant instruments for financing.

Zakat

Islamic capital structure, with its inclusion of *zakat*, differs vastly from traditional capital structure models. *Zakat*, the third pillar of Islam, 'is corporate taxation levied on wealth that remains idle and unused by the business for the whole Islamic calendar year' (Al-Ajmi, Hussain, and Al-Saleh, 2009). Various models have been proposed to incorporate *zakat* payments into the capital structure combination of debt and equity. The inclusion of *zakat* payments could negate the benefits of the tax shield offered by conventional debt, thereby making equity more attractive than debt. Firms in some Muslim countries (Saudi Arabia, Bahrain, Kuwait, Qatar, Oman, and the United Arab Emirates) are required to pay *zakat* on their net worth. *Zakat* is levied at 2.5 per cent of the total *zakat* base. The *zakat* base includes paid-up capital, retained earnings, long-term debt, notes payable, advance used for financing fixed assets, and adjusted net income. The *zakat* base includes most of the debt instruments used by traditional firms to take advantage of the debt tax shield. Thus, the incorporation of *zakat* makes equity a more attractive source of funding for *shariah*-compliant firms.

Sukuk

Although the issuance of *sukuk* (Islamic bonds) is very limited and minimally active in the secondary market, the implications of *sukuk* for the capital structure of *shariah*-compliant firms are significant. *Sukuk*, a hybrid instrument that pays dividends instead of interest, allows both investors and the firm to stay within the parameters of the *shariah*. The recent development of the *sukuk* market has added a new dimension to the field of Islamic capital structure, and also provides *shariah*-compliant firms an alternative form of non-equity financing. To illustrate, in the period from 2001 to 2007, 417 firms in Malaysia issued a total of USD 61 billion in *sukuk*. Empirical studies have found that large firms have easy access to *sukuk*, and firms that have used *sukuk* are more likely to issue *sukuk* in the future. Additionally, *shariah*-compliant firms prefer *sukuk* over normal bonds, and the issuance of *sukuk* impacts both normal bonds and traditional bank loans.

Debt maturity

Gunn and Shackman (2014) conducted a cross-country comparison using 658 firms across 16 Muslim and non-Muslim countries. The results showed no significant differences between the total debt ratios of the firms in the Muslim and non-Muslim countries. However, they found a significant difference in the choice of short-term and long-term debt between Muslim and non-Muslim countries. Firms in Muslim countries showed strong preference for short-term debt. This result suggests that *shariah*-compliant firms in Muslim countries do have other options to raise capital to maintain leverage ratios similar to those of firms in non-Muslim countries. However, heavy dependence on short-term debt indicates that these firms in Muslim countries are missing out on the advantage of stability offered by long-term debt, which makes them vulnerable in times of financial distress or credit crunch (Gunn and Shackman, 2014).

In addition to religion, national culture also has an influence on firms' capital structure choices (Lam, Zhang, and Lee, 2012; Antonczyk and Salzmann, 2014; Ramirez and Kwok, 2009). As national culture is vastly influenced by the religious view of the majority of the population, it is believed that Islam as a religion probably has an indirect effect of promoting a culture of less risk-averse managers. The true influence of Islam on firms' capital structure choices probably cannot be readily observed by the traditional methodology of identifying the difference in leverage ratios between conventional and *shariah*-compliant firms in the same country.

Conclusion

The optimal capital structure for firms has been a matter of debate for almost half a century. During this period, significant progress has been made in understanding the capital structure decisions of conventional firms. However, researchers have yet to reach a consensus about the optimal capital structure for *shariah*-compliant firms. Many Islamic scholars believe that interest-based debt financing, a major component of capital structure, is the root cause of all financial crises. Due to the prohibition of interest (*riba*) in Islam, some researchers believe that there should not be any place for debt in *shariah*-compliant firms' capital structures. However, many Islamic scholars, as well as some regulatory agencies, have agreed to allow up to 33 per cent of debt for *shariah*-compliant firms. The question we face now is how, in the real world, do *shariah*-compliant firms decide the composition of their capital structure? What should be their target level of debt, and can they maximize their value by using no debt at all?

This chapter has attempted to review the capital structure decision of *shariah*-compliant firms from an Islamic finance perspective. From this review, it is clear that there is a need to develop new theories to explain capital structure for *shariah*-compliant firms. The existing theories may be necessary but are not sufficient to explain the financing choices of *shariah*-compliant firms. Many consensuses are necessary before we can expand our understanding of this topic. For instance, is *sukuk* considered to be debt or debt-like? What is the treatment of *sukuk* in terms of tax saving? Is there a tax exemption for returns received from *sukuk*? How do *shariah* restrictions impact the performance and valuation of *shariah*-compliant firms? Perhaps there are too many vague interpretations that require clarification before we can reach an understanding to the level that has been achieved for conventional finance.

References

AAOIFI (2010). Accounting and Auditing Standards for Islamic Financial Institutions, Accounting and Auditing Organization for Islamic Financial Institutions, Manama.

Abraham, A. (2013). Foreign ownership and bank performance metrics in Saudi Arabia. *International Journal of Islamic and Middle Eastern Finance and Management*, *6*(1), pp. 43–50.

Aggarwal, R., and Yousef, T. (2000). Islamic banks and investment financing. *Journal of Money, Credit and Banking*, *32*(1), pp. 93–120.

Ahmed, H. (2007). *Issues in Islamic corporate finance: capital structure in firms* (Research Paper), No 70, Occasional Papers, The Islamic Research and Teaching Institute (IRTI). Jeddah, Saudi Arabia: Islamic Development Bank.

Al-Ajmi, J., Hussain, H., and Al-Saleh, N. (2009). Decisions on capital structure in a *zakat* environment with prohibition of *riba*. *The Journal of Risk Finance*, *10*(5), pp. 460–476.

Alti, A. (2006). How persistent is the impact of market timing on capital structure? *The Journal of Finance*, *61*(4), pp. 1681–1710.

Anderson, R., and Carverhill, A. (2011). Corporate liquidity and capital structure. *Review of Financial Studies*, *25*(3), pp. 797–837.

Antonczyk, R., and Salzmann, A. (2014). Overconfidence and optimism: The effect of national culture on capital structure. *Research in International Business and Finance*, *31*, pp. 132–151.

Chay, J., Park, S., Kim, S., and Suh, J. (2015). Financing hierarchy: Evidence from quantile regression. *Journal of Corporate Finance*, *33*, pp. 147–163.

Chittenden, F., Hall, G., and Hutchinson, P. (1996). Small firm growth, access to capital markets and financial structure: Review of issues and an empirical investigation. *Small Business Economics*, *8*(1), pp. 59–67.

De Jong, A., Verbeek, M., and Verwijmeren, P. (2011). Firms' debt–equity decisions when the static tradeoff theory and the pecking order theory disagree. *Journal of Banking & Finance*, *35*(5), pp. 1303–1314.

Eckbo, B., and Masulis, R. (1995). Seasoned equity offerings: a survey. In R. Jarrow, V. Maksimovic, and W. Ziemba (Eds), *Handbooks in Operation Research and Management Science* (7, pp. 1017–1072). North Holland: Elsevier.

Fama, E., and French, K. (2002). Testing trade-off and pecking order predictions about dividends and debt. *Review of Financial Studies*, *15*(1), pp. 1–33.

Fama, E., and French, K. (2005). Financing decisions: Who issues stock? *Journal of Financial Economics*, *76*(3), pp. 549–582.

Frank, M., and Goyal, V. (2003). Testing the pecking order theory of capital structure. *Journal of Financial Economics*, *67*(2), pp. 217–248.

Frank, M., and Goyal, V. (2008). Trade-off and pecking order theories of debt. In B. Espen Eckbo (Ed.), *Handbook of Empirical CORPorate Finance: Empire Corporate Finance* (2, pp. 135–202). North Holland: Elsevier.

Graham, J., and Leary, M. (2011). A review of empirical capital structure research and directions for the future. *Annual Review of Financial Economics*, *3*(1), pp. 309–345.

Gunn, T., and Shackman, J. (2014). A comparative analysis of the implications of the Islamic religion on corporate capital structures of firms in emerging market countries. *International Journal of Islamic and Middle Eastern Finance and Management*, *7*(3), pp. 277–287.

Hassan, N., Shafi, R., and Mohamed, S. (2012). The determinants of capital structure: Evaluation between shariah-compliant and conventional companies. *International*

Conference on Innovation, Management and Technology Research. DOI: 10.1109/ICIMTR.2012.6236389.

Jensen, M., and Meckling, W. (1976). Theory of the firm: Managerial behavior, agency costs and ownership structure. *Journal of Financial Economics, 3*(4), pp. 305–360.

Korajczyk, R., Lucas, D., and McDonald, R. (1990). Understanding stock price behavior around the time of an equity issue. In R. G. Hubbard (Ed.), *Asymmetric Information, Corporate Finance, and Investment* (pp. 257–277). Chicago: University of Chicago Press.

Kraus, A., and Litzenberger, R. (1973). A state-preference model of optimal financial leverage. *The Journal of Finance, 28*(4), pp. 911–922.

La Rocca, M., La Rocca, T., Gerace, D., and Smark, C. (2009). Effect of diversification on capital structure. *Accounting & Finance, 49*(4), pp. 799–826.

Lam, S., Zhang, W., and Lee, R. (2012). The norm theory of capital structure: International evidence. *International Review of Finance 13*(1), pp. 111–135.

Leary, M., and Roberts, M. (2008). The pecking order, debt capacity, and information asymmetry. *Journal of Financial Economics, 95*(3), pp. 332–355.

Lemmon, M., and Zender, J. (2010). Debt capacity and tests of capital structure theories. *Journal of Financial and Quantitative Analysis, 45*(5), pp. 1161–1187.

Lemmon, M., Roberts, M., and Zender, J. (2008). Back to the beginning: Persistence and the cross-section of corporate capital structure. *The Journal of Finance, 63*(4), pp. 1575–1608.

Michaelas, N., Chittenden, F., and Poutziouris, P. (1999). Financial policy and capital structure choice in UK SMEs: Empirical evidence from company panel data. *Small Business Economics, 12*(2), pp. 113–130.

Modigliani, F., and Miller, M. (1958). The cost of capital, corporation finance and the theory of investment. *The American Economic Review, 48*(3), pp. 261–297.

Modigliani, F., and Miller, M. (1963). Corporate income taxes and the cost of capital: A correction. *The American Economic Review, 53*(3), pp. 433–443.

Myers, S. (1984). The capital structure puzzle. *The Journal of Finance, 39*(3), pp. 575–592.

Myers, S. (2003). Financing of corporations. *Handbook of the Economics of Finance*, 1(A), pp. 215–253.

Myers, S., and Majluf, N. (1984). Corporate financing and investment decisions when firms have information that investors do not have. *Journal of Financial Economics, 13*(2), pp. 187–221.

Omet, G. (2006). Ownership structure and capital structure: Evidence from the Jordanian capital market (1995–2003). *Corporate Ownership and Control, 3*(4), pp. 99–107.

Petersen, M., and Rajan, R. (1994). The benefits of lending relationships: Evidence from small business data. *The Journal of Finance, 49*(1), pp. 3–37.

Rahman, A. (2010). Financing structure and insolvency risk exposure of Islamic banks. *Financial Markets and Portfolio Management, 24*(4), pp. 419–440.

Ramirez, A., and Kwok, C. (2009). Multinationality as a moderator of national institutions: The case of culture and capital structure decisions. *Multinational Business Review, 17*(3), pp. 2–28.

Shyam-Sunder, L., and Myers, S. (1999). Testing static tradeoff against pecking order models of capital structure. *Journal of Financial Economics, 51*(2), pp. 219–244.

Wright, S. (2004). Measures of stock market value and returns for the U.S. nonfinancial corporate sector, 1900–2002. *Review of Income and Wealth, 50*(4), pp. 561–584.

Zaher, T., and Kabir Hassan, M. (2001). A comparative literature survey of Islamic finance and banking. *Financial Markets, Institutions and Instruments, 10*(4), pp. 155–199.

4

ISLAMIC VENTURE CAPITAL FINANCING

Ali Ashraf and M. Kabir Hassan

Introduction

In this chapter, we discuss Islamic venture capital financing, an emerging concept in Islamic finance. We start with a brief description of various sources for start-up financing, define some key terms, and talk about the conventional venture capital life cycle. We then discuss the theory and practice of Islamic venture capital financing, and present a real-life case study on an Islamic venture capital fund.

Venture financing: some definitions

Venture capital financing is the process of investing in start-up businesses where investors lock in their investment for longer period. The person or individual or firm that engages in such investment activity is cited as *venture capitalist,* and the start-up business or venture receiving initial investment is called the *venture firm* or *venture business* or *business venture* (the terms are synonymous). In starting a new business or new venture, an entrepreneur can raise initial capital in three possible ways:

- *From the founder/ friends/ family:* The entrepreneur may start with her own investment or initial capital from friends or family; this is the most frequent source for start-up ventures.
- *From angel investors: Angel investors* or *business angels* are high net-worth individuals who are willing to invest in start-ups for a longer time horizon; they may have entrepreneurial experience in the same or a related industry.
- *From venture capital funds:* These are mutual funds managed by professional investment managers. Fund investors are mostly institutional investors and

pension funds that are willing to lock in capital for the long term in various start-up projects or ventures.

'Business angels' and 'angel investors' are terms that have recently become popular within the investment industry (Morrissette, 2007); angels are also known as *private investors* or *informal investors*. In addition to much needed capital, angel investors can bring in additional resources such as management expertise, brand recognition, market and sales distribution prowess, or technology sharing. More recently, angel investors have been forming investment platforms that provide certain support services for business angels in the selection and management of their venture investments. One popular example is the "Dragons' Den" or "Shark Tank" television show, where the "dragons" or "sharks" are the angel investors willing to invest in new ventures.

Conventional venture capital finance

Investing in new ventures is generally riskier than investing in established companies and requires investing for a longer time horizon. A venture capitalist is willing to accept several failures for each successful venture; the possibility of enormous returns on winning ventures compensates for the many likely failed ventures (Sahlman, 1994).

The venture capital fund (VCF) is one of the major types of private equity that are not traded on exchanges; it provides the benefit of risk diversification for the venture capitalists or investors in the VCF as the fund invests in a pool of new ventures. The VCF can take equity interest in a business venture in any stage: at idea stage or seed stage, an early stage, formative stage, or later stage. Although VCFs invest in start-up ventures for the longer time frame, they are different from business angels because of their sources of funding, investment size, and investment objectives. Table 4.1 compares business angels and VCFs.

History of venture capital finance

The first formal venture capital firm traced back in history was the American Research and Development Corporation (ARD), which started in 1946 after World War II. Until 1960, when the ARD-backed business venture Digital Equipment Corporation (DEC) became a success, the concept of venture capital was not well known among the majority of US investors (Bygrave & Timmons, 1992). In recent times, NASDAQ has seen the market capitalization of venture capital firms grow up to USD 5,205 billion in the year 2000.

Different types of venture capital financing

A venture capitalist can invest at different stages of the life cycle of a business or entrepreneurship. The following list is based on the stages of Kaplan & Strömberg (2002):

TABLE 4.1 Differences between business angels and venture capitalist funds

	Business angels	*Venture capital fund*
Funding source	Angel's own money	Investors
Number of deals per year	One every two years	Five to ten per year
Typical investment per company	Average US$ 50,000 to US$ 75,000	Average US$ 4 million
Company stage	Small, startup, early stage	Larger, expansion stage
Geographic focus/ orientation	Usually one or two hours from home	Usually nationwide/ regional
Sources of deals	Other angels, friends, business contacts	Proposals submitted, other venture capital funds
Decision makers	Experienced individuals, entrepreneurs	Fund managers, committees
Involvement	Hands-on	Strategic, board seat

Source: Morrissette (2007).

1. In *seed-stage financing,* the venture capitalist provides long-term capital at the idea generation stage, usually to support research and development of products and services.
2. In *early-stage financing,* investment takes place before the company starts its commercial production and sales of its products or services.
    a. In *start-up financing*, investment helps the start-up prepare for operations such as product development or initial marketing.
    b. In *first-stage financing,* the capital is used to start commercial production of goods or services.
3. *Formative-stage financing* may include investing either at seed stage or at early stage.
4. In *later-stage financing*, the investment capital is used after the business starts its commercial productions, but before any initial public offering (IPO).
    a. *Second-stage financing* refers to financing a business during its initial expansion phase; at this stage, it may be producing and selling its products and services, but it is struggling to earn consistent profits.
    b. *Third-stage financing* is generally used to finance major expansion projects. Examples are building, modifying, or reconstructing a physical plant or facility, or major improvement in an already existing manufacturing process or marketing strategy.
    c. *Mezzanine financing* is also called *bridge financing*; it refers to providing capital to business to support the expansion of the business before it can raise additional capital through an IPO.

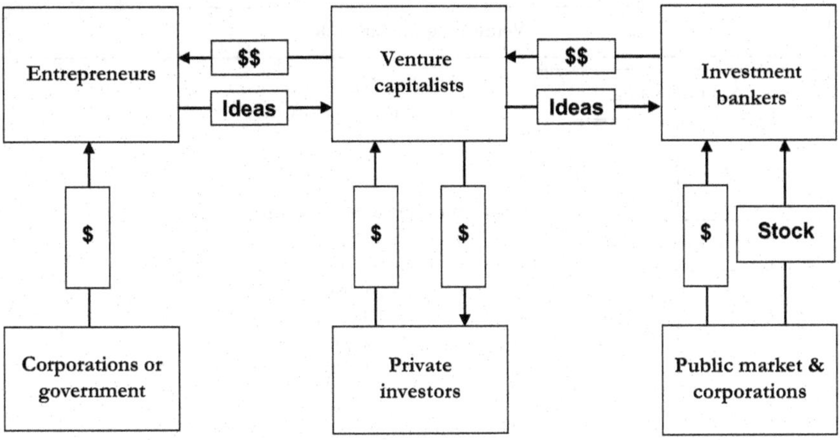

FIGURE 4.1 How the venture capital industry works
Source: Harvard Business Review (1998).

5. *Second-stage* and *third-stage financing* are also known as *expansion-stage financing.* Financing across various stages, from seed phase to mezzanine phase, is also referred to as *balanced stage financing.*

How does the venture capital industry work?

Figure 4.1 depicts the process of how venture capital works, and how a venture capitalist adds value to the business process as a whole. A *start-up firm* or a *distressed business* can look for additional equity investment from two possible sources: venture capital investment or government participation. In a venture capital fund, high-net-worth individuals or financial institutions provide the funding to invest in a large pool of venture investments, and the investors are willing to lock in their investment for a longer time horizon until the business becomes *profitable* or *marketable* through investment banks through either *private placement* or *IPOs* (Harvard Business Review, 1998).

The venture capital life cycle

Figure 4.2 presents a basic model of the diverse functions that venture capital fulfills at different stages of the venture capital cycle. In the first phase, the *fundraising stage*, the venture capitalist decides on the sources of the funds and their structures. In the second phase, the venture capitalist analyzes suitable investments and decides on the modalities, i.e. how the investment will take place, whether through common stock or other instruments. In the third phase, the

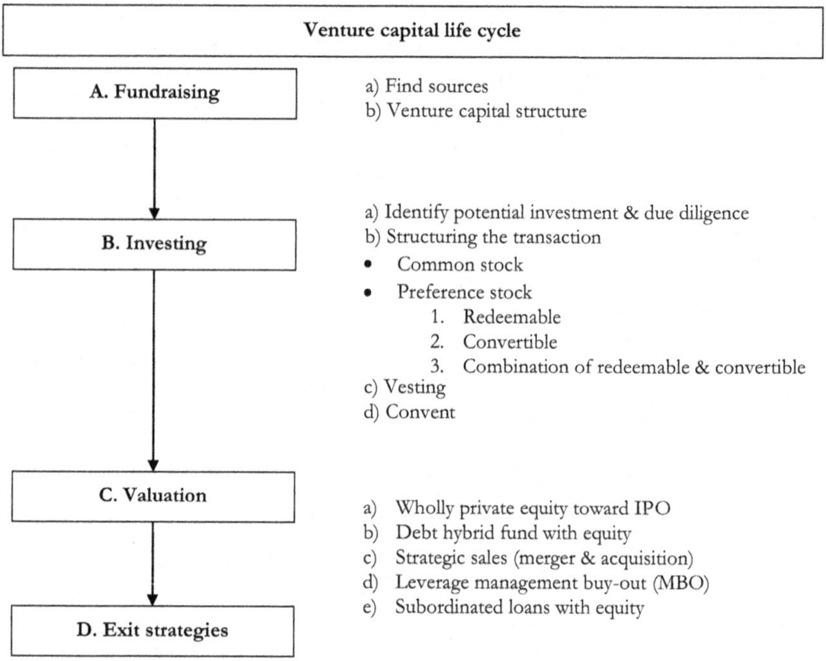

FIGURE 4.2 Venture capital life cycle
Source: Al-Rifai and Khan (2000).

venture capitalist assesses the intrinsic value of the investment before deciding on the exit strategy. In the fourth and final stage, the venture capitalist designs the exit strategy or strategies (Al-Rifai & Khan, 2000).

Types of liquidation/divestment

The last and most crucial phase of venture capital financing is called the exit phase, where the venture capitalists decides on the exit strategy, which can vary according to situational needs. In this phase, the venture capitalist is cashing out or liquidating the investment in order to realize the profit or gain, and often the exit strategy is stated in the contract terms. A venture capitalist can use a single or a combination of more than one exit strategies (Clement & Valerie, 2001):

1. Through *IPO:* By selling the shares in the venture in the capital market
2. Through *company buyback:* By repurchasing the shares in the venture from the capital market
3. Through *trade sale:* By selling the common stocks in the venture to another company
4. Through *write-off:* By liquidating the venture

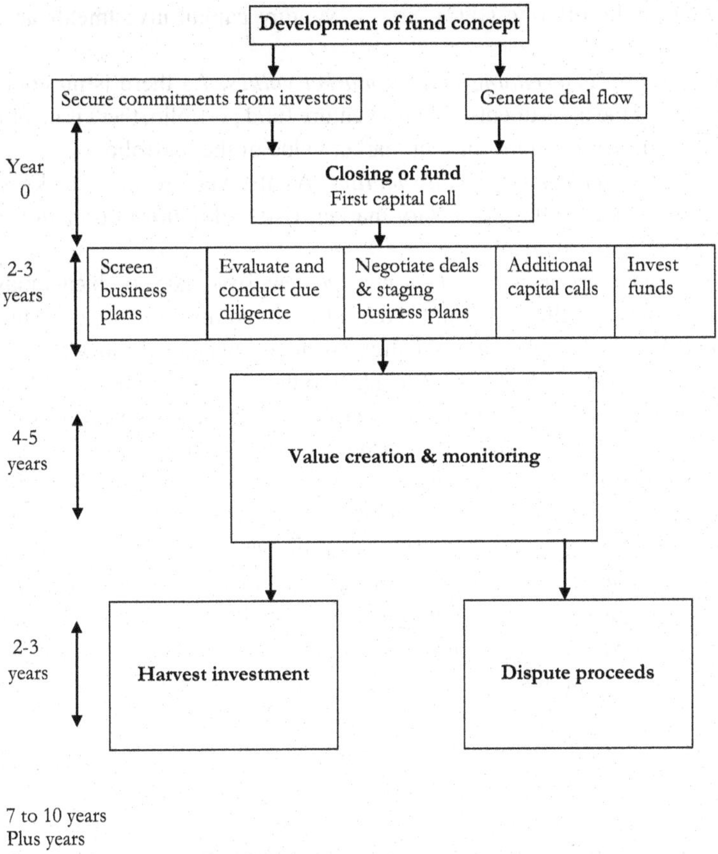

FIGURE 4.3 Venture capital investment process
Source: Ashraf (2009).

5. Through *secondary sale:* By selling the shares in the venture to another venture capital investor
6. Through *reorganization:* By restructuring the venture

In Figure 4.3 an at-a-glance overview is given of the venture capital investment process.

Investment characteristics of venture capital finance

The following are unique characteristics of venture capital investment:

- *Lack of liquidity:* Liquidation of each venture within a portfolio is dependent on the fund manager's ability and success in creating a buyout or issuing an initial public offering (IPO). So, the venture capital investments are rather illiquid.

- *Difficulty in determining current market values:* As there is no continuous trading of the investments within a venture fund portfolio, there is no objective way of determining the current market value of the portfolio.
- *Lack of historical return information:* As the venture firm stocks are not actively traded in the secondary market, risk and return information for the ventures is not available.
- *Entrepreneurial or management mismatches:* Two major problems may arise during the early life of a firm: (1) the entrepreneur may not be a good manager, and (2) as the business grows, entrepreneurs or managers who succeeded with small ventures may not be able to adapt to the demands of larger companies.
- *Compensation of fund managers:* Fund managers are generally rewarded by the size of the fund they are managing rather than by the performance of their funds. This type of incentives package encourages the fund managers to increase their investment size rather than to focus on performance, and that can create agency conflict within the venture capital fund.
- *Extensive operations analysis and advice:* More than financial engineering skill is required from the fund managers. Apart from extensive investments analysis, extensive operating management experience and industry know-how is also required.

Table 4.2 shows the main points of comparison between traditional corporate finance and venture capital.

Recent developments in venture capital financing

Trend to global diversification

In recent times, venture capital investing has expanded its investment frontiers and fund managers actively seek for investment opportunities across the globe to diversify their investment portfolio and seek higher returns. Since 1971, increasing numbers of venture capital investments are taking place across borders. Domestic investments usually perform better than international investments of similar size. The further away the investments are, the lower the returns. Difference in culture, business, and regulatory environment between the host and investing countries also affect profitability. Although returns on both domestic and global deals have declined since late 1990s, fund managers are still interested in investing in other countries, for two main reasons. First, there is the benefit of global diversification, and, second, the market for domestic deals is becoming increasingly saturated (Kenney et al., 2007).

Islamic approach to venture capital financing

In this part of the chapter we introduce the emerging concept of Islamic venture capital investment. We present a brief discussion of the wide range of financial

TABLE 4.2 Principal comparison points between traditional corporate finance and venture capital

	Feature	*Corporate finance*	*Venture capital*
1	Liquidity of shares	Shares are traded or liquid	Shares are less traded or illiquid
2	Management oversight	Investors do not actively participate	Investors actively engage in management
3	Market for corporate control	High	Low
4	Accessibility of capital	Capital easily accessible from market by issuing bonds or additional equity	*Early stage:* Capital can be raised from investors with high industry skills. *Later stage:* Capital can be raised by issuing IPOs or private placement
5	Project evaluation techniques	A wide variety of evaluation techniques	As companies do not pay dividends, only cash-flow-based models are used
6	Investment decisions	Single-stage	Multi-stage

IPO, initial public offering.

services provided by Islamic banks and then talk about the rationale of Islamic venture capital financing.

Why do we need Islamic venture capital financing?

In practice, Islamic banks (IB) overuse fixed-income instruments like *murabaha* and *ijarah* (see list below). There is a strong economic rationale for using equity financing in Islamic finance, as debts are usually associated with short-term investments and equity investments are long-term and necessary for economic growth. However, Islamic banks are generally reluctant to engage in long-term profit-sharing investments because of the uncertainty and risk involved.

One way to increase the use of profit-sharing modes of financing is to providing equity investment through alternate equity-based institutions, and venture capital financing can fill in this space. Equity investments from equity funds and venture capital firms can play a key role in financing for the start-up, and small and middle-sized firms (SMEs) that need funds for growth, and for firms in financial distress.

Figure 4.4 presents a snapshot of the variety of Islamic financing modes. Islamic finance offers a wide range of financing modes that caters to different needs of Islamic customers and businesses. Among these three basic categories, the *participatory mechanism* can be divided into two basic categories:

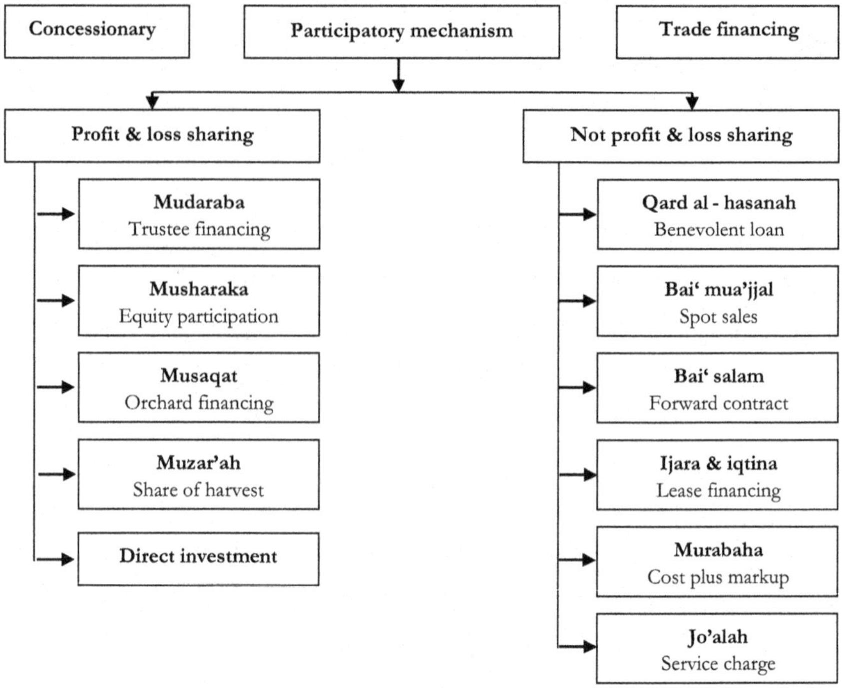

FIGURE 4.4 *Sharia'h*-compliant financing modes
Source: Kazarian (1993) and Iqbal and Mirakhor (1987).

- *Profit and loss sharing (PLS) instruments:* examples are *mudaraba* (a profit-and-loss sharing partnership arrangement between an investor and the business where investor provides capital either in cash or asset, and receiving business provides labor. So, in essence, *Mudaraba* is one special case of *Musharakah* where one party provides labor, instead of capital) and *musharaka* (a partnership structure in Islamic finance in which partners share the profit and loss of the business), which are equity instruments.
- *Mark-up/ fixed-income instruments:* examples are *murabaha* (a cost-plus financing in Islamic finance where the seller buys an asset and then sells at a profit, rather charging an interest) and *ijarah* (Islamic financing is similar to lease in conventional financing that leads to purchase of the asset eventually), which are debt instruments.

Between these two broad categories of Islamic financing modes, Islamic scholars often prefer PLS as "the essence of Islamic financing". One important feature of these PLS instruments is that they are all equity instruments. The economic impact of such equity instruments in the development of SMEs can be far reaching. As these equity instruments aim at equity interest in the development of new entrepreneurship, they are likely to share the risk and returns of these businesses in the longer time horizon. In addition, equity participation in terms of *musharaka* signifies that the equity investor in effect participates in the management decision making of the business, which also allows transfer of technology and development of human capital in the long run (Hassan, 2000).

However, over the last three decades, since the beginning of their operations, Islamic banks have become increasingly dependent on fixed-income or mark-up-based instruments, which are by their nature debt instruments. To meet different business needs of Islamic clients, Islamic banks have been using these debt instruments in innovative ways. For example, *murabaha* is used in different forms in trade financing, working-capital financing, and even for investment banking. *Ijarah* and *istisna* are used in long-term financing such as capital budgeting, project financing, and even in investment banking in creating *sukuk* (Islamic bonds that are structured in a special way to generate returns to investors, but are not based on prohibited Riba or Interest) (Hassan, 2005).

Although Islamic banks have innovated different uses of these debt instruments for various purposes, the bottom line remains the same: by no means can these innovations in debt instruments replace the need for equity instruments. We can analyze the need for higher participation in equity in Islamic Businesses from two perspectives:

1. *From the perspective of Islamic businesses or clients:* Islamic businesses and clients have obvious preferences about equity modes as opposed to debt instruments. As debt instruments require fixed debt servicing periodically, that increases the financial risks for Islamic businesses in both the short and the long term. On the other hand, equity modes, which are much more participatory in nature, may help them effectively share both risk and return with the financing partner.
2. *From the perspective of Islamic banks:* For Islamic banks which already depend heavily on debt instruments in making investments or loans, effective equity participation in Islamic banks or financial institutions can minimize risks by diversifying the investment types in their lending portfolio.

Although these economic rationales behind the preference for PLS instruments are well recognized and well documented throughout the existing literature on Islamic finance, Islamic banks have historically been hesitant to use equity instruments. They often cite different reasons for their non-preference for equity investments that are similar to the risk features of conventional equity investments, such as higher cost of closer monitoring, high risk of moral hazard, information asymmetry, longer time horizons, illiquidity, and a higher rate of failure (Dar & Presley, 2000).

Islamic VCFs, designed, structured, and operated in an Islamic *shariah*-compliant manner, can bridge the gap between the need of Islamic businesses for equity investment and the hesitancy on the part of Islamic banks towards participatory investment.

Similarity between conventional VCFs and Islamic VCFs

Since the objectives of an Islamic VCF are similar to those of its conventional counterpart, we may think of an Islamic VCF as a variant of a conventional VCF; however, we need to be aware of two operational aspects:

1. *Technical or operational matters* relating to running the institution efficiently enough to yield acceptable rates of return for the investors. This is similar for both conventional and Islamic VCFs. Both types of VCF use similar techniques and tools to reduce risks, manage the firms portfolio operations, evaluate ventures, carry through proceedings for IPOs, etc. The technical aspects can be value-neutral and can be adapted for Islamic VCF.
2. *Contractual engagements or transactions* between the venture capital firm and the business. Unlike the case for the technical aspects of operations, conventional and Islamic VCFs differ in the contracts used by agents involved in different transactions, because the contracts of an Islamic VCF are governed by *shariah* rules and regulations which are different from those of conventional financial contracts.

Islamic venture capital framework

In essence, the Islamic equity financing modes *mudaraba* and *musharaka* can be used in their purest form in Islamic venture capital financing. The overall business process of Islamic venture capital finance can be derived from the venture capital cycle, ensuring that each phase of the process complies with Islamic *shariah* principles. A graphic representation of the model is shown in Figure 4.5.

Although the basic business model of the Islamic VCF emulates the stages of the conventional VCF, there are significant difference in each of these phases as all financing instruments and contracts need to be *shariah*-compliant and should serve the core values of Islam. As such the model identifies the following broader steps:

1. *Raising funds* from possible sources through *shariah*-compliant modes of contract
2. *Investment analysis* through a combination of *shariah* screening and business/economic feasibility analysis
3. *Equity participation* in providing finance and management
4. *Exit strategies* based on liquidating investments through *shariah*-compliant ways

The venture capital cycle: an Islamic approach

In a VCF, the fund managers raise equity capital from institutional investors and high-risk-taking wealthy individual investors who participate as the *limited partners*. The VCF managers then make investments in a portfolio of business

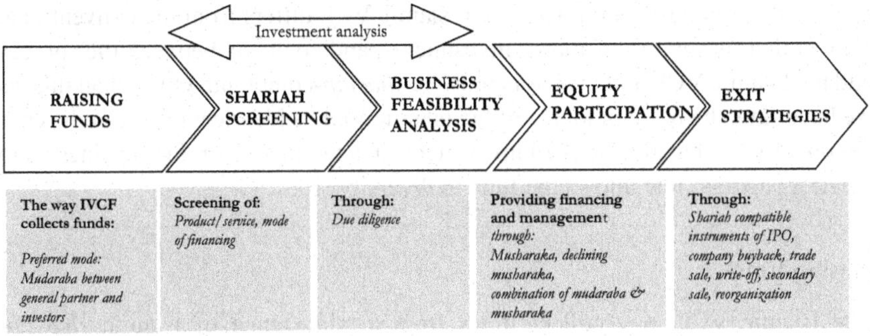

FIGURE 4.5 Business process of Islamic VCF
Source: Ali Ashraf (2009).

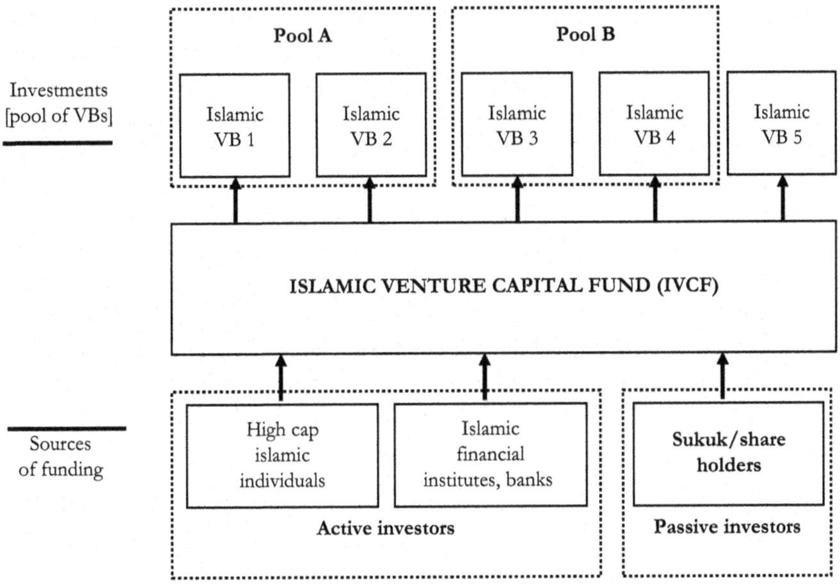

FIGURE 4.6 Fund management framework of Islamic VCF. VB, venture business
Source: Ashraf (2009).

ventures. So, the risk of failure in individual ventures is diversified in the VCF structure as number of ventures or businesses are pooled together. In addition to institutional and individual investors, VCFs can also collect funds from *funds of funds*. Management responsibility lies with the fund managers or private equity experts, who act as *general partners.* The Islamic VCF model extends the conventional VCF model; Figure 4.6 elaborates the broader model for fund collection and investment disbursement of the Islamic VCF.

The important aspect on which the Islamic VCF differs from the conventional VCF is that its sources of funds, investments, and contracts between the sources and the Islamic VCF and investors must be *shariah*-compliant. Other than this, as we have said, the basic rationale of the Islamic VCF is identical to that of the conventional VCF that aims to pool investments in a number of venture businesses to create a portfolio that allows the fund to diversify risks.

Raising funds

The Islamic VCF may collect funds from a wide range of Islamic *shariah*-compliant individuals and institutional investors, for example Islamic banks, *takaful* (an Islamic shariah compliant alternative of conventional Insurance that avoid *riba* (usury) and *gharar* (unnecessary risk taking)) companies, and other Islamic financial institutions through *mudaraba* (the entrepreneurial partner who provides expertise and management) contracts where Islamic VCF will act as *mudarib* and other investors or partners act as silent partners or *rab-ul-mal* (the investor who provides capital to Mudarib in a Mudaraba contract). Such *mudaraba* contracts may include different clauses or covenants so long as the contract clauses do not contradict *shariah* principles and have been agreed upon in advance (Hassan, 2000). Table 4.3 elaborates the basic structure of the *mudaraba* contract that Islamic VCF and investors may engage in.

The Islamic VCF can raise funds in different stages and lock them in for a long time like a conventional VCF. To restrict activities as a *mudarib*, the *mudaraba* contracts can include certain clauses and covenants with the consent of the investor and the Islamic VCF. For example, the remuneration of the *mudarib* can be either fixed or flexible. A combination package of fixed and flexible compensation is permissible if the contracts are separate contracts. Obligations may include proper attention to duty on part of one of the parties. If a failure is identified due

TABLE 4.3 *Shariah* compatibility of features of contracts between Islamic VCFs and Islamic investors

Feature	*Islamic alternative*
Limited partnership	*Mudaraba* contract
Funds raised in stages	Acceptable
Long-term contracts (funds locked in)	Acceptable
Cancelation of contract	Acceptable
Covenants imposed on general partners	Acceptable
Compensation to general partners	
– Fixed (wages or percentage of capital)	– Allowed
– Flexible (percentage of profit)	– Allowed
– Fixed and flexible	– Acceptable if contracts are separate

Source: Ahmed (2007).

to negligence and inaction of the agent, a demand for compensation can be made with the dissolution of the contract (Kharofa, 2000).

Selection and structuring of investments

The next stage for the Islamic VCF is selecting suitable businesses, and again this is similar to the conventional VCF. However, the IVCF performs an extra screening phase in selecting suitable businesses, called *shariah screening*. The new venture needs to operate in *shariah*-compliant ways and the products and services should not include any "non-permissible" or *haram* elements as identified in Islamic jurisprudence. After this initial *shariah* screening, the normal economic and technical criteria for selecting projects for investment may be used (Hassan, 2002).

Analysts often use the net present value (NPV) technique in computing the intrinsic value of potential investments, and consider a discount rate commensurate with the risk of the project. An IVCF may consider a firm's cost of equity as a relevant discount rate if the project is fully funded by equity (i.e., no debt at all).

Arrangement between the IVCF and the venture capital business

Once the Islamic VCF has selected a venture for investment, it signs a contract with the new venture; this is a *musharaka*-type contract that allows the manager of the Islamic VCF to actively participate in the management of the business venture. Table 4.4 summarizes the *shariah* compatibility of features of contract between Islamic VCFs and Islamic venture businesses.

Conventional equity investments such as private equity and venture capital investing are permissible so long as they follow the restrictions imposed by Islamic jurisprudence. Common stockholders are considered as the residual owners of the business and do not enjoy any special rights; in the case of bankruptcy or liquidation, common stockholders are paid after all other stakeholders. Such a system works better in conjunction with equality of ownership, but this is not the case for the majority of venture capital deals, as these firms prefer to be minority investors. Equity ownership is consistent with the profit-sharing principles of Islamic jurisprudence, and common stocks are *shariah*-compliant contracts as long as the business excludes any prohibited activities. Although Islamic contracts allow a great deal of flexibility regarding the distribution of different rights between the two parties, Islamic principles do not allow conventional *preferred stocks*. Preferred stockholders get priority over common stockholders during liquidation of a business, and they may have additional rights such as decision-making management control or the ability to receive dividends. Islamic scholars argue that preferred stock is a debt instrument in disguise, as it allows investors to preserve the face value of their original investment or provides a guaranteed return. Besides, the existence of a liquidation preference artificially favors one party at the expense of another.

TABLE 4.4 *Shariah* compatibility: contract features of Islamic VCF and Islamic venture business

Features	*Islamic alternative*
Criteria for selection firms to invest in	– Screening for compatibility with Islam – Economic
Equity contracts	*Musharaka* contract
Preferred stocks (for VCF)	No
Control rights different from ownership	Acceptable
Cash flow rights different from amount invested	Acceptable (different profit-sharing ratios)
Liquidation rights	Acceptable
Entrepreneurs compensation	– Acceptable
– Fixed (wages)	– Acceptable
– Flexible (percentage of profit)	– Acceptable if contracts are separate
– Fixed and flexible	
Vesting	Acceptable
Covenants	Acceptable

Source: Ahmed (2007).

The control rights over the firm can be different from the ownership stakes in the firm; an Islamic VCF may have a stronger voice in running the affairs of the firm relative to its shares in the venture business. The cash flow rights of the VCF can be larger than the amount invested; that is, the profit sharing ratio in favor of the VCF can be larger than its share in the capital as long as the parties involved have agreed upon it.

Entrepreneur/manager compensation schemes can be either fixed or flexible; in the latter the entrepreneur gets compensation as a percentage of profits. Contracts can include both *positive* and *negative* covenants that can guide the activities of the entrepreneur/manager.

Vesting, in terms of giving more control rights and/or share of profits to the entrepreneur as an incentive scheme, does not contradict the principles of *shariah*. Such vesting can be introduced in the contract in a couple of ways: either the financing and vesting features can be incorporated in a comprehensive contract that outlines the conditions under which certain clauses become operative, or else contracts for limited term periods can be signed, with successive contracts that will include newer terms dependent on the performance of the venture.

Figure 4.7 elaborates a *declining musharaka* contract between the Islamic VCF (equity provider) and its client the Islamic venture business (equity recipient), where the Islamic VCF, as a general partner, actively participates in the management of the venture in addition to providing the investment (Hassan, 2000).

In a *musharaka structure*, a single round of financing would involve the following steps:

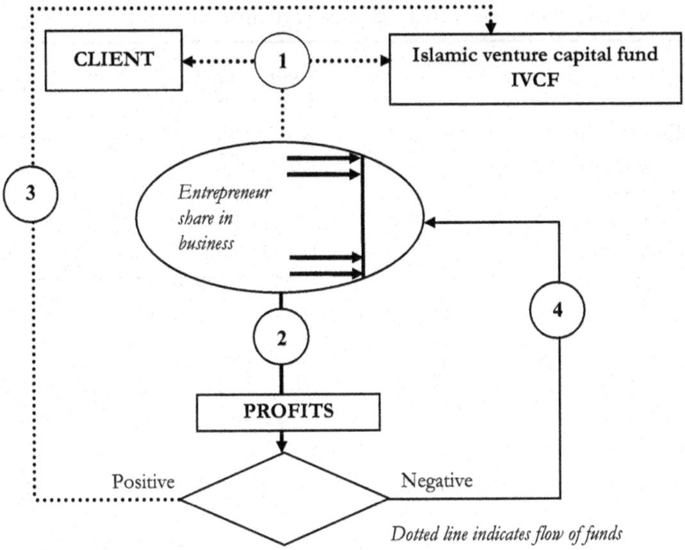

FIGURE 4.7 Venture financing through declining musharaka
Source: Ashraf (2009).

1. To begin with, the venture capitalist or VCF manager will discuss the business with the entrepreneur and both of them will agree to contribute capital to the business.
2. In addition to providing the capital, the VCF manager will also actively participate in managing the business and its operation, and the terms of engagement will be determined at the beginning.
3. The business can generate both positive and negative profits, as success in the business is not guaranteed, and the venture capitalist contract with the entrepreneur will be a profit and loss sharing contract.
4. If the business earns a positive profit, then profits will be shared between the entrepreneur and VCF in a pre-agreed ratio.
5. If the business is facing a loss or profits are negative, the loss will be shared between the entrepreneur and VCF as well, as agreed in the initial contract. This will effectively reduce their asset value but make their respective shares in the business unchanged.

Managing investments

In managing investments, IVCFs can participate in the board of directors of the firm and monitor the decision-making process on a regular basis, and also provide technical and managerial skills to the venture business. Management participation may engage in periodic evaluation of the performance of the venture business and ensure that there is no informational asymmetry between the VCF

TABLE 4.5 *Shariah* compatibility: management participation

Features	*Islamic alternative*
Participating in board	Acceptable
Management can be changed	Acceptable
Staged Financing	Acceptable
Providing non-financial services	Acceptable
Assistance in working capital needs	Using Islamic financial instruments

Source: Ahmed (2007).

and the business itself. The IVCF can include the option of removal of the manager of the venture business if the manager's performance does not meet certain criteria.

To reduce the concerns of moral hazard issues and informational asymmetry, the Islamic VCF manager and the entrepreneur can agree to use the *staged financing model* in which they will hold each other accountable during the different phases of financing. This can be done in two possible ways (Wang & Zhou, 2004; Landier, 2002):

1. A comprehensive signed contract may define the conditions of the funding at different stages. These conditions may relate to the needs and performance of the venture business.
2. Contracts may be signed periodically and new terms and conditions be negotiated at the time of signing the new contracts.

Table 4.5 summarizes Islamic *shariah* compatibility in relation to management participation issues.

Exiting investments

IVCFs can use a combination of different exit strategies: IPO, company buyback, trade sale, write-off, secondary sale, and reorganization (Clement & Valerie, 2001) (Table 4.6). All of these exit options can be acceptable from the *shariah* point of view if implemented in compliance with *shariah* norms, i.e., they must avoid *riba*, *maya-sir* (or *Maisir*, refers to gambling that is prohibited in Islam), *darar* (harmful activities that are prohibited in Islam), and other prohibited practices (Hassan, 2002). As such, the use of the specific possibilities must be included in the initial contract signed.

Case study of an IVCF

Injazat Technology Fund (ITF) is a venture capital firm registered in Bahrain and based in Dubai, United Arab Emirates. The objective of ITF is to invest in the

TABLE 4.6 *Shariah* compatibility: exit strategies

Feature	*Islamic alternative*
Initial public offering	Acceptable
Acquisition	Acceptable if the other party agrees
Secondary sale	Acceptable if the other party agrees
Buyback	Acceptable
Write-off	Acceptable

Source: Ahmed (2007).

emerging technology and telecom sector of the Gulf member countries through *shariah*-compliant principles. Its mission is to maximize the returns to its investors by nurturing growing companies while reducing overall risk by investing in a diversified portfolio of technology companies in the Middle East and North Africa (MENA) region.

Raising funds

ITF raised the funds through private placement; it is a five-year closed-end fund with a capital of US$ 50 million. The Islamic Corporation for the Development of the Private Sector (ICD), and the Gulf Finance House (GFH) are the major sponsors; each of them holds 25 percent of the equity in the fund. The remaining 50 percent of capital was raised from wealthy individuals and other institutional investors such as the Dubai Islamic Bank, Saudi Economic and Development Company, and Iran Foreign Investment Corporation (IFIC).

ITF raised the funds for investment in various stages; the investors are aware of the high risks of the fund and expect a high return. Investors as general partners oversee the operations of the ITF by being represented on its Board, and as a legal entity ITF gets paid for the management of funds in the form of a fixed fee and a flexible proportion of the realized profits. ITF, in turn, hires managers and professionals to manage its operations, and the employees receive fixed wages. General partners have imposed several conditions/restrictions on the activities of ITF, including diversification, limits to the amount of debt and amount of maximum investment in a single project, types of investment in certain sectors, and involvement of the managers in other activities.

Selecting and structuring investment

ITF uses several criteria in the selection process for projects; for example: the intellectual property rights content, technology content, management team, market potential of the product, etc. The ITF selection process goes through three major steps. First, it screens the projects to ensure compliance with the policies of the fund, such as the type of product and the place of operations. Next, it conducts preliminary assessment to ascertain the merits of the project; ITF management visits the project site and meets with the firm management. If the project appears satisfactory then it goes through the third and last stage of screening and due diligence.

ITF is very selective in awarding funding to new ventures. At the end of the selection process, the fund invests in about 5 percent of all applications. Having made its selection, it engages in a comprehensive contract with the venture. The fund expects a return of 20–25 percent from its investments. ITF usually has a minority stake (less than 50 percent) in its portfolio companies, but the contract gives it many control rights including management and *veto rights*. The contract contains both positive and negative covenants with which the manager of the portfolio company must comply.

A key condition in the contract is the nature of financing if the firm needs funds for working capital. If the portfolio firm needs funds, ITF tries to arrange funding from Islamic financial institutions. ITF does not practice vesting in terms of transferring control/ownership rights to the entrepreneur depending on performance, as the entrepreneur already has a relatively large share in the partner or venture company to start with.

Managing investments

ITF actively participates in the management and business operations of its venture firms. ITF oversees the operations of the venture firm to ensure that the firm is managed professionally and efficiently so that it can reach the ITF's objectives. ITF's representation in the board of its portfolio companies is on a pro rata basis. ITF usually has at least two members (or 30 percent) on the boards of the companies, one being a senior management professional of ITF and the other chosen from the general partners. While the ITF does not get directly involved in the production and distribution aspects of the venture firm, it may assist in strategy, marketing, networking, and accessing additional financing.

ITF uses various financial indicators to assess the performance of the venture firm. It monitors sales, costs, and net profit figures on a monthly basis. Other than board meetings, which are held every two months, there are frequent meetings between the officials of the ITF and the venture firm. The management of the latter has to submit reports in reporting formats suggested by ITF.

Exiting investments

The optimal investment period before exiting is three to five years. The criteria used to decide the time of exit are capital appreciation and/or maturity for IPO. The subscription agreement gives ITF a dominant control in deciding when to exit. Table 4.7 summarizes ITF's approach to exit strategy.

Although ITF considers an IPO as the preferred exit strategy, it does not regard IPO as a practical exit strategy as the stock markets in the region in general and the

TABLE 4.7 Comparison of *shariah*-compliant exit options in order of preference (1 highest, 5 lowest)

	IPO	*Acquisition*[1]	*Secondary sale*[2]	*Buyback*[3]	*Write-off*[4]
Overall preferred option	1	2	4	3	5
Ease in the operational sense	4	2	3	1	5
Ease in the legal sense	3	2	4	1	5
Ease from *shariah* point of view	3	1	2	4	5

IPO, initial public offering; VCF, venture capital fund.
1 Private sale of entire firm.
2 VCF sells its share only.
3 VCF sells its share to entrepreneur.
4 Offload a project that is not performing well.

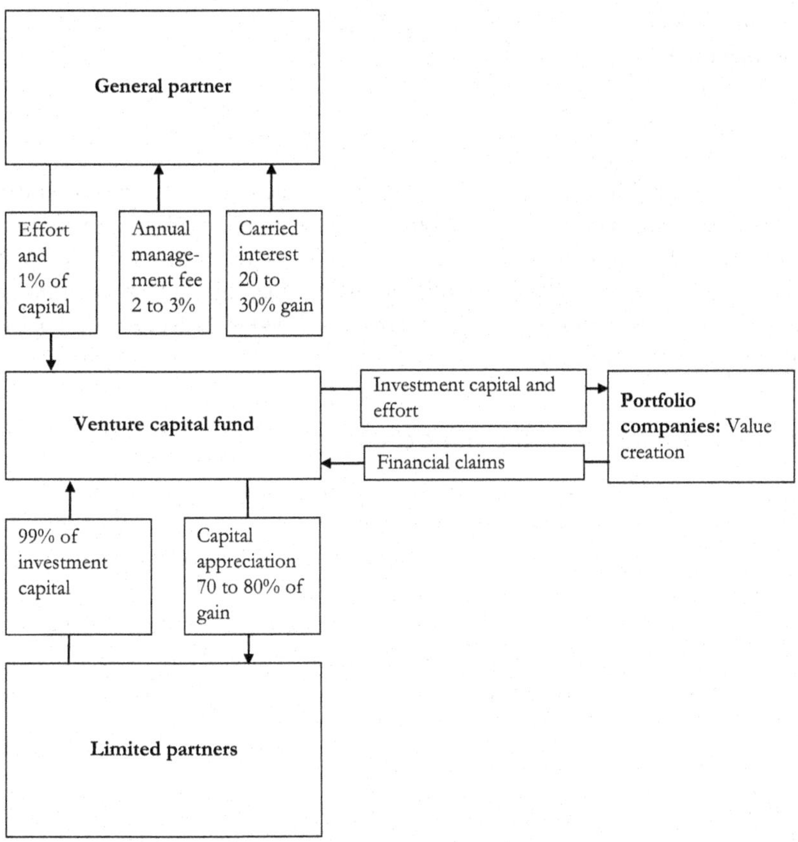

FIGURE 4.8 Organizational structure of venture capital investment

United Arab Emirates in particular are relatively small and dormant. Instead, ITF regards buyback as the key exit strategy, and this option is usually include in the subscription agreement. One possible way of buyback is to use the diminishing *musharaka* principle. Among all the alternatives, *write-off* is the least preferred option in all cases.

Economic and developmental impact of IVCFs

Role of IVCF as a financial intermediary

Although Islamic banking has expanded rapidly over the last four decades, because of various operational hazards and other problems Islamic banks overuse debt instruments despite the fact that equity financing is the essence of Islamic financing. IVCFs can play a significant role as a financial intermediary by bridging the gap between the demand side of equity financing, Islamic businesses, and the supply side, Islamic financial institutions, Islamic banks, Islamic mutual funds, individuals and other funds. The Islamic VCF structure allows Islamic banks and other financial institutions to minimize their operational risks and costs below what the individual Islamic bank would incur if participating in a direct equity investment in SMEs.

Risk diversification

Islamic banks and financial institutions have become overly dependent on debt-based investments; equity participation provides the opportunity to diversify the overall risk of their investment/lending portfolio significantly. Venture capital investing provides these Islamic institutions with equity investment opportunities. Similarly, for Islamic businesses already overburdened with debts, equity participation would provide relief.

Increasing values along the value chain

By its nature, venture capital financing is possible in any phase of the business life cycle. A VCF has significant flexibility in making strategic investments. Depending on the economic analysis and business feasibility, a VCF may take equity interest in different stages of the value chain of a particular industry. For example: a VCF may identify a sick business in the garments industry that requires second-stage financing. As the VCF performs due diligence and feasibility analysis, it foresees that if a knitwear unit were added along the value chain, the business could again be profitable (Ashraf, 2009).

Synergy

As the Islamic VCF undertakes equity investments in a pool of venture capital/business in different industrial sectors or segments, experience along the value chains of industrial segments of one industry may have significant synergy effects on the VCF managers. This could increase the business expertise of VCF managers in providing further equity financing to other units, and this may enhance the successes of the venture businesses in the long run (Gompers et al., 2009).

Development of human capital

The impact of venture capital on the development of human capital in SMEs is well documented. Since venture capital financing puts in management and technical expertise along with financing, for startup business through sick businesses, it can add significantly to the development of entrepreneurship and human capital. As the structure of the Islamic VCF allows it to pool a number of venture businesses in diversified industrial segments, the developmental impact on human capital will be occur in diversified industrial segments of an economy.

Scope of future growth and global integration

With globalization, financial innovations are taking place across the globe. Financial systems around the world are becoming increasingly integrated. For the Islamic banking sector, the Islamic VCF can provide an alternative platform to integrate global Islamic funds or allow equity participation from Islamic banks in one country to businesses in other Islamic countries. That way Islamic VCFs can also become a much broader tool in integrating equity investments across Islamic financial systems globally and help global Islamic banks to diversify risk in their investment portfolios. Different Islamic VCFs in different countries can be interlinked through some Islamic funds of funds (which may emulate conventional fund of funds), connected through *shariah*-compliant modes of contracts such as the *mudaraba* mode with funds other than Islamic VCFs as silent partners and Islamic VCFs remaining as general/ management partners.

Recommendations for Islamic VCFs

Venture capital financing is an emerging concept in Islamic financing. Equity investment participations in the startup or middle stages of a business can be beneficial for the businesses, the financial institutions, and the overall economy as whole.

For Islamic banks, which are overdependent on debt-based, less-risky investment and loan portfolios, the Islamic VCF provides an opportunity to take part in risky equity investments for the longer term through an alternative investment vehicle. VCFs generally specialize in analyzing, selecting, managing, and investing in new ventures; they also take part in managing the daily operations of the new ventures, and invest in a pool of new ventures. So, for Islamic banks and other financial institutions, the Islamic VCF provides excellent alternative way to diversify their portfolio.

Besides the obvious benefit of diversification, Islamic banks can benefit from investing through Islamic VCFs in two other ways. First, many of these banks face the problem of excess liquidity. Venture capital investments provide an opportunity to utilize these funds better by channeling them into long-term and potentially high-yield instruments. Second, an encouraging development in the venture capital industry has been the emergence of a large secondary market for trading limited partner interests.

The US venture capital sector continues to outperform other asset classes over the long term. Importantly, these venture capital returns do not correlate perfectly to other sector returns such as public equities and real estate returns. Therefore, diversifying into venture capital presents an opportunity to increase returns without an equivalent increase in risk.

References

Ahmed, H. (2007). Issues in Islamic corporate finance: Capital structure in firms. *Jeddah: Islamic Research and Training Institute, Islamic Development Bank Group.*

Ashraf, A. (2009). Islamic approach to venture capital finance: An alternative to financing MME. *Second International Conference on Inclusive Islamic Financial Sector Development.*

Buchner, A., Espenlaub, S., Khurshed, A., & Mohamed, A. (2018). Cross-border venture capital investments: The impact of foreignness on returns. *Journal of International Business Studies, 49*(5), 575–604.

Bygrave, W., & Timmons, J. (1992). *Venture Capital at the Crossroads.* Harvard Business School Press.

Dar, H. A., & Presley, J. R. (2000). Lack of profit loss sharing in Islamic banking: Management and control imbalances. *Economic Research Paper No. 00/24,* Department of Economics, Loughborough University.

Farid, A., & Madehah, F. (2007). *The potential of Musha?? rakah as an Islamic financial structure for venture capital funding in Malaysia.* Doctoral dissertation, Durham University, UK.

Gompers, P., & Lerner, J. (1999). *The Venture-Capital Cycle.* Cambridge; The MIT Press.

Gompers, P., Kovner, A., & Lerner, J. (2009). Specialization and success: Evidence from venture capital. *Journal of Economics & Management Strategy, 18*(3), 817–844.

Kaplan, S. N. & Strömberg, P. (2002). Characteristics, contracts, and actions: Evidence from venture capitalist analyses. *Journal of Finance, 59*(5), 2173–2206.

Kenney, M., Haemmig, M., & Richard, W. G. (2007). *The Globalization of the Venture Capital Industry.*

Kerr, W. R., Lerner, J., & Schoar, A. (2011). The consequences of entrepreneurial finance: Evidence from angel financings. *The Review of Financial Studies, 27*(1), 20–55.

Landier, A. (2002). *Start-up Financing: From Banks to Venture Capital.* The University of Chicago, Graduate School of Business.

Morrissette, S. G. (2007). A profile of angel investors. *The Journal of Private Equity,* 52–66.

Oseni, U., Hassan, K., & Matri, D. (2013). An Islamic finance model for the small and medium-sized enterprises in France. *JKAU: Islamic Economics, 26*(2), 153–180.

Sahlman, W. A. (1990). The structure and governance of venture-capital organization. *Journal of Financial Economics,* 27, 473–521.

Sahlman, W. A. (1994). Insights from the venture capital model of project governance. *Business Economics*, 35–37.
Wallmeroth, J., Wirtz, P., & Groh, A. P. (2018). Venture capital, angel financing, and crowdfunding of entrepreneurial ventures: A literature review. *Foundations and Trends in Entrepreneurship*, *14*(1), 1–129.
Wang, S., & Zhou, H. (2004). Staged financing in venture capital: Moral hazard and risks. *Journal of Corporate Finance*, *10*(1), 131–155.

5

IPO UNDERPRICING, REGULATION, SENTIMENT AND *SHARIAH* SCREENING IN BANGLADESH

Mamunur Rashid, Varun K. Sibdoyal, Md. Shafiul Islam and Ahsanur Rahman

Introduction

'Initial public offering' (IPO) can be defined as the first-time sale of securities (Brau and Fawcett 2006) by a private company with the intent of becoming public (Brau and Fawcett, 2006; Brav, Brav and Jiang, 2009; Caglio, Hanley and Marietta-Westberg, 2011; Ghosh, 2004; Ritter and Welch, 2002; Tinic, 1988). The IPO acts as a portal through which a company can bolster its liquidity, enabling it to raise colossal amounts of capital and allowing it to trade its securities publicly (Brau and Fawcett, 2006; Brav et al., 2009; Bubna and Prabhala, 2006; Chemmanur and Fulghieri, 1999). On the downside, the IPO often entails a lengthy process and also naturally portrays itself as a risky procedure given the uncertainty that revolves around the long-term performance of the offers. More importantly, however, this finance-raising activity has more often than not been clouded by underpricing. IPO underpricing occurs when the offer price is below its first day trading price, triggering an abnormal initial return. Primary markets all over the world are subject to numerous anomalies, but the most pertinent one seems to be IPO underpricing.

This chapter acknowledges the haziness that surrounds the determinants of IPO underpricing and aims at shedding light on this matter by trying to narrow down the gap between theory and practice. 'Investor sentiment' is the behavioural change among investors due to overly optimistic or pessimistic expectations (Hirshleifer, 2001). With investor decisions being greatly a function of investor sentiment, managers often take advantage of the misevaluations that result from irrational decisions (Baker and Stein, 2004). Different studies on investor sentiment try to explore the difference between the actual and normative manner of investor behaviour (Ritter, 2003a; Subrahmanyam, 2007). Investor sentiment has been found to have a potential impact on IPOs (Agarwal, Liu and Rhee, 2008;

Bradley, Gonas, Highfield and Roskelley, 2009; Leite, 2005; Narayanasamy, Rashid and Ibrahim, 2018; Narayanasamy and Rashid, 2015), the direction and magnitude of which will be looked into in this chapter.

Regulators, on their part, are responsible for building a mechanism that will facilitate better functioning of the IPO markets. Book building, for instance, is one of several methods that can be used to value an IPO and is in fact considered the most efficient one. In principle, book building can alter the incentives of both investors and investment banks participating in the IPO process. These changes can be positive or negative. Discretion in allocation gives investment banks greater credibility in extracting information because it offers investors the incentive to engage in more aggressive information gathering prior to an issue. On the other hand, discretion can also offer opportunities for abuse. Investment banks may use the flexibility in allocation to dispense favours to specific parties (Mahmud, 2009). Lastly, the longer the time gap between the opening and trading dates in days, the more the chances are that the securities will move away from a rational price as the investor gets more time to digest new information circulating in the market.

The average initial return in the UK and in Singapore, Thailand, Malaysia and India ranges from 16 to 93 per cent (Loughran, Ritter and Rydqvist, 1994). Bangladesh seems to be an outlier, with an average initial return of 116 per cent (Islam, Ali and Ahmad, 2010a; Islam and Munira, 2004). The same scenario can be inferred by comparing the levels of IPO underpricing in New Zealand and Japan, which stand at 26 per cent (Firth 1997) and 10–15 per cent (Cai and Wei, 1997) respectively, to that in Bangladesh, with the maximum return being 285 per cent. While it could be argued that Chinese IPO underpricing also stands at around 267 per cent, the latter is rationalised by Chinese financial regulation and risk (Tian, 2003). While most underpriced stocks initially instilled hope in the market through their excessive abnormal return, they underperform in the long run, in turn undermining the rationality of the investors (Yong, 2007). While the presence of IPO underpricing and its effects are well grounded both theoretically and empirically, there is indeed a paucity of literature that digs deeper to identify and analyse the factors that influence IPO underpricings.

The Bangladesh capital market is relatively small compared to regional markets. In such a setting, investors need to be protected so that the economy is ultimately safeguarded. With its majority Muslim population, the country has recently (in 2014) introduced *shariah* screening, and for this very reason IPO underpricing needs to be assuaged to foster better market stability. This chapter tries, first, to differentiate between the IPO regulations of 1998 and 2006, to find out whether any possible relationship may exist between the new, 2006 regulations and IPO underpricing, and also to find out the major differences between the two sets of IPO regulations. Secondly, the *shariah* screening era (2014 onward) is considered in order to investigate its importance for IPO underpricing. For the capital market of Bangladesh to witness and be home to stability, the difference between the New Issue Rules of 1998 and 2006 must account for efficiency, just pricing and optimal quality of information. Only then can the capital market in question be insulated against anomalies in the likes of IPO underpricing.

This chapter also aims to shed light on the influence of investor sentiment, the hot issue phenomenon, and IPO regulation on the level of underpricing in the Bangladesh capital market. The ratio of public over- or undersubscription is considered as the proxy to investor sentiment. The market is considered to be hot when there are a more than median number of issues from the financial sector, such as banks, insurance, investment and leasing companies. Cross-sections of IPO underpricing before and after the implementation of the 2006 IPO regulations were examined to investigate the influence of IPO regulation on IPO underpricing. Our results reveal an interesting picture of the role of investor sentiment and the need for government control of the primary market in a developing country.

Review of the literature

The issuance of publicly traded stocks is regarded as a milestone for any company (Ellis, Michaely and O'Hara, 1999). While it is indeed optimal to keep the company private in some stages, the subsequent progress of the firm is usually accompanied by changes in the ownership structure. Going public becomes optimal when outside investors possess a comparative advantage in collecting information that is useful to future capital budgeting decisions (Maug, 2001). In addition, public trading is a value-creating activity to the firm, inspiring confidence from the investors, customers, suppliers, and employees as well (Chemmanur and Fulghieri, 1999). An IPO may also act as an exit mechanism from venture capitalists (Jeng and Wells, 2000), thus enabling entrepreneurs to regain control of their companies (Black and Gilson, 1998). A firm might also wish to go to public if that would give it a first-mover advantage in the industry it is operating in (Ritter and Welch, 2002).

IPO underpricing is said to be one of the top ten puzzles in the financial world (Brealey and Myers, 1991). IPO underpricing is far from being a phenomenon observed in financial markets of only emerging countries; quite the contrary, this anomaly has manifested itself in financial markets all over the world regardless of the economic power or sophistication of the market (Ghosh, 2004). Indeed, a handful number of prior studies have shown that the distribution of initial returns is highly skewed with a positive mean (Ritter, 1991). Such findings suggest that there is a player in the IPO process who is incentivised to underprice (Mahmud, 2009). Despite such incentives, most IPOs underperform in the aftermarket and in the long run (Ibbotson and Jaffe, 1975; Ritter, 1991). Further, Firth (1997) noted that the subsequent price performance of IPOs is in fact poor and that investors who bought IPOs at the close of trading on the first day would have lost around 14 per cent against the benchmarked matched companies over a three-year period. Cai and Wei (1997), for their part, find that the post-issue operating performance of underpriced IPOs is also poor, and within five years after the offering, ordinary income to total assets drops significantly from 3.0 per cent to 1.6 per cent. Such underperformance in the aftermarket hampers the underwriter's reputation and also the further capital-raising ability of the issuing firm. While informed investors skip underpriced IPOs to avoid the poor long-run, aftermarket performance, uninformed ones find it an incentive for short-term gain. In a nutshell, the excess initial returns become insignificant, if not negative, once the aftermarket performance is taken into account (Yong, 2007).

While underpricing could be explained by specific factors in different financial markets, IPO underpricing in general is a function of an array of factors. Low and Yong (2011) found a strong negative relationship between the cost of capital and oversubscription, the latter usually serving as a proxy for investors' demand for the IPO. The upfront payments involved in applying for IPOs that are tied up due to lengthy offer periods result in increases in the opportunity cost of the investors' capital, thus hampering interest in the IPO. Another determining factor is the pricing method used in valuing the IPO. Low and Yong (2011) suggest that high IPO oversubscription is prevalent where the fixed price method is used. Chowdhry and Sherman (1996) go further by suggesting that the contrary holds true for the book-building method, where IPO underpricing is mitigated by the greater delay in setting the price. This allows investors to adjust their offer size and price (Low and Yong, 2011). While the level of underpricing is dependent on the level of oversubscription, the latter is further dependent on the time period between the last day of IPO application and the listing day. A shorter period would dampen the oversubscription, which would in turn constrict the level of underpricing (Low and Yong, 2011). The size of a firm going for an IPO is also a variable whose interaction with underpricing is such that the larger it is, the lower the uncertainty and risk for potential investors. This is because larger firms with more diversified product lines and monitoring procedures have better access to investment capital and resources (Kiymaz, 2000).

The level of IPO underpricing is also a function of the type of investor the issuing firm is targeting. Daily et al. (2003) suggest that the issuers tend to set a relatively low price when they aim to encourage retail investors to participate in the subscription. Conversely, firms looking to attract institutional investors tend to set higher offer prices. In support of the foregoing, Gompers and Metrick (2001) indicate that institutional investors are known to avoid low price shares. Benveniste and Spindt (1989) goes counter to the proposition formulated by Gompers and Metrick (2001) by advancing that the presence of institutional investors might lead to greater underpricing given the compensation required for the valuable information they provide and their contribution to better marketing of the IPO. Table 5.1 elaborates on various theories and factors that explain IPO underpricing.

Sentiment and underpricing

There are two major reasons that justify the applicability of investor sentiment in emerging capital markets. The first is that most emerging capital markets are

TABLE 5.1 Theories explaining IPO underpricing

Theory	*Description*	*Sources*
The winner's curse (oversubscription)	If uninformed investors end up obtaining all the shares they ask for, only to find later that informed investors are refraining from buying these very shares, the former are said to be victims of the 'winner's curse'. This may be the result of overconfidence on the part of individual investors.	Rock (1986)
Dynamic information acquisition	When book building is used, underwriters may underprice IPOs to motivate regular investors to accurately measure their valuations during the pre-selling period, which can then be used to assess the issue price.	Benveniste and Spindt (1989), Hanley and Hoberg (2010).
Signalling	The 'lemons' problem arises when the issuer is more informed than the investor. To stand out from lower-quality issuers, high-quality ones use underpricing as a signalling tool.	Ritter and Welch (2002), Grinblatt and Hwang (1989), Welch (1989)
Information cascades	Sometimes an investor may decide to buy or not to buy a share only by observing the pattern of other investors' buying or selling, even if the former has positive or negative information regarding that particular issue.	Bikhchandani et al. (1992), Yong (2007)
Prospect theory	Issuers are more interested in a rise in their future wealth than in instant profits. IPO companies therefore regard not only the shares they sell in the IPO, but also those they hold, which benefit from the large initial price run-up.	Loughran and Ritter (2002)
Lawsuit avoidance	A fall in price after an IPO can entail investor litigation, which in turn motivates the issuer and underwriters to underprice their IPOs; this acts as a shield from future class action lawsuits by reducing the chance of investors' losing money.	Lowry and Shu (2002)
Marketing event	Publicity is generated by an excess initial return on the first day of trading. Additional interest can be generated through such publicity and thus increase market revenue from greater brand awareness.	Chemmanur and Fulghieri (1999), Demers and Lewellen (2003)

home to small and unstable companies. The second reason, which stems from the first one, is that the onus on these markets to keep the interest of retail investors is much larger (Baker and Wurgler, 2002; Daniel, Hirshleifer and Teoh, 2002; Lamont and Stein, 2005). Sentiment is primarily driven by investor psychology (Ritter, 2003a), which encloses the mood at the time of investment, the choice of investment, as well as mistakes made by the investors (Ritter, 2003a; Subrahmanyam, 2007). While investor sentiment has significant bearing on the effective management of the stock market (Daniel et al., 2002), there are scant studies linking investor sentiment to IPOs in emerging markets, thus opening the door for managers to mislead investors by taking advantage of sentiment-biased markets (Baker, Wurgler and Yuan, 2012; Kaniel, Saar and Titman, 2004).

Islam, Ali and Ahmad (2010b) found that the offer size as well as the size of the company has significant positive impact on the degree of underpricing at the Dhaka Stock Exchange (DSE), Bangladesh. The timing of the offers and the years of operation before listing into the DSE, however, were found to have no significant effect on the degree of underpricing. Psychological bias, skill shortage and knowledge gap on the part of the investor also leads them toward irrational decision making and is partially responsible for mispricing. The presence of information asymmetry and ignorance of the fixed-price method caused much of the underpricing in earlier times, back in the 1990s. Therefore, investor sentiment plays a major role in determining the level of underpricing. Multiples of over- and undersubscription show investor demand for that particular stock, and the higher the demand, the higher the underpricing. Underpricing is also negatively related to the gap between the opening date and the trading date. Indeed, Chowdhry and Sherman (1996) suggested that the longer this gap, the more uncertainty surrounds the IPO. With a view to compensating for such delays, firms often apply for a share-pricing discount, which in turn has a bearing on IPO underpricing. Another possibility advanced by Chowdhry and Sherman (1996) relates to the fact that a longer gap is equivalent to more time being available to investors for them to revise their expectations about the future value of the firm and hence affect the level of underpricing. It can therefore be inferred that the longer the time period, the lower the underpricing. Investors as well can be affected by rumours and thus make suboptimal judgments, the gravity of which is directly related to the length of the period.

Hot issues and underpricing

Ritter (1998) finds that another anomaly that surrounds any IPO market is the tendency for the market to undergo periods of concentrated activity whereby the number of new issues coming into the market is higher in certain periods as compared to the average. These periods of high activity are referred to as 'hot markets'. Indeed, a hot IPO market is characterised by an unusually high volume of offerings, severe underpricing, frequent oversubscription of offerings, a preponderance of smaller issues, and, to a certain extent, by concentrations in particular industries. (Ritter, 2003b) documents that in 1999 and 2000 only, 803 companies went public in the

United States, raising about $123 billion, and leaving about $62 billion on the table in the form of initial returns. (Lowry, 2001) shows that fluctuations in IPO volume are related to three distinct factors: variations in investor optimism, changes in a private firm's aggregate demand for capital, and changes in the adverse selection cost of issuing equity. More companies tend to raise first-time public equity when private firms' total demand for capital is higher, the adverse costs of issuing equity are lower, and investor optimism in the markets is flying high so that they are willing to overpay for IPO firms. Lee, Shleifer and Thaler (1991) provide additional evidence that IPO volume is positively related to the level of investor sentiment. (Loughran et al. 1994) go further by claiming that issuers 'time' their IPOs to coincide with periods of excessive optimism, consistent with the finding in Lee et al. (1991) that more companies go public when investor sentiment is high. Such overly optimistic expectations are said to create 'windows of opportunity' during which many firms rush to the market. This, however, results in disappointing returns to long-term investors when the issuers fail to live up to the overly optimistic expectations.

Shariah-compliant IPOs

A plethora of studies investigate the presence of underpricing in *shariah*-compliant IPOs. IPO underpricing is said to have occurred when the first day trading price of an issue is significantly higher than its offer price. Apart from the inclusion of IPO underpricing as an indication of the presence of sentiment, several behavioural biases are found to be determining the underpricing of such IPOs (Abdul-Rahim and Yong, 2008, Abdul-Rahim and Yong, 2010). Of particular interest, a relatively higher return among Malaysian non-private-placement IPOs compared to the same from privately placed IPOs exhibits the presence of 'winner's curse' (see Table 5.1) and the bandwagon effect (Yong, 2011). The overall extent of underpricing has been decreasing from almost close to 100 per cent (94.91 per cent reported by Yong and Isa, 2003) to below 30 per cent over the course of two decades (Nashirah and Uzaki, 2013). Similar trends are reported for the long-term performance of the *shariah*-compliant IPOs in Malaysia, which have experienced a 16.81 per cent of return over the market (Nashirah, 2016). Immediate post-list trading performance and a great portion of trading day underpricing is explained by increased investor demand (Yong, 2011). However, the same demand is profit-oriented while institutional investors are brought into the picture (Alqahtani and Boulanouar, 2017). Therefore, the demand during IPO period, particularly in the post IPO period, is profit-centric for IPOs concentrated with larger amounts of institutional investment. Higher demand is also driven by greater information asymmetry (Tajuddin et al., 2015).

IPO regulation in Bangladesh

IPO regulation differs from country to country. It is indeed the major responsibility of the regulators to ensure the safety of the investors in the whole IPO process. Investors are highly dependent on the information provided in the IPO prospectus that are open to the public and made compulsory by regulators. High quality and immediate availability of information is therefore a must to stabilize market conditions and bring trust among the investors, which eventually will result in the mollifying of market anomalies. For the aforementioned to occur, strong effective regulations must prevail and be enforced.

The Bangladesh capital market is a relatively small market compared to those of neighbouring countries. However, the country's two burses, the Dhaka Stock Exchange (DSE) and the Chittagong Stock Exchange (CSE), reported stable performance even after the global financial crisis of 2007–2008. These markets are mostly uncorrelated to those of the developed countries, which may explain why the market has a history of uninterrupted operations even across the financial turmoil that shook the world as of late (Hassan, 2001). Historically, the only alternative available for a firm contemplating a public issue was to make a fixed-price offering. The firm going public would set a price and open the issue for subscription. Allocations were made on a strictly proportionate basis. Recently, however, the Bangladesh Securities and Exchange Commission has introduced the book-building method to ensure pricing efficiency. A comparison of the regulations is shown in the appendix in Table 5.A1.

In 2006, the country introduced a new public issue rule, the IPO Rules 2006, with a view to increasing public interest in IPO markets and public safety in terms of the availability of information on the new issues to investors. The new set of regulations has very much increased the availability of information as they require increased publication and dissemination of a prospective company's prospectus as well as the nature of its intended business. Further, the lapse of time between approval of the company's prospectus and the opening of the subscription list has been lengthened from 10 days to now 25 days. With regard to the board of directors, it is worth noting that the lock-in period has remained unchanged at three years from the later of the date of publication of the prospectus and the date of commercial operation. Additional disclosure is now required pertaining to management information, one instance being the disclosure of the remuneration of the top five salaried officers of the company as compared to only three in the IPO Rules 1998. On a similar line, companies going for an IPO are now required to show the net tangible assets per share being issued, with a view to improving disclosures regarding company asset information. Regarding disclosures, companies are no longer required to provide all the information relating to the underwriter of the issue. Disclosures have also been amped-up regarding the leverage condition, whereby companies have to describe the terms, structure, and conditions of any debt securities that they may have issued or be planning to issue within six months. The IPO Rules 2006 is also more comprehensive in terms of documents required to be exhibited. Taken together, companies contemplating an IPO are now bound by more disclosures in terms of administrative documents as well as more information regarding the financial health of the company. The IPO Rules 2006 can therefore be said to bolster transparency and thus aim to reduce the information asymmetries present between a company and its prospective shareholders.

Empirical design of the study

The primary objective of the present study is to investigate factors affecting IPO underpricing in Bangladesh during several time periods, such as before and after the IPO regulation of 2006 and after the introduction of *shariah* screening in the stock exchanges. In order to differentiate between the two sets of IPO regulations and the *shariah* screening, the study considered four time periods: (1) IPOs from 2002 until 2006, and again from 2006 until 2009, to see the impact of IPO regulation; and (2) IPOs from 2010 until 2014, and again from 2014 until 2017, to see the impact of *shariah* screening. Including an equal number of IPOs for each period (40 before 2006 and 40 after 2006 until 2009), a total of 80 companies were considered for the first panel of analysis. For the second set of analysis, the study used a total of 114 IPOs from 2010 until 2017, of which 49 IPOs were registered during 2010–2014, ie.e the period before *shariah* screening.

A multivariate regression technique was used to identify significant factors explaining the changes in the IPO underpricing. IUP_i, the IPO underpricing for company *i,* was the percentage change in the difference between first day closing pricing, P_i, and offer price, OP_i. REG_i is a dummy variable where companies listed before regulation of 2006 were coded as '0' and otherwise as '1'. Other variables considered in the model are given below in Equation 5.1. Because the number of book-building IPOs was extremely limited, all the IPOs used in this study were fixed-price IPOs. Table 5.2 shows the descriptions of the variables.

$$(5.1)\quad IUP_i = \alpha + \delta_i SUB_i - \theta_i DAY_i + \beta_i CAP_i - \gamma_i REG_i + \varnothing_i ISL_i + \varphi_i HOT_i + \varepsilon$$

The difference between P_i and OP_i becomes larger when the offer price is fixed lower than expected and/or when the investors are ready to pay a high price on the first day of trading, positively influenced by company achievement. Investors are ready to pay a higher price in the first day of trading for companies that already exhibit oversubscription. An overly subscribed issue indicate optimistic investor behaviour towards the company and presents a good image to potential investors. Issues with a longer delay between subscription opening and the first trading day are able to attract many informed investors, as during the period between the subscription and trading dates the investors are able to collect relevant information and can reach a close-to-just-value decision. Hence, the delay (in days) should reduce underpricing and thus carries a negative sign. Companies with a larger issue size are able to attract more investors as in many developing countries IPOs are considered to be a profitable investment. The size of the issued capital also indicates the strength of the company in undertaking new investment opportunities.

New regulation of an IPO market, such as the one in 2006 in Bangladesh, aims at achieving higher levels of public confidence in new-issue investments. The regulations of 2006 entail ensuring a supply of quality information that will enable investors to make informed decisions. Hence, any new issue that has to comply with the new regulations – that is, any issue registered after 2006 – should show

TABLE 5.2 Description of the variables

Notation	*Description*
IUP	IPO underpricing: natural log of the percentage difference between first day closing trading price and offer price of the issue.
SUB	Oversubscriptions: total amount of public subscriptions divided by total public offer.
DAY	Difference (delay) in opening and trading dates in days: natural log of the difference between subscription opening and trading dates in days.
CAP	Size dummy for issued capital: '1' if the issued capitalwais larger than the median of the issued capital of all issues, '0' otherwise.
REG	Dummy for regulation: '1' if companies were listed before new regulations in 2006 and '2' if the companies were listed after 2006.
ISL	Dummy for *shariah* screening: '1' if companies were registered before 2014 when *shariah* screening was absent in Bangladesh, and '2' for companies with post-2014 registration.
HOT	Dummy for hot issue market based on type of company: '1' if the new issue was from financial companies such as banks, insurance or investment firms, and '0' if the issue was from non-financial firms.

reduced underpricing. Hence, in Equation 5.1 *REG* is shown as having a negative relationship with IPO underpricing. We also tested for the presence of the hot issue concept in IPO markets in Bangladesh. By hot issue market we normally mean a time when there is a more than median number of issues being registered. Here, *HOT* is another proxy for hot issue market, based on type of company. New issues from the financial industry are considered to be very valuable in Bangladesh. Investors of new issues believe that the long-term performance of issues from financial firms will exceed that of non-financial firms, and therefore that it is wise to pay a high price for financial-industry shares on the first trading day. As a result, hot issues, or issues from the financial industry, are normally underpriced.

Shariah screening in the Bangladesh market should not be misunderstood with *shariah*-compliant IPOs. By the year 2017, *shariah* screening in Bangladesh was three years mature. The first *shariah* screening in the country started with the Dhaka Stock Exchange on 10 January 2014, and is denoted 'DSEX'. The DSEX uses S&Ps *shariah* screening methodology. Since IPOs in Bangladesh are not particularly meant to follow *shariah* screening methodology, and since most of the non-financial companies are *shariah*-compliant (Rashid et al., 2017), this study investigates how the information content from the start of the *shariah* screening has influenced IPO underpricing.

Findings

Table 5.3 presents the descriptive statistics of the variables used in the analyses. Underpricing has been a common phenomenon in the Bangladesh IPO market.

TABLE 5.3 Descriptive statistics (average)

REG	*IUP*	*SUB*	*DAY*	*HOT*	*CAP*	*No. of IPOs*
From 2002 until 2006	2.87	18.84	74.83	0.85	0.625	40
After 2006 until 2009	1.28	11.44	87.73	0.68	0.375	40
From 2010 until 2017	2.00	15.10	73.10	0.34	0.46	114
From 2014 until 2017	2.56	25.10	76.21	0.12	0.61	49

Note: Averages were calculated before transforming to natural log (if applicable).

TABLE 5.4 Correlation coefficients

	IUP	*CAP*	*REG*	*HOT*	*DAY*	*SUB*	*ISL*
IUP	1	0.03	0.086	−0.092	−0.042	0.397**	0.079
CAP		1	0.043	−0.025	−0.05	0.006	0.152*
REG			1	−0.242**	0.680**	0.260**	0.312**
HOT				1	−0.375**	−0.371**	−0.462**
DAY					1	0.409**	0.503**
SUB						1	0.545**
ISL							1

Note: '**' Correlation is significant at the 1% level, '*' at the 5% level.

Average IPO underpricing has ranged from the maximum of 287 per cent during 2002–2006 to the minimum of 128 per cent during the 2006–2009 period. During the *shariah* screening era (since 2014), underpricing has been on the rise. Public subscription (*SUB*) has been way higher in the most recent years. During 2006–2009, IPOs took 88 days to appear on the market (trading day), whereas in recent years the delay has been 76 days. Most financial-industry IPOs took a much longer time to come to trading. On average, IPOs took 12–15 weeks to get to trading. New issues from financial sectors were treated more positively than other sectors during the 2002–2009 period. However, financial-sector IPOs have seen a decline in the most recent years. Median issued capital from recent years is returning to its position of 15 years ago, with a higher amount of issued capital in recent years.

Table 5.4 shows the correlation coefficients with their respective significance values among different variables. A look at the first row (with *IUP* at left) is enough to get a clear picture of the table. Apparently, when considered individually, only subscription is positively connected to underpricing. Other variables do not show significant relationship with *IUP*. However, significant interrelationships among the other explanatory variables suggest a need for further investigations.

Table 5.5 shows the outputs of the multiple regression analysis. The outputs are divided into three panels: impact of regulation, impact of *shariah* screening, and

TABLE 5.5 Determinants of IPO underpricing

Variables	*Impact of regulation*			*Impact of shariah screening*		*Total sample (2002–2017)*
	Before (2002–2006)	*After (2006–2009)*	*Total (2002–2009)*	*Before (2002–2014)*	*After (2014–2017)*	
SUB	0.404***	0.439***	0.401***	0.06***	0.04***	0.051***
DAY	−0.260*	−0.222*	−0.252***	−0.34***	−0.528	−0.34***
REG			−0.184*	0.69*	$	0.716**
CAP	0.125	0.083	0.159*	0.29	−0.46	0.048
HOT	−0.14	0.320**	0.206**	−0.02	#	−0.103
ISL						−0.473
F value	3.576,	7.523,	11.29,	4.33,	8.65,	8.56,
	$p = 0.015.$	$p = 0.000$	$p = 0.000$	$p = 0.000$	$P = 0.000$	$p = 0.000$
R^2	0.29	0.501	0.45	0.179	0.571	0.237

Notes: Dependent variable = IUP (natural log of IPO underpricing), values are standardized beta coefficients. '***' presents significance at 1%, '**' at 5% and '*' at 10% level. Outputs for 'After Shari'ah screening (2014–2017)' are not shown due to limited observations. # = Most companies in post-*shariah* period were non-financial firms. Hence, categorisation based on financial and non-financial firms to identify hot market phenomenon was less important for this model, thus was not used in the model. $ = all IPOs in post-*shariah* screening period followed the new IPO regulation, thus was not used in the model. SUB = Public over-subscription, DAY = Delay between issue open date and first trading dates, REG = dummy variable for new and old regulation (cut-off period 2006), CAP = dummy variable for median issued capital, HOT = dummy variable to identify hot market phenomenon based on type of industry (financial versus non-financial), ISL = dummy variable to identify pre- and post-*shariah* screening period (cut-off period 2014).

the total sample. New regulations were introduced in 2006, and *shariah* screening started officially from January 2014. Looking at the overall results, public subscription was the most influential and robust determinant of IPO underpricing in Bangladesh. Higher public subscription increases the IPO underpricing. Despite its strong statistical significance, the strength of the coefficient has been lower in the most recent years, as indicated by lower coefficients. Delay in appearing in the market has also been robust in explaining the changes in IPO underpricing. Interestingly, longer delay translates into smaller underpricing. Regulation poses an interesting challenge. Before 2010 – from 2002–2009 – the new regulations helped to reduce underpricing. However, in more recent years, the regulations are not helping much, which may indicates a need to update the regulations. The size of issued capital, where it is larger than the median issued capital, is only significant during the new regulation era – up until 2009. Similarly, the hot market phenomenon is only significant during the new regulation era. Being a financial company will increase the degree of IPO underpricing. Being in the Islamic *shariah* screening era does not carry any significant weight in the overall sample. The coefficient is negative, indicating a decrease in underpricing if the issue comes during the *shariah* screening era.

Discussion and conclusion

IPOs are underpriced globally. Average underpricing in Bangladesh reaches 200 per cent or even more. This acts as an incentive for a group of 'seasonal/ habitual IPO investors' to invest in IPOs. However, establishing a fair price for an IPO is a prerequisite for an efficient price recovery system in a developing capital market. With that in mind, the Government of Bangladesh introduced new public issue rules in 2006, which replaced the earlier rules of 1998. The new regulations are intended to ensure the diffusion of new information to the investors that will be used to make informed decisions. In addition, from 2014, *shariah* screening activity started in the country, indicating a stronger demand for Islamic capital market activities in this majority Muslim country.

This chapter has investigated the determinants of IPO underpricing in Bangladesh, considering the data of 149 fixed-price IPOs registered during the period 2002–2017. Public oversubscription, the delay between the issue opening and the first trading day, and the new regulations of 2006 have significantly contributed to existing understanding of IPO underpricing. Higher public oversubscription and shorter time taken to open trade for investors signal greater underpricing. Public oversubscription has increased tremendously in recent years – from almost 19 times during 2002–2006 to 25 times during 2014–2017. Regulation can play an important role in controlling public oversubscription to fixed-price IPOs.

Companies often take an average of 73–87 days to open secondary market trading; financial companies take even longer. While taking a shorter time is good for the issuing firms as they can collect funds faster, in the IPO process taking a shorter time is a sign of market development. However, in markets with limited investors' education programmes, a shorter time taken to begin open trading will allow less information to pass to the investors for an informed decision of their IPO investment. Regulation should fix the time to be taken from the opening day of the issue until the day it can start trading in the open market, in order to control the level of underpricing. Theoretically, a larger amount of information and being given a longer time for decision making should enable investors to find a fair price. In addition to this, investors heavily rely on sentiment when buying new issues. For instance, issues with higher issued capital and greater public oversubscription are the companies for which retail investors are ready to pay more, eventually leading to great underpricing. Hence, restructuring regulation may help to cut the degree of underpricing in Bangladesh.

The present study has found that the new regulations helped to reduce underpricing until 2009. In more recent IPOs, the new regulations have seemed inadequate to ensure that a fair price is offered to investors. IPO regulation in Bangladesh needs to be updated with respect to the new *shariah* screening criteria and other recent changes in the IPO market. The hot market phenomenon has not been seen in recent IPOs. Being a non-financial company tends to result in higher underpricing. People in general tend to overestimate their ability to earn a higher return in the first day of trading even though it may or may not happen for any IPO. They look at the trading behaviour of others, and contribute to large public subscriptions. Information cascades theory shows that investors follow how fellow investors make decisions, which gives rise to volume purchasing of IPOs by retail investors when the market is hot. A balance of financial and non-financial IPOs within a specific time period may help to reduce this tendency.

Note: This study faced multiple challenges with data and models. In the absence of a structured database, all data were collected manually by the researchers. There were multiple missing data, resulting in a limited choice of variables. Due to the limited number of book-building IPOs, a comparison of these with fixed-price IPOs was not possible. Future studies will be able to use much longer datasets with more determinants.

References

Abdul-Rahim, R., & Yong, O. 2008. Initial returns of Shariah-compliant IPOs in Malaysia. *Capital Markets Review* 16(2): 270–279.

Abdul-Rahim, R., & Yong, O. 2010. Initial returns of Malaysian IPOs and shariah-compliant status. *Journal of Islamic Accounting and Business Research* 1(1): 60–74.

Agarwal, S., Liu, C., & Rhee, S. G. 2008. Investor demand for IPOs and aftermarket performance: Evidence from the Hong Kong stock market. *Journal of International Financial Markets, Institutions and Money* 18(2): 176–190.

Alqahtani, F., & Boulanouar, Z., 2017. Sharia compliance status and investor demand for IPOs: Evidence from Saudi Arabia. *Pacific-Basin Finance Journal* 46(2017): 258–268.

Baker, M., & Stein, J. C. 2004. Market liquidity as a sentiment indicator. *Journal of Financial Markets* 7(3): 271–299.

Baker, M., & Wurgler, J. 2002. Market timing and capital structure. *The Journal of Finance* 57(1): 1–32.

Baker, M., Wurgler, J., & Yuan, Y. 2012. Global, local, and contagious investor sentiment. *Journal of Financial Economics* 104(2): 272–287.

Benveniste, L. M., & Spindt, P. A. 1989. How investment bankers determine the offer price and allocation of new issues. *Journal of Financial Economics* 24(2): 343–361.

Bikhchandani, S., Hirshleifer, D., & Welch, I. 1992. A theory of fads, fashion, custom, and cultural change as informational cascades. *Journal of Political Economy* 100(5): 992–1026.

Black, B. S., & Gilson, R. J. 1998. Venture capital and the structure of capital markets: banks versus stock markets. *Journal of Financial Economics* 47(3): 243–277.

Bradley, D. J., Gonas, J. S., Highfield, M. J., & Roskelley, K. D. 2009. An examination of IPO secondary market returns. *Journal of Corporate Finance* 15(3): 316–330.

Brau, J. C., & Fawcett, S. E. 2006. Initial public offerings: An analysis of theory and practice. *The Journal of Finance* 61(1): 399–436.

Brav, A., Brav, O., & Jiang, W. 2009. The choice of going public and going private: evidence from UK. Working paper, Columbia University.

Brealey, R., & Myers, S. 1991. *Principles of Corporate Finance*. New York: McGraw Hill.

Bubna, A., & Prabhala, N. R. 2006. When bookbuilding meets IPOs. Working paper, Indian School of Business and University of Maryland.

Caglio, C., Hanley, K. W., & Marietta-Westberg, J. 2011. Going public abroad: The role of international markets for IPOs. Working paper, US Securities and Exchange Commission, Washington D.C.

Cai, J., & Wei, K. C. 1997. The investment and operating performance of Japanese initial public offerings. *Pacific-Basin Finance Journal* 5(4): 389–417.

Chemmanur, T. J., & Fulghieri, P. 1999. A theory of the going-public decision. *Review of Financial Studies* 12(2): 249–279.

Chowdhry, B., & Sherman, A. 1996. The winner's curse and international methods of allocating initial public offerings. *Pacific-Basin Finance Journal* 4(1): 15–30.

Daily, C. M., Trevis Certo, S., Dalton, D. R., & Roengpitya, R. 2003. IPO underpricing: A meta–analysis and research synthesis. *Entrepreneurship Theory and Practice* 27(3): 271–295.

Daniel, K., Hirshleifer, D., & Teoh, S. H. 2002. Investor psychology in capital markets: Evidence and policy implications. *Journal of Monetary Economics* 49(1): 139–209.

Demers, E., & Lewellen, K. 2003. The marketing role of IPOs: evidence from internet stocks. *Journal of Financial Economics* 68(3): 413–437.

Ellis, K., Michaely, R., & O'Hara, M. 1999. *A Guide to the initial Public Offering Process*. Citeseer.

Firth, M. 1997. An analysis of the stock market performance of new issues in New Zealand. *Pacific-Basin Finance Journal* 5(1): 63–85.

Ghosh, S. 2004. Revisiting IPO underpricing in India. Available at SSRN: http://ssrn.com/abstract=703501 or http://dx.doi.org/10.2139/ssrn.703501.

Gompers, P. A. & Metrick, A. 2001. Institutional investors and equity prices. *The Quarterly Journal of Economics* 116(1): 229–259.

Grinblatt, M., & Hwang, C. Y. 1989. Signalling and the pricing of new issues. *The Journal of Finance* 44(2): 393–420.

Hanley, K. W., & Hoberg, G. 2010. The information content of IPO prospectuses. *The Review of Financial Studies* 23(7): 2821–2864.

Hassan, M. K. 2001. Bangladesh capital market development: Issues, problems and policy formulation. International Monetary Fund.

Hirshleifer, D. 2001. Investor psychology and asset pricing. *The Journal of Finance* 56(4): 1533–1597.

Ibbotson, R. G., & Jaffe, J. F. 1975. "Hot issue" markets. *The Journal of Finance* 30(4): 1027–1042.

Islam, M. A., Ali, R., & Ahmad, Z. 2010a. An empirical investigation into the underpricing of initial public offerings in the Chittagong stock exchange. *International Journal of Economics and Finance* 2(4): 36–46.

Islam, M. D. A., Ali, R., & Ahmad, Z. 2010b. Why IPOs are underpriced? Evidence from Dhaka Stock Exchange, Bangladesh. Available at www.researchgate.net/profile/Md_Aminul_Islam3/publication/228358023_Why_IPOS_are_Underpriced_Evidence_from_the_Dhaka_Stock_Exchange_Bangladesh/links/0046352d4176a397cc000000.pdf, accessed January 2018.

Islam, M. S., & Munira, S. 2004. IPO flipping and its determinants in Bangladesh. *Dhaka University Journal of Business Studies* 25(1). Available at www.researchgate.net/profile/Mohammad_Islam38/publication/249404410_IPO_Flipping_and_its_Determinants_in_Bangladesh/links/55a79bd808ae345d61db5ea1/IPO-Flipping-and-its-Determinants-in-Bangladesh.pdf, accessed as January 2018.

Jeng, L. A., & Wells, P. C. 2000. The determinants of venture capital funding: evidence across countries. *Journal of Corporate Finance* 6(3): 241–289.

Kaniel, R., Saar, G., & Titman, S. 2004. Individual investor sentiment and stock returns. *Journal of Finance* 63(1): 273–310.

Kiymaz, H. 2000. The initial and aftermarket performance of IPOs in an emerging market: evidence from Istanbul stock exchange. *Journal of Multinational Financial Management* 10(2): 213–227.

Lamont, O. A., & Stein, J. C. 2005. Investor sentiment and corporate finance: micro and macro. *American Economic Review* 95(4): 147–151.

Lee, C. M., Shleifer, A., & Thaler, R. H. 1991. Investor sentiment and the closed-end fund puzzle. *The Journal of Finance* 46(1): 75–109.

Leite, T. 2005. Returns to sentiment investors in IPOs. *Economics Letters* 89(2): 222–226.

Loughran, T., Ritter, J. R., & Rydqvist, K. 1994. Initial public offerings: International insights. *Pacific-Basin Finance Journal* 2(2–3): 165–199.

Loughran, T., & Ritter, J. R. 2002. Why don't issuers get upset about leaving money on the table in IPOs? *The Review of Financial Studies* 15(2): 413–444.

Low, S. W., & Yong, O. 2011. Explaining over-subscription in fixed-price IPOs – Evidence from the Malaysian stock market. *Emerging Markets Review* 12(3): 205–216.

Lowry, M. 2001. Why does IPO volume fluctuate so much? *Journal of Financial Economics* 67(1): 3–40.

Lowry, M., & Shu, S. 2002. Litigation risk and IPO underpricing. *Journal of Financial Economics* 65(3): 309–335.

Mahmud, M. A. F. 2009. IPO underpricing and short run performance in Bangladesh: Determinant attribution and explanation. Working Paper, University of Dhaka, Bangladesh.

Maug, E. 2001. Ownership structure and the life-cycle of the firm: A theory of the decision to go public. *European Finance Review* 5(3): 167–200.

Narayanasamy, C., & Rashid, M. 2015. Unexplained volume and after-market divergence of opinion of fixed IPOs. *Taylor's Business Review* 5(1): 31–49.

Narayanasamy, C., Rashid, M., & Ibrahim, I. 2018. Divergence of opinion and moderating effect of investors' attentions in IPO market: Malaysian evidence. *Review of Behavioral Finance* 10(1): 105–126.

Nashirah, A. B. B. 2016. Long term performance of Islamic share price for initial public offerings (IPOs) in Malaysia: Evidence from sharia-compliant companies listed on the Malaysian stock exchange (2006–2010). *International Journal of Management Science and Business Administration* 2(6): 55–66.

Nashirah, A. B. B., & Uzaki, K. 2013. An empirical study of initial public offerings underpricing for shariah-compliant companies: the case of Malaysian market. *International Journal of Economics, Business and Finance* 1(9): 262–274.

Rashid, M., Hassan, M. K., Amin, N., & Samina, Q. S. 2017. Shari'ah compliant companies in Bangladesh. *Journal of Islamic Economics Business and Finance* 13(2): 129–143.

Ritter, J. R. 1991. The long-run performance of initial public offerings. *Journal of Finance* 46(1): 3–27.

Ritter, J. R. 1998. Initial public offerings. *Contemporary Finance Digest* 2(1): 5–30.

Ritter, J. R. 2003a. Behavioural finance. *Pacific-Basin Finance Journal* 11(4): 429–437.

Ritter, J. R. 2003b. Investment Banking and Securities Issuance. In Constantinides, G. M., Harris, M., & Stulz, R.M. (Eds), *Handbook of the Economics of Finance* 1(Part A): 255–306.

Ritter, J. R., & Welch, I. 2002. A review of IPO activity, pricing, and allocations. *The Journal of Finance* 57(4): 1795–1828.

Rock, K. 1986. Why new issues are underpriced. *Journal of Financial Economics* 15(1–2): 187–212.

Subrahmanyam, A. 2007. Behavioural finance: a review and synthesis. *European Journal of Financial Management* 14(1): 12–29.

Tajuddin, A. H., Mohd-Rashid, R., Abdullah, N. A. H., & Abdul-Rahim, R. 2015. An empirical examination of over-subscription in the Malaysian IPO market. *International Journal of Economics and Management* 9(Special Issue): 81–102.

Tian, L. 2003. Financial regulations, investment risks, and determinants of Chinese IPO underpricing. Available at http://citeseerx.ist.psu.edu/viewdoc/summary?doi=10.1.1.581.2724, accessed January 2018.

Tinic, S. M. 1988. Anatomy of initial public offerings of common stock. *Journal of Finance* 43(4): 789–822.

Welch, I. 1989. Seasoned offerings, imitation costs, and the underpricing of initial public offerings. *The Journal of Finance* 44(2): 421–449.

Yong, O. 2007. A review of IPO research in Asia: What's next? *Pacific-Basin Finance Journal* 15(3): 253–275.

Yong, O. 2011. Investor demand, size effect and the immediate post-listing behaviour of Malaysian IPOs. *Universiti Tun Abdul Razak E-Journal* 7(2): 23–32.

Yong, O., & Isa, Z. 2003. Initial performance of new issues of shares in Malaysia. *Applied Economics* 35: 919–930.

Appendix

TABLE 5.A1 Differences between IPO rules 1998 and IPO rules 2006

Criteria	*IPO Rules 1998*	*IPO Rules 2006*
Availability of information		
Publication of prospectus	Prospectus has to be published in two daily newspapers within 10 days of receiving the consent of the SEC	Prospectus has to be published in four daily newspapers (two English and two Bengali) within the time specified in the letter of consent issued by the SEC
Prospectus delivery requirements	Prospectus has to be widely disseminated and has to be available in the issuer's office, office and websites of the SEC and the exchanges and other marketing intermediaries	Prospectus has to be widely available in the issuer office, stock exchanges, SEC and all related offices. The issuer has to post the prospectus on its website and the website of SEC and stock exchanges within three days of receiving the consent from the SEC and has to post it until the compilation of the offering
Limitations on the use of prospectus	Occurrence of any events: the issuer must notify the general public through at least two daily newspapers	Occurrence of any events: the issuer must notify the general public through at least four national daily newspapers
Description of the business	n/a	All the subrules of 1998 regulation are included and a new rule added that the issuer must give information about production capacity and current utilisation
Distribution		
Opening of subscription list	After completion of the period, the issuer will inform the SEC within 20 days regarding the following matters: date of completion; total number of securities sold and the amount received from the sale; the amount paid as commission	After completion of the period, the issuer will inform the SEC and the stock exchanges within five working days regarding the following matters: total number of securities sold and the amount received form the sales; the amount paid to the banker to the issue as commission
Availability of securities	In case of oversubscription, a lottery must be conducted in the presence of representatives of the stock exchanges and applicants, if any	In case of oversubscription, a lottery must be conducted in the presence of representatives of the issuer, the stock exchanges and applicants, if any

(*continued*)

TABLE 5.A1 (Cont.)

Criteria	*IPO Rules 1998*	*IPO Rules 2006*
Placement	Any issuer may make placement with investors, both foreign and local, and the amount so placed, including the names and addresses of such investors, must be disclosed in detail in the financial structure section of the prospectus	n/a
Subscription		
Opening of subscription list	The subscription list will be opened and the sale of securities will start after *10 days* of publication of the prospectus and it will remain open for not more than 15 days	The subscription list will be opened and the sale of the securities will start after *25 days* of publication of the prospectus and it will remain open for the period as specified by the SEC
Prospectus delivery requirements	No sale of the securities or no money will be taken from any person regarding such sale until *10 days* after the prospectus has been published	Within *25 days* of publication of the prospectus, no sale of securities or no money taken from any person regarding such sale
Limitation on the use of prospectus	If any event occurs, the offering will be terminated and amendments of the prospectus has been filed with and declared effective by the SEC	If any events occurs, the offering will be suspended until an amendment signed by all the directors, CEOs of both the issuers and the issue managers has been filed and declared effective by the SEC
Plan of distribution	All the information about the underwriter of the issue must be given in the prospectus including underwriters' names and addresses, amount of securities pledged to be taken by each underwriter, term of underwriting agreement, amount of commission to be paid, etc.	n/a
Approval rejection and review	In case the application is incomplete, the SEC will inform the applicant in writing of the incompleteness generally within *15 working days* of receiving of such application	In case the application is incomplete, the SEC will inform the applicant in writing of the incompleteness generally within *28 working days* of such application

TABLE 5.A1 (Cont.)

Criteria	*IPO Rules 1998*	*IPO Rules 2006*
Risk factor		
Cover page	The following statement must be written, 'If you have any queries about this document, you may consult with your stock broker/ dealer, bank management, lawyer, professional accountant or other professional advisor'	The following statement must be written, 'if you have any queries about this document, you may consult issuer, issue manager and underwriter'
Risk factors and management's preparation regarding risk	1. No recent receipt of revenues 2. Poor financial conditions 3. Industry and currency risk 4. Market- and technology-related risk 5. Potential or existing government regulation 6. Potential changes in global or national policies 7. No operating history	1. Interest rate, exchange rate and industry-related risk 2. Market- and technology-related risk 3. Potential or existing government regulation 4. Potential changes in global or national policies 5. History of non-operation, if any 6. Operational risk
Directors and officers	n/a	All the rules of 1998 are included in this regulation except one: the 2006 regulation states that if any shareholders owns more than 50% shares, and if s/he becomes a loan defaulter according to CIB report, then it must be mentioned in the prospectus
Involvement of officers and directors in certain legal proceedings	In the prospectus, any bankruptcy petition filed by or against any company of which any officer or director or nominee of the company filing the prospectus was a director, officer or general partner *at the time of the bankruptcy or within 2 (two) years prior to that time*	Any bankruptcy petition filed by or against any company of which any officer or director of the issuer company filing the prospectus was a director, officer or partner *at the time of bankruptcy*
Board of directors and management information		

(*continued*)

TABLE 5.A1 (Cont.)

Criteria	*IPO Rules 1998*	*IPO Rules 2006*
Directors and officers	The sponsors' share capital will be subject to a lock-in of three years from the date of publication of prospectus or commercial operation whichever comes later. This is not applicable for foreign sponsors either in a joint venture company or 100% foreign-owned company	Name with position, educational qualification, date of joining the company and least 5 years experience of: CEO, CFO, company secretary, advisers, DMD and all departmental heads
Lock-in provision	n/a	a. The Sponsors' share capital at the time if public offering shall be subject to lock-in period of three years from the date of issuance of prospectus or commercial operation, whichever comes later
	n/a	b. If any person, other than directors and those who hold 5% or more, who have owned the shares of the company within immediately
	n/a	c. Preceding 2 years of public offering, shall be subject to;lock-in period of one year from the date of issuance of prospectus or commercial operation, whichever comes later
Management information		
Certain relationships and related transactions	The prospectus must contain a description of any transaction or proposed transaction between the issuer and any of the following persons, giving the name of the person involved in the transaction, relationship with the issuer and nature of interest in the transaction:	The prospectus must contain a description of any transaction or proposed transaction between the issuer and any of the following persons, giving the name of the person involved in the transaction, relationship with the issuer and nature of interest in the transaction:
	1. Any director or executive officer of the issuer	1. Any director or executive officer of the issuer
	2. Any nominee for directors or officer	2. Any director or officer
	3. Short bio-data of each director	n/a

TABLE 5.A1 (Cont.)

Criteria	*IPO Rules 1998*	*IPO Rules 2006*
Executive compensation	The amount of remuneration paid to each of the *top three officers* of the company in the last year and the name and designation of each officer	The amount of remuneration paid to the *top five salaried officers* of the issuers in the last accounting year and the name and designation of each officer
Ownership of the company's securities	There must also be a table in the prospectus showing the number of shares of the company's securities owned by each of the top three officers, each director, and all officers as a group, indicating the percentage of outstanding shares represented by the shares owned	There must also be a table in the prospectus showing the number of shares of the issuer's securities owned by each director, each of the top ten salaried officers, and all officers as a group, indicating the percentage of outstanding shares represented by the shares owned
Asset information		
Tangible assets per share	n/a	The prospectus shall show the net tangible asset backing per unit of the securities being offered at the date of last statement of financial position or referred to in the prospectus
Pricing		
Determination of offering price	n/a	If the issue price of the ordinary share is higher than the par value thereof, justification of the premium should be stated
Underwriting		
Plan of distribution	All the information about the underwriter of the issue must be given in the prospectus including underwriters name, address, amount of securities pledged to be taken by each underwriter, term of underwriting agreement, amount of commission to be paid, etc.	n/a

(continued)

TABLE 5.A1 (Cont.)

Criteria	*IPO Rules 1998*	*IPO Rules 2006*
Listing		
Market for the securities being offered	If the securities being offered have been approved for listing on the stock exchange, the name of such stock exchange must be given in the prospectus; any conditions that need to be met by the company before trading on such stock exchange must be explained	The issuer must apply to all the stock exchanges in Bangladesh within seven working days from the date of consent accorded by the commission to issue the prospectus
Compulsory listing of securities	All public limited companies must enlist with at least one recognised stock exchange	n/a
Leverage condition		
Debt securities	The terms and conditions must be described of any debt securities that the company may have issued or be planning to issue, including the date of redemption, whether such debt securities are convertible to equity, rate of interest payable and any other rights given to holders of such securities	The terms and conditions must be described of any debt securities that the company may issued or planning to issue *within six months*, whether such debt securities are convertible to equity, rate of interest payable and any other rights given to holders of such securities
Debenture trustee	The public company issuing debentures shall appoint a debenture trustee and the trustee must be either a bank, a financial institution or an insurance company	The public company issuing debentures shall appoint a debenture trustee and the trustee must be either a bank, a financial institution, an insurance company or any other entity registered by the SEC to act as trustee
Non-resident Bangladeshis (NRBs)		
Subscription by and refund of NRBs	The value of securities applied for such person may be paid in TK or US Dollar or UK Pound Sterling at the rate of exchange mentioned in the securities application Form	The value of securities applied for such person may be paid in TK or US Dollar or UK Pound Sterling or Euro at the rate of exchange mentioned in the securities application Form

TABLE 5.A1 (Cont.)

Criteria	*IPO Rules 1998*	*IPO Rules 2006*
Availability of securities	10% of all issues shall be reserved for NRB and the remaining 90% shall be open for subscription by the general public	10% of all issues shall be reserved for NRB and 10% for mutual funds and collective investment schemes registered with the commission and remaining 80% shall be open for subscription by the general public
Documents		
Exhibits	The following documents should be filed as exhibits to the Application for public offering:	The following documents should be filed as exhibits to the Application for public offering:
	1. Memorandum and Articles of Association – in original attested by the Managing Director	1. Memorandum and Articles of Association- certified by the Register of Joint Stock Companies and Firms(RJSC) and attested by the Managing Director/CEO
	2. Certificate of Incorporation and Certificate of Commencement of Business- Photocopy attested by the Managing Director	2. Certificate of Incorporation and Certificate of Commencement of Business- certified by the RJSC and attested by the MD/CEO
	3. Land Title Deed- photocopy attested by the Managing Director	3. Land Title Deed with current rent receipts- photocopy attested by the MD/CEO
	4. Due Diligence Certificate form the Investment Advisor- in original	4. Not included
	5. Due Diligence Certificate form Underwriter-in-original	5. Due Diligence Certificate (using formal included in Annexure C) from the Manager to the issue- in original
	6. Due Diligence Certificate from Underwriter	6. Due Diligence Certificate (using formal included in Annexure D) from Underwriter-in original
	7. Due Diligence Certificate from Debenture Trustee- in original	7. Due Diligence Certificate form Debenture Trustee, in original, as prescribed by the Commission
	n/a	8. Copy of return of allotment and particulars of directors certified by the RJSC and attested by the MD / CEO

(*continued*)

TABLE 5.A1 (Cont.)

Criteria	*IPO Rules 1998*	*IPO Rules 2006*
		9. Banker's certificate/ bank statement showing deposit of an amount equivalent to the paid-up capital/ auditor's certificate in that regard attested by the MD/CEO 10. Undertaking of the issuer company and its directors for obtaining CIB Report from Bangladesh Bank- attested by the MD/CEO 11. Copies of valid licence from the regulatory authority, where applicable- attested by the MD/ CEO 12. Deed of Trust (in case of debt securities) attested by the MD/CEO 13. Credit rating report, if applicable- attested by the MD/CEO
Financial conditions		
Plan of operation and discussion of financial conditions	1. If issuer has not started its commercial operation then the company's plan of operation for the next 12 months has to be described in the prospectus 2. If the issuer has been in operation for more than 2 years, then he has to give information about the company's financial conditions, changes in financial conditions and the result of operations for the last 2 years 3. Any VAT, Income tax, Customs duty or other tax liabilities which are not yet paid, stating why they are not paid and the sources from which these will be paid	1. If issuer has not started its commercial operation, the company has to describe the plan of operations for the period required to start commercial operation in the prospectus. 2. If the issuer has been in operation then he has to give information about the company's revenue, financial conditions, changes in financial conditions and the result of operations for the last 3 years 3. Any VAT, Income tax, Customs duty or other tax liabilities which are not yet paid, stating why they are not paid, prior to the issuance of the prospectus
Financial statement requirement	n/a	Selected ratios on liquidity, operating, and probability have to be disclosed in the prospectus

SEC, Bangladesh Securities and Exchange Commission; n/a, not applicable/available; CIB, Credit Information Bureau of Bangladesh Bank; CEO, chief executive officer; CFO, chief financial officer; DMD, deputy managing director.

6

SUKUK

Introduction and global performance

Rasidah Mohd-Rashid and Ahmad Hakimi Tajuddin

Meaning of "Islamic bonds"

The first public issue of *sukuk* was in 1998, and the years 2001 to 2003 saw the formation of the Islamic capital market with the issuance of the *Shariah* Standard No. 17, Investment *Sukuk*, by the Accounting and Auditing Organization for Islamic Financial Institutions (AAOIFI). In Malaysia, the *sukuk* market funding concept emerged when one of the private sector corporations, Shell Malaysia, raised RM12 million (US$40 million) using *sukuk* through the Kuala Lumpur Stock Exchange (now Bursa Malaysia). Both equity and debt securities are bought and sold in capital markets. The Islamic capital markets differ from conventional markets in that the sale and purchase of interest-bearing debt securities is prohibited. One of the non-interest-bearing instruments used in Islamic capital markets for debt obligations is *sukuk*.

Sukuk is the Arabic term for Islamic securities. It is the plural of the Arabic *sakk*, which means "certificate." The term *sukuk* is broadly translated as "Islamic bonds," although the correct translation is "Islamic investment certificates" (Tahmoures, 2013). Sometimes, the Islamic securities that grant investors a share of an asset are known as *sukuk sanadat*, and ownership includes the cash flow and risks associated with the bonds. AAOIFI has officially defined *sukuk* as certificates of equal value representing undivided shares in ownership of tangible assets, usufruct and services (AAOIFI, 2008). Usufruct gives the right to an individual to earn profits from the property of others or from collective ownership, that is, a number of people own an asset which is not public property and no individual could claim ownership for a part of the asset. The International Islamic Financial Market (IIFM) in 2010 defined *sukuk* as "commercial papers that provide investors with ownership in underlying assets". Therefore, *sukuk* provide a stable income and ownership in the transaction since it has an underlying tangible asset. Meanwhile, the Islamic Financial Services Board (IFSB) defined *sukuk* as certificates that provides proportion of undivided ownership in a tangible asset, business venture (*mudaraba*) or pool of main tangible assets.

Sukuk are often referred to as "Islamic bonds" due to some similarities between *sukuk* and bonds, especially in terms of financial process. In fact, some studies say that *sukuk* mimic the financial features of bonds in addition to being compliant with Islamic finance principles (Lahsasna & Lin, 2012). The features of *sukuk* that differ from those of conventional securities are as follows:

- For *sukuk*, the purpose of raising funds should be specified in terms of assets. That means the funds raised through *sukuk* should provide identifiable assets.
- The funds raised from the issuance of *sukuk* must be related to the purpose for which they are used.
- *Sukuk* backed by assets grant the right for a proportion of ownership of the assets set aside for the funding. The transfer of ownership would be upon the maturity of the *sukuk.*

Some Islamic countries require firms to comply with the international definitions, such as the Qatar Financial Center, which in the *Islamic Finance Rulebook* (section 6.2.2) requires the authorized firm to comply with AAOIFI standards. In Malaysia, the Securities Commission of Malaysia has issued a guideline on the offering of Islamic securities. *Sukuk* in the Malaysian market is defined as documents or certificates that represent the value of the underlying assets. In Bahrain, *sukuk* are defined as certificates that give a proportion of ownership in the tangible assets, usufruct, services or investment activity. *Sukuk* can be issued either for long-term or short-term maturity. The first short-term *sukuk*, known as *salam sukuk* (see below, 'Types and valuation of *sukuk*'), were issued by the Bahrain Monetary Agency in 2001 for 30- and 91-day periods. In Malaysia, the Central Bank of Malaysia issues short-term *ijarah sukuk* for a one-year maturity period. Short-term investment based on *shariah* principles in Malaysia is traded through the Islamic Interbank Money Market (IIMM).

Types and valuation of *sukuk*

AAOIFI has issued standards for 14 types of *sukuk* and their possible structures, which underscores the variations in *sukuk* (Ainley et al., 2007). Based on approval and assessment of the details by the Securities Commission, Islamic structured financial instruments or *sukuk* can be developed centered on various Islamic contracts, such as *mudaraba* (profit and loss sharing contracts), *musharaka* (partnership and joint stock ownership), *ijarah* (leasing), *murabaha* (installment), *istisna* (futures) and *salam* (advance purchase).

Sukuk al-murabaha *(cost-plus or deferred-payment* sukuk*)*

Murabaha contract debt papers are one of the most popular forms of Islamic financing methods used in Malaysia. This is due to the more liberal interpretation of *fiqh* (Islamic law) by Malaysian jurists permitting the sale of debt *(bai al-dayn)* at a negotiated price. This is an agreement between a seller and buyer for the delivery of an asset. The buyer of the *murabaha* certificates is the *sukuk* holder and the seller of the certificates is the issuer of the certificates. The *murabaha* facility involves the purchase of assets on behalf of the client (issuer) by the financiers, such as banks, and the immediate sale of those assets back to the client (issuer) at a price mark-up with cost and profit margin on a deferred-payment basis as agreed upon by both parties.

The purpose of this form of *sukuk* is to attract investment capital from investors to purchase the *murabaha* assets or commodity. At the same time, the realized funds are the purchasing cost of the commodity under the concept of cost plus sale. This transaction to settle the purchase price is securitized under the issuance of *murabaha*. In Malaysia, the *murabaha sukuk* is considered as a short-term debt security; its tradability depends on the underlying asset that may be a permissible debt form like a *murabaha* receivable (Thomas et al., 2006). The *murabaha* concept was used in the year 2000 by Arcapita Bank in Bharain for a five-year maturity period and the amount issued was US$200 million. The structure of the *murabaha sukuk* is illustrated in Figure 6.1.

Sukuk salam *(advance purchase)*

The objective of the issuance of this form of *sukuk* is to channel capital from the investor to support the short-term period purchase of a commodity. In this contract, an asset is delivered to a buyer or client on a future date in exchange for full advance spot payment to the seller. In other words, *salam* is structured

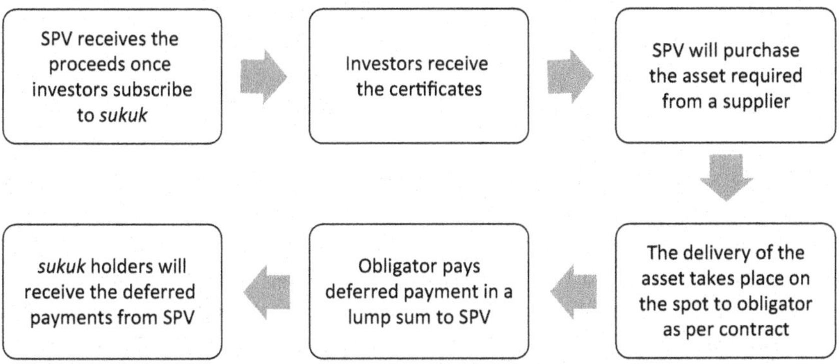

FIGURE 6.1 *Sukuk* based on *murabaha* contract. SPV, special purpose vehicle

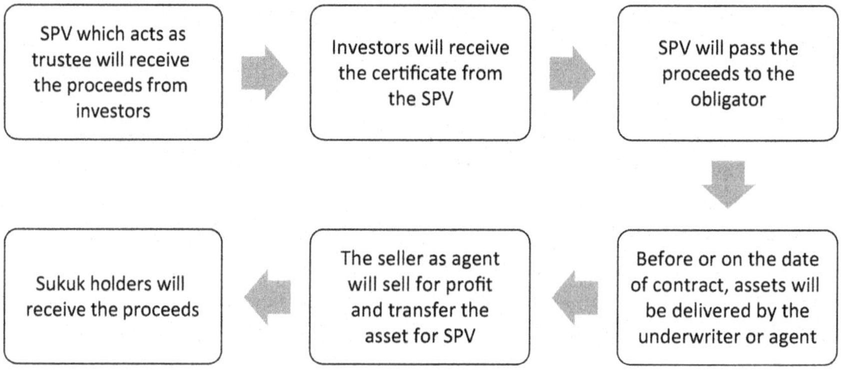

FIGURE 6.2 *Sukuk* based on *salam* contract

based on the concept of advance payment, which is allowed in *sharia*. Hence, *sukuk* holders' (investors') funds are used to make payment on assets from an obligator in the future. Thus, this *salam* contract requires an agent who will sell the future assets. This is because the investors want money in return for their investment instead of the assets themselves (Sukor, 2008). The funds from the sale are returned to the *sukuk* holders. This comprises the cost of the asset plus profits. In *salam sukuk*, the agent can be appointed by a "special purpose vehicle" (see below, under '*Sukuk mudaraba*') and can be a separate underwriter. *Salam sukuk* are used by companies that have short-term liquidity problems. The Central Bank of Bahrain often issues *salam sukuk* on a monthly basis with three-month maturity periods. The process of the *sukuk* is shown in Figure 6.2.

Musharaka *(joint venture)*

The *musharakah* contract is based on a joint venture business activity where all the partners provide labor, expertise and capital. The losses and profits are shared among all parties based on agreed-upon ratios. *Musharakah* has a similar concept to that of *mudaraba* in that it operates on a profit and loss sharing basis. However, it differs from *murabaha* as investors have the right to be involved in the investment decision-making process. Further, *musharaka sukuk* can also be traded in the secondary market.

The objective of *musharaka* is to channel investment funds from investors to finance business ventures. The transactions are based on the approved *sharia* concept of partnership contracts (profit and loss sharing). *Musharakah* is regarded as a high-risk tool due to the uncertain returns to the financier (bank), as they depend on the success of the business involved (Hunt-Ahmed, 2013). Basically, the *musharaka* investors are the owners of the business venture and have the right to profits based on pre-agreed profit sharing ratios. However, the losses are shared based on the equity participation. Unlike conventional financing, the financier (bank) of *sukuk* under these two concepts also faces an equity risk in addition

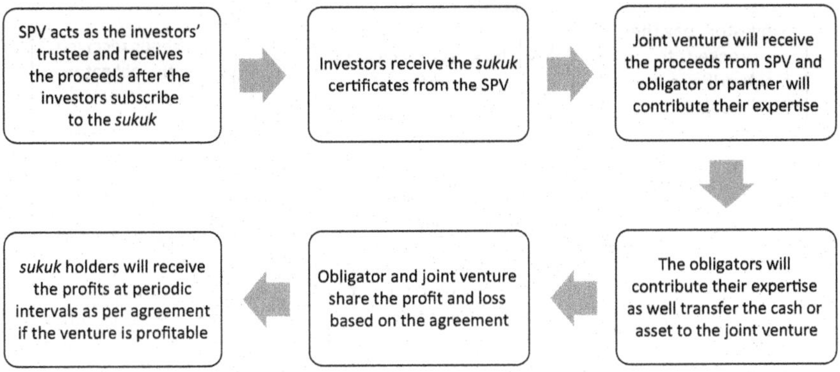

FIGURE 6.3 *Sukuk* based on *musharakah* contract

to the credit risk. Figure 6.3 illustrates the process after the *musharaka* contract takes place.

Sukuk mudaraba *(profit and loss sharing)*

Mudaraba is a contract of investment structure based on the approved Islamic concept of profit and loss sharing. The purpose of *mudaraba* is to raise public funds for major projects which require huge capital. This type of *sukuk* represents ownership of units of equal value in the *mudaraba* equity and the returns are allocated according to the percentage of ownership of shares. In *mudaraba*, the client is the owner of the equity with equal value that is registered in the name of holders on the basis of undivided ownership of shares in the *mudaraba* equity. Furthermore, the holder of *sukuk* is a silent partner (*rab al-mal*) who does not participate in the management of the underlying asset or project. On the other hand, the working partner (*mudarib*) plays a role as the *sukuk* obligator. When the investment activity reaps profits, the profits will be shared between both parties based on an initial agreement. Normally, the *sukuk* obligators are entitled to a fee or share of the profits (Hunt-Ahmed, 2013). A "special purpose vehicle" (SPV), also known as a "special purpose entity" (SPE), is a silent partner in the *mudaraba* contract which pools the funds from investors and represents the *sukuk* holders. Figure 6.4 summarizes the *mudaraba sukuk* contract structure.

Ijarah *(leasing)*

The main concept of *ijarah* is that the *sukuk* holders or investors are the owners of the asset and have the right to receive a profit when that asset is leased; that is, they are given the right to use an asset for a fee. The process of *ijarah* contract begins when a company requires an asset but is incapable of purchasing it. Therefore, the company enters into an *ijarah* contract that allows the asset to be

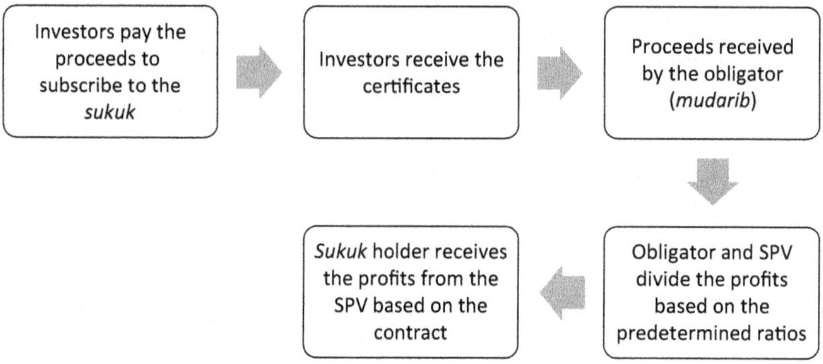

FIGURE 6.4 *Sukuk* based on *mudaraba* contract

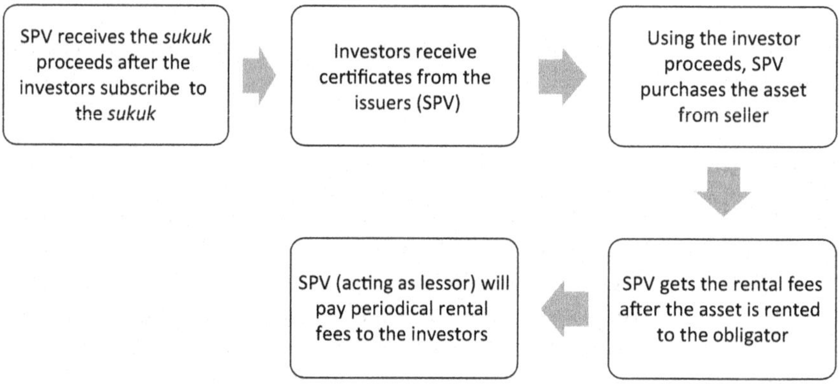

FIGURE 6.5 *Sukuk* based on *ijarah* contract

purchased by investors and then leased to the company for a fixed period of time. According to AAOIFI, this contract gives the owners (*sukuk* holders) the right to own the real estate, receive the rent and dispose of their *sukuk* in a manner that does not affect the rights of the lessee. The holders of such *sukuk* will bear all costs of damage to the real estate and its maintenance. Figure 6.5 illustrates how the the *ijarah* contract works after the contract is signed.

Istisna *(purchase order)*

Istisna is a contract between a buyer and contractor whereby the manufacturer (issuer) promises to complete a construction project by a future date. In the contract, both parties agree on a certain fixed price and the product specifications. If the identified project is not completed, or completed but the outcome does not meet the contract specifications, the buyer can withdraw from the contract. Alternatively, the issuer can sell the uncompleted asset to the financiers (bank).

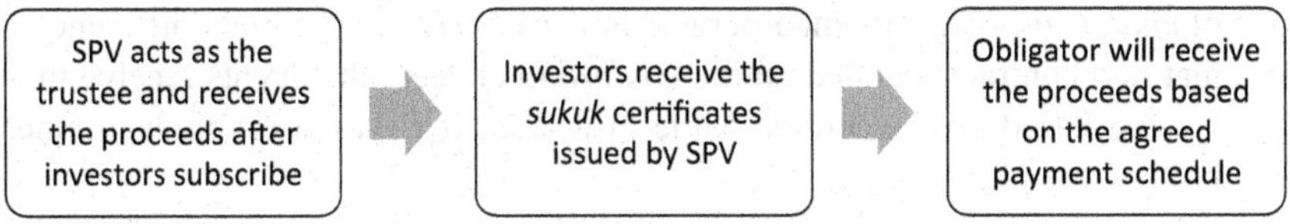

FIGURE 6.6 *Sukuk* based on *istisna* contract

Then the bank can resell the identified assets to the issuers, based on deferred-payment terms. Therefore, the *istisna* contract will securitize the issuer's obligation to settle the purchase price. *Shariah* does not allow the sale of these debt certificates to a third party at any price other than their face value. Usually, the *istisna* contract is suitable for financing large infrastructure projects. The process of *istisna sukuk* is shown in Figure 6.6.

New types of sukuk

Based on the requirement of corporations, government or investors, the *Sharia* Board has developed new financial products.

- The hybrid *sukuk* is a combination of different types of *sukuk* that has emerged from the significant growth in *sukuk* issuance. The limitations faced in the issuance of *ijarah sukuk*, due to insufficient tangible assets, resulted in hybrid *sukuk* to meet the demands of the investors. The hybrid *sukuk* combines *murabaha*, *ijarah* and *istisna* concepts and allows better securities for fund mobilization. Thus, there is a deviation from the strict requirement for *sukuk* transactions to have tangible assets. Therefore, in the case of a pool of hybrid securities, there is a requirement that at least 51 percent of the *sukuk* transactions must comprise tangible assets. Further, there is the prohibition of *riba* on the debt created by the *istisna*- and *murabaha*-based sale. Thus, the requirement is that at least 51 percent of the pool of hybrid *sukuk* should comprise *ijarah*, since that does provide for underlying tangible assets in the transaction.
- *Convertible sukuk* allow the holders to convert from *sukuk* to equity shares. The main underlying assets of the *sukuk* are the shares, and the *sukuk* coupon payments are not guaranteed but based on the dividend income of the underlying assets. The first in the world to issue the convertible *sukuk* was the Malaysian Khazanah Nasional Berhad. This *sukuk* had a five-year maturity period. The amount issued in October 2006 was US$750 million and the *sukuk* gave holders the right to convert their securities to ordinary shares in Telekom Malaysia at a fixed price of RM 1.00.
- With *wakala sukuk*, the agent (*wakeel*) makes investment decisions for the investors. The agent receives a fee for expertise and managements skills. *Wakala* contracts are of interest where there are no tangible underlying assets. In fact, *wakala sukuk* are used for assets to be collected. The features

of *mudaraba sukuk* are incorporated in *wakala sukuk*. The main difference is that in a contract founded on the *mudaraba* concept the agents receive their portion based on the profits, while in *wakala* it is based on predetermined profit share ratios.

- *Sukuk bai bithaman ajil* (BBA) are based on "cost plus profit" that has been agreed upon by both parties. The purpose of the *sukuk* is to meet the need for working capital, refinance debt or other financial requirements related to everyday activities. Although no physical asset exists in the transaction, the *mudaraba* interbank investment is used to satisfy the requirement of "existing" asset under the *sukuk* issuance. The underlying asset in BBA is used only to perform the purchase and sale of contracts (*bai inah*). Throughout the *sukuk* tenure, the seller has the ownership, which it is transferable upon maturity of the contract. However, most *sharia* scholars do not agree with this concept and it is available only in the Malaysian market.
- "Green *sukuk*" are for investments in environmental projects. Green *sukuk* represent three investments trends: (1) socially responsible investments (SRI), (2) Islamic mutual funds and (3) *sukuk*. Green *sukuk* are driven by factors such as the need to create jobs, sustainable investments related to renewables and support for green technology. The Malaysian government was the first to support Islamic finance related to green technology in 2010 by establishing a US$250 million fund for extending loans. Malaysia was also the pioneer in establishing the green *sukuk* framework in 2014 by expanding the SRI framework. The year 2014 also witnessed the partnership signed between Dubai and the World Bank to promote and launch green *sukuk* for projects related to infrastructure and clean energy.

In conclusion, there are different types of sukuk based on the purpose, contract, scheme and issues. The most familiar *sukuk* contracts are of the *musharaka* type, which is used for financing ventures, while in Malaysia the dominant *sukuk* contract type is the *ijarah*.

Recent global growth of *sukuk*

Malaysia was the first country to issue Islamic bonds, which it did in the year 1983. The first *sukuk* product introduced was the Government Investment Issue (GII), but this was not tradable as it was not allowed by the *Sharia* Council because the product itself lacked *sharia* compliance. In 1990 Islamic bonds received a boost when Shell from Malaysia issued *sukuk* for US$30 million. The kick-off of Islamic bonds began in 2001 when Kumpulan Guthrie and the Bahrain government issued *sukuk* based on the *ijarah* concept. Since then, the *sukuk* market has been growing rapidly. As of 2017, the largest *sukuk* issued are in the form of *murabaha,* accounting for 30% of the market share, followed by hybrid *sukuk murabaha/mudaraba* (24%) and *sukuk ijarah* (18%). Figure 6.7 shows the amount of *sukuk* issuance during the period 2001–2017.

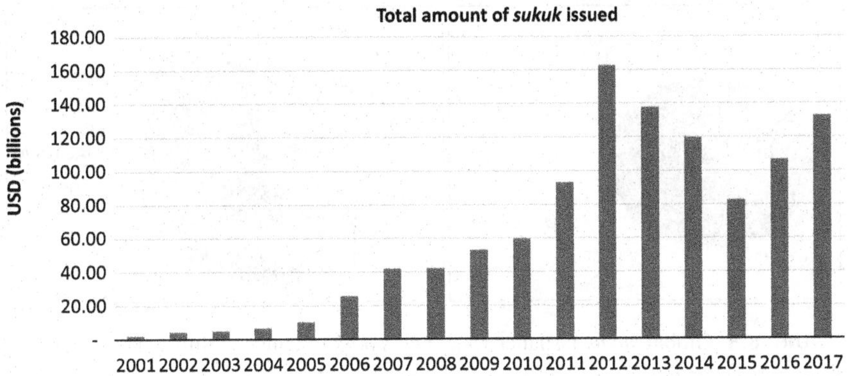

FIGURE 6.7 Total amount of *sukuk* issued
Source: Bloomberg.

The 2008 global fiscal crisis pushed investors to seek safer instruments and this greatly boosted the demand for *sukuk*, which peaked at nearly US$162.4 billion (including the Malaysian GII in 2012). Despite obstacles such as disputes over different *shariah* schools of thought, underdeveloped secondary markets, and limited supply, there were factors that contributed towards the growing popularity of *sukuk* as a debt instrument. These include a thriving Islamic funds industry catered to by large pools of Muslim wealth and abundant liquidity, indicating that demand still exceeded supply. However, the *sukuk* market showed downward trends in the years 2013, 2014 and 2015 with *sukuk* issuance declining to $137.38 billion, $119.49 billion and 82.41 billion, respectively. In 2016, the global *sukuk* market witnessed a rebound after three consecutive years of decline following its peak in 2012. Global *sukuk* issuance posted a solid growth of 29% from the previous year to reach $106.39 billion in 2016.

The next year, 2017, showed strong performance of *sukuk* issuance with an increase by 24%, reaching $132.46 billion, underpinned primarily by the jumbo issuances of some Gulf Cooperation Council (GCC) countries. To date, the largest international *sukuk* issue was by the government of Saudi Arabia, with US$9 billion sovereign issuances as well one of the largest domestic *sukuk* totaling US$15.7 billion in 2017. According to S&P Global Ratings, these performances were driven by good liquidity conditions in the GCC and, more generally, globally, as well as activity by some countries with the goal of further developing their Islamic finance industries.

As of 2017, *sukuk* issuances reached US$1,082 billion, with 84% from the Asian countries, 15% from European countries and 1% from African countries, as shown in Figure 6.8. Within Asia, the largest *sukuk* issuance was by the Malaysian market, with total value of $614 billion, accounting for 57% of total issuances compared to others countries with only 43% or $468.43 billion.

The second largest *sukuk* issuance in Asia was by the GCC countries, with total issuances of 14% or $145.78 billion for the period 2001 to 2017 (Figure

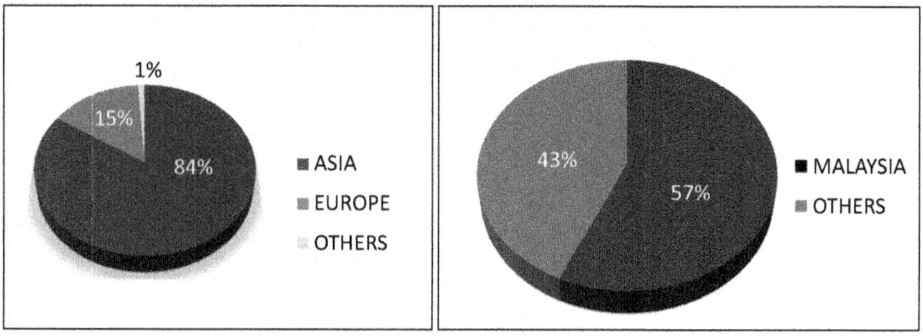

FIGURE 6.8 Global *sukuk* issuance (*left*) and *sukuk* issuance within Asia (*right*)
Source: Bloomberg.

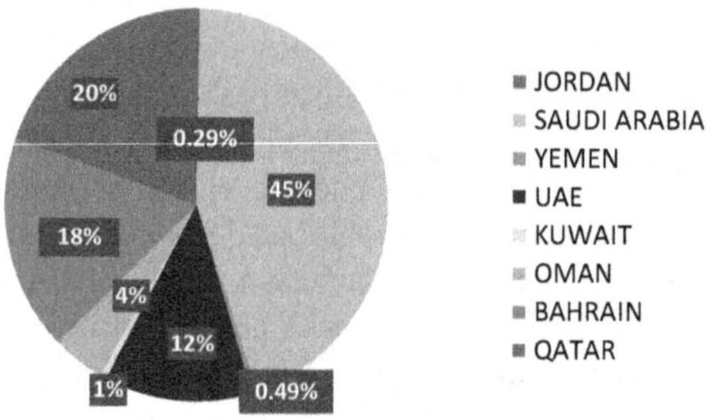

FIGURE 6.9 Total *sukuk* issuance in the Middle East
Source: Bloomberg.

6.9). The largest *sukuk* issuance in the Middle East was from Saudi Arabia, which totaled US$64.9 billion, constituting 45%. This was followed by Qatar, Bahrain, United Arab Emirates and Oman with total issuances constituting 19.5%, 17.71%, 12.49% and 4.44%, respectively. Others countries such as Kuwait, Yemen and Jordan showed total issuances of less than 1%. Total issuances for Kuwait, Yemen and Jordan constituted 0.56%, 0.49% and 0.29%, respectively.

Global *sukuk* outstanding increased to a record US$498.86 billion as at 31 December 2017, a 28% rise from US$389.33 billion at end 2016. Malaysia's secondary *sukuk* outstanding was US$226.28 billion, or 45% of the total *sukuk* outstanding (Figure 6.10).

Malaysia also developed itself as an offshore *sukuk* hub for other countries. *Sukuk* denominated in Malaysian ringgits (MYR) have been issued by foreign issuers in the past, including the Gulf Investment Corporation, National Bank of Abu Dhabi and Noble Group. At present, Malaysia is developing itself as a multi-currency *sukuk* center. In fact, two Malaysian entities issued the first

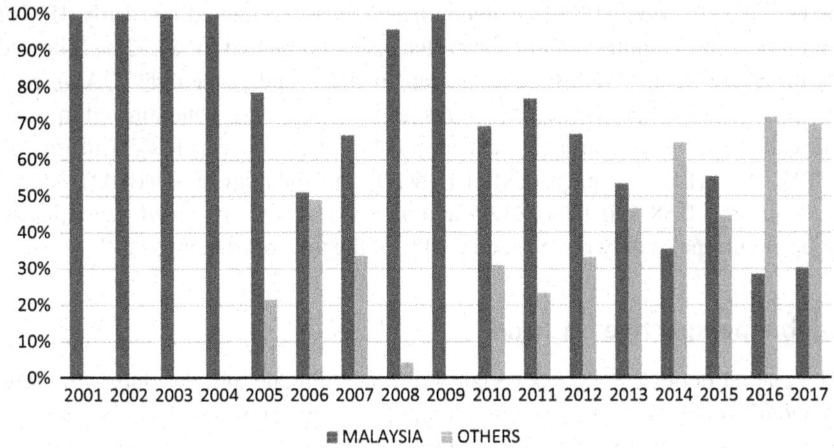

FIGURE 6.10 Total *sukuk* outstanding: Malaysia vs others from 2001 to 2017
Source: Bloomberg.

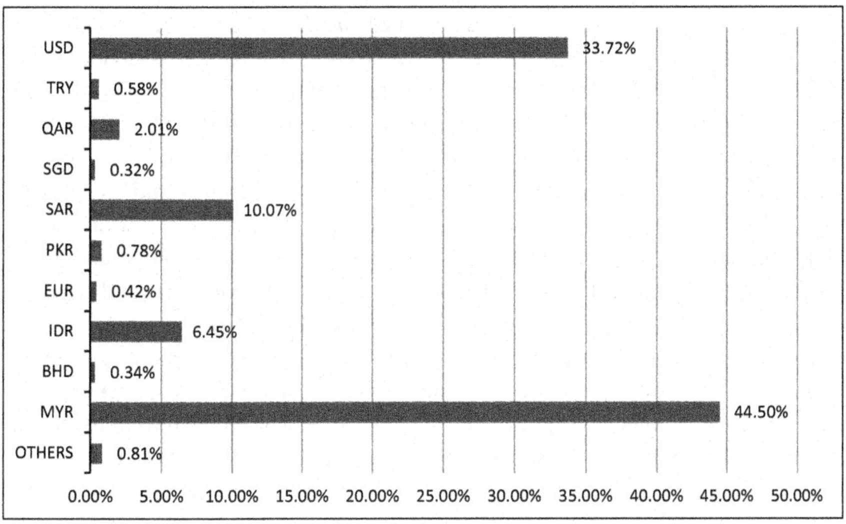

FIGURE 6.11 Global *sukuk* outstanding by currency
Source: Bloomberg.

Chinese yuan (CNH)-denominated *sukuk*. Danga Capital's issuance of three-year CNH-denominated *sukuk* in 2011 was followed by Axiata's two-year CNH-denominated *sukuk* in 2012. The CNH *sukuk* was also designed to take advantage of the regional demand for the renminbi.

Malaysia continues to dominate the local currencies or MYR-denominated *sukuk* market, as shown in Figure 6.11. The figure also shows global *sukuk* outstanding by currency. At end 2017, MYR-denominated *sukuk* accounted for nearly 45% of total *sukuk* outstanding, US$-denominated *sukuk* accounted for 33.72%, followed by the Saudi riyal (SAR), Indonesian rupiah (IDR) and Qatar riyal (QAR), constituting 10.07%, 6.45% and 2.01%, respectively. The rest, denominated in other currencies, are less than 1%, such as the Pakistani rupee (PKR), Turkish lira (TRY), euro (EUR), Singapore dollar (SGD) and Bahraini dinar (BHD), constituting 0.78%, 0.58%, 0.42%, 0.32% and 0.34%, respectively. *Sukuk* denominated in other currencies only represented 0.81% of the total outstanding.

Global perspective on *sukuk*

The market outlook for *sukuk* certainly is uncertain due to tight global liquidity, geopolitical risks and slow progress in the development of new Islamic products. Recently some of the non- Islamic countries such as Hong Kong have been attracted to *sukuk* issuances. With greater awareness created of the Islamic products, more non-core Islamic finance countries could also be enticed to *sukuk*. Under tight liquidity conditions, if the cost of funding increases, *sukuk* will become more expensive for issuers and accordingly this will affect the liquidity of the market as well the demand for *sukuk*. However, since *sukuk* have a standard or fixed rate to hedge against foreign currency risk, that would support their issuance. Based on geopolitical risks, such as when Qatar faced sanctions in June 2017, investors' perceptions would be unfavorable towards the GCC as a whole. Qatar faced a major outflow of foreign deposits in 2017, estimated atabout Us$21 billion. However, the government mitigated the outflow by injecting funds amounting to US$39 billion in that year. This could affect the progress of *sukuk* and ultimately their growth prospects in 2018. Therefore, global harmonization among the markets should be directed towards boosting the issuance of *sukuk* and restoring investors' interest. One of the ways to strengthen *sukuk* issuance is standardization of the different schools of thought of *sharia* scholars on *sharia*-compliant status. Ultimately, we can see a boost for *sukuk* issuance if the gap between demand and supply is bridged. High-quality and liquid assets are believed to protect investors and significantly support *sukuk* issuance. Further, the development of new products should not be ignored since it could meet the needs of global investors. For example, the green *sukuk* product has attracted Quantum Solar Park in Malaysia to issue the first ever green *sukuk* of US$250 million. Given several landmark issuances from Turkey, the United Arab Emirates, Saudi Arabia, Malaysia and others in 2017, the growth prospects of *sukuk* are bright and the interest shown in Islamic products is envisaged to attract more global investors.

Bibliography

Accounting and Auditing Organization for Islamic Financial Institutions (AAOIFI) (2008). *Guidance statement on accounting for investments and amendment*. Financial Accounting Standard 17. Manama, Bahrain: AAOIFI.

Adam, N. J., & Thomas, A. S. (2004). *Islamic Bonds: Your Guide to Issuing, Structuring and Investing in Sukuk*. London: Euromoney Books.

Ainley, M., Mashayekhi, A., Hicks, R., Rahman, A., & Ravalia, A. (2007). Islamic *Finance* in the UK: *Regulation* and *Challenges*. London: Financial Services Authority.

Aljazira Capital (2010). *The Financing Role of the Saudi Capital Market*. Retrieved from www.aljaziracapital.com.sa/report_file/ess/eco-4.pdf.

Bank Negara Malaysia, Annual Reports – several years. Retrieved from www.bnm.gov.my/files/publication/ar.

Capital Market Issues According to Islamic Jurisprudence. Resolutions of the Securities Commission Shariah Advisory Council. Securities Commission, Kuala Lumpur. Retrieved from www.sc.com.my/main.asp.

Godlewski, C. J., Turk-Ariss, R., & Weill, L. (2013). Sukuk vs. conventional bonds: A stock market perspective. *Journal of Comparative Economics*, *41*(3), 745–761.

Haneef, R. (2009). From asset-backed to asset-light structures: The intricate history of sukuk. *ISRA International Journal of Islamic Finance*, *1*(1), 103–126.

Hunt-Ahmed, K. (2013). Contemporary Islamic *Finance*: Innovations, *Applications*, and *Best Practices*. New York & Chichester: John Wiley & Sons.

International Islamic Financial Market (IIFM) (2010). *Sukuk report*, various issues. www.iifm.net/market-research. Nasdaq Dubai.

International Islamic Financial Market (IIFM) (2017). Sukuk report: A comprehensive study of the global sukuk market. Nasdaq Dubai.

International Organization of Securities Commissions, IOSCO (2005). *Islamic Capital Markets: Fact Finding Report*. Madrid, Spain: International Organization of Securities Commissions.

Lahsasna, A., & Lin, L. S. (2012). Issues in Islamic capital markets: Islamic bond/sukuk. In 3rd International conference on Business and Economic Research. Proceeding. 12–13 March 2012. Bandung, Indonesia.

Memon, N. A. (2009). Sukuk structures and markets. *Journal of Islamic Banking and Finance* (July–September), 64–76.

Rating Agency Malaysia (RAM) Ratings newsletters, various issues. Retrieved from www.ram.com.my/news-events/.

Securities Commission of Malaysia. Guidelines on the Offering of Islamic Securities. Retrieved from www.sc.com.my/main.asp?pageid=448.

Shabnam, M. (2009). Function of wa'ad in asset-backed sukuk. *ISRA Bulletin*, (4), 7–10.

Sukor, M. E. A., Muhamad, R., & Gunawa, A. Y. (2008). Malaysian Sukuk: Issues in accounting standards. *Shariah Journal*, *16*(1), 63–74.

Tahmoures, A. A. (2013). Compare and contrast sukuk (Islamic bonds) with conventional bonds, are they compatible? *Journal of Global Business Management*, *9*(1), 44–52.

Thomas, A., Cox, S., & Kraty, B. (2006). *Structuring Islamic Finance Transactions*. London: Euromoney Books.

Wilson, R. (2008). Innovation in the structuring of Islamic sukuk securities. *Humanomics*, *24*(3), 170–181.

7

SUKUK

Meaning, valuation, benefits and challenges

Mustapha Abubakar and Nasiru Abdullahi

Meaning of '*sukuk*'

There are different accounts of the history of the origin of *sukuk.* According to some reports, the history of *sukuk* can be traced back as far back as the era of the second caliph, Umar b. al-Khattab (A.D. 634–644) (Rohim & Shereeza, 2013). According to others, the word '*sukuk*' has been recognised to be in existence during the period of Caliph Mu'awiyah (A.D. 661–680) (Zulkhibri, 2015). Furthermore, it has also been reported that the sale of *sukuk* was recorded in the era of Marwan b. al-Hakam (A.D. 684–685), but the practice was objected to by some of his companions and was therefore outlawed (Zulkhibri, 2015).

The use of the word '*sukuk*' can be traced back to traditional Islamic literature as a word used in place of a certificate for goods or foodstuffs (*sakk al-bada'i*). *Sukuk* is the plural of s*akk*, which means a legal document, deed, or check. From another perspective, *sukuk* or *sikak* is also the plural of *sakk* meaning to strike or to hit; this meaning is related to striking a seal on a document, hence also the meaning of legal instrument or deed. The word translates literally as 'written document'.

Thus, by origin the word *sukuk* is an Arabic word for certificates related to financial dealings, but can now be seen as an Islamic equivalent of conventional bonds and has been defined variously in the literature. Its first definition was as a system of paying the wages of government officers, who would later exchange the certificates in line with their day-to-day consumption of goods or foodstuffs. From this was derived its second definition as 'certificates of equal value representing individual shares in ownership of tangible assets, usufructs and services or (in the ownership of) the assets of particular projects or special investment activity'. (Norton Rose Fulbright, 2018). In a third definition, the Islamic Financial Services Board defines *sukuk* in the following terms: '*sukūk* (plural of *sakk*), frequently referred to as "Islamic bonds", are certificates with each *sakk* representing a proportional undivided ownership right in tangible assets, or a pool of predominantly tangible assets, or a business venture (such as a *mudārabah*)' (IFSB, 2009). Finally, *sukuk* can be defined as commercial papers providing investors with ownership in underlying assets. They are asset-backed trust certificates evidencing ownership of an asset or its usufruct. Their additional feature is that they provide a stable income and comply with the principles of *shariah*.

In all the above definitions, the central theme seen is that *sukuk* represent financial transactions in which assets are pooled and certificates representing interests in the pool are issued to investors. Thus, *sukuk* are used to mobilise resources, and are beneficial to investors on the one hand and fund users on the other, through their provision of liquidity to corporations and other users of funds. It is noteworthy here from the definitions that, although *sukuk* represent a share of the ownership of underlying assets or projects, they are negotiable or tradable. However, it is not tradable if the trade would create any debt obligations. In addition to their compliance with *shariah* principles, the main features that differentiate *sukuk* from conventional bonds are their link to the underlying asset. Furthermore, the remuneration of the *sukuk* holders is not based on debt and interest payments of the issuer, but depends on the income generated by the asset underlying the *sukuk*.

Recent trends and mega *sukuk* project globally

Sukuk issuance has become an attractive alternative financing option to many countries in Africa, Europe and Asia.

Recent trends in corporate *sukuk* issuances globally indicate a fluid mix of varying features with respect to issuers, tenors, currency of issue as well as structures among others. According to the International Islamic Financial Market

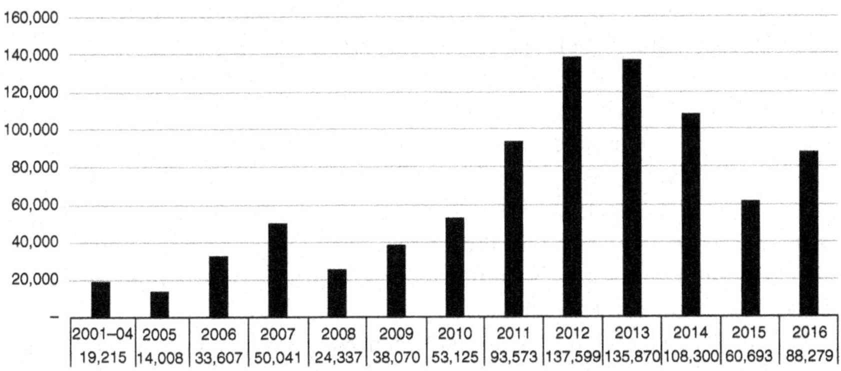

FIGURE 7.1 Global corporate *sukuk* issuances – selected value leaders (2014 > USD 200 million, tenor > 1 year)

Source: IIFM Sukuk Database 2016. Permission to use chart obtained from IIFM.

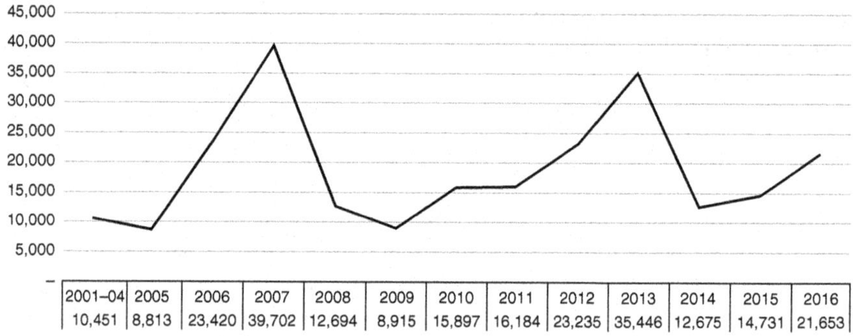

FIGURE 7.2 Global corporate *sukuk* issuances (Jan 2001–Dec 2014) – all tenors, all currencies, in USD millions

Source: IIFM Sukuk Database 2016. Permission to use chart obtained from IIFM.

(IIFM) annual report of 2016, landmark corporate *sukuk* issuances were made by different corporate entities in Malaysia, Pakistan, United Arab Emirates, Qatar and Saudi Arabia. Malaysia is regarded as the hub of Islamic capital markets among Muslim countries because of the regularity in its *sukuk* issuances. The tenors for the issues made range from a minimum of 5 years to perpetuity. The issues made were combinations of international and domestic offerings having minimum amounts of USD 202 million or equivalent and maximum of USD 1,500 million. The underlying structures for the issues were *mudharaba, murabaha, ijarah, musharaka* and *wakala* (Figure 7.2).

Valuation of *sukuk*

Corporate *sukuk* as well as public *sukuk* carry pre-fixed rates of return. This is comparable to the profit rates in deferred-payment *murabaha* and rentals in *ijarah*, which are all pre-fixed. Nevertheless, as mentioned by s*hariah* scholars, parties in contractually partnership-based modes should not specify any pre-fixed return or guarantee of the investment. Accordingly, AAOIFI offered some specific standards on *sukuk.* The standard specified that the *sukuk* prospectus should not contain any clause that states an issuer's liability to compensate certificate holders for the nominal value except in negligence and torts, and a guarantee given by the issuer of a fixed percentage of profit. In reality, however, the actual structure of *sukuk* and the way in which they are marketed assure the subscribers and holders of a fixed return rate, which is similar to other fixed-income securities in the conventional interest-based structure.

As *sukuk* issuance globally is new when compared to conventional bonds, they suffers some basic challenges with respect to many issues associated with them. One of these issues is how they are valued to reflect Islamic principles as a departure from existing conventional bond instruments. It should be noted here that the current mechanism for *sukuk* valuation is based on a conventional benchmark rate such as the London interbank offered rate (LIBOR) or its euro equivalent (EURIBOR).

The difficulties encountered in determining *sukuk* prices identified in the literature are many. The first is the limited number of participants in the market, which results in less liquidity occasioned by absence of market depth. The second is the absence of a clear pricing mechanism that is risk-based in *sukuk*. The third is the absence of an appropriate risk mitigation strategy for *sukuk* that will accommodate instability in the market value of instruments due to fluctuations in benchmark rates. The fourth is the dearth of appropriate mechanisms for validation of a standard price, needed for the purpose of information dissemination.

In consideration of the above-mentioned factors as part of the difficulties associated with coming up with an ideal mechanism for valuation, there have been some limited efforts by researchers to suggest some mechanisms that will address appropriate valuation of *sukuk*. An alternative approach is that *sukuk* returns are made through periodic income from leases, profits from operations, or sales of assets such as property, equipment or joint venture business. In a real sense, the incomes from leases and profits from operations or sales are structured to obtain the equivalent of a constant annual interest rate, which therefore does not fall into the category 'interest payments'. It can, however, be argued here that under this mechanism a problem arises as to how an appropriate daily *sukuk* pricing can be achieved, which could facilitate its trading and ensure a robust secondary market.

Naifar and Mseddi (2013) have proposed a pricing methodology for *sukuk ijarah*, the most utilised form of *sukuk*, by presenting a model that prices *sukuk* in consideration of their inherent default risk. Thus the model is premised on factors such as probability of default, rates of recovery, maintenance cost and damage to real estate for the purpose of determining a fair expected price.

The valuation is based on two segments of cash flow, identified as the variable leg and the default leg. The variable segment is obtained from the present value of all the rental payments made by the special purpose vehicle (SPV) to the *sukuk* holders/investors. It can be expressed as:

$$V_{variables} = \sum_{i-1}^{n} Rent_i \, P(t,T) Q(t_i) C(t_{i-1}, t_i), \tag{7.1}$$

where V is the present value of the variable segment and $Rent_i$ represents the rental incomes of the assets, which are assumed to be made up of the variables:

$P(t, T)$ as the discount functions for a rental income from valuation date to rental payment date,

$Q(t_i)$ as the probability of no default (survival probability),

$C(t_{i-1}, t_i)$ representing the accrual function denoting the fraction of year between date $i–1$ and i, and

n as the specified period of time.

The default segment is given by the expected amount received by the *sukuk* holders in the case of a credit event

$$V_{Default} = \int_{0}^{r} (1-R)P(t,T)(1-Q(t))dt, \tag{7.2}$$

where *Default* is the present value of default segment,

R represents the recovery rate, and

d_t is the length of the time interval.

Now the value of *sukuk ijarah* is simply determined as the difference between the two segments as follows:

$$V_{sukuk} = \sum_{i=1}^{n} P(t,T)Q(t_i)C(t_{i-1,}t_i) - \int_{0}^{r} (1-R)P(t,T)(1-Q(t))dt \tag{7.3}$$

Values for the discount function and survival probability are to be determined using Monte Carlo or bootstrap methods to simulate possible realisations of interest rate and intensity of default.

In another work, Yunita (2015) proposed a fair market value model of *sukuk ijarah* and *mudaraba* in Indonesia. According to the proposed model, a fair value of *sukuk* is determined on the basis of some assumptions, which are: periodic payment of rental costs, the repurchase price, costs that are related to expenses used during the *sukuk* period of the assets and transaction costs at the time of bond issuance in capital markets, and the fee given to the SPV at the beginning of the contract. The formula is given as:

$$\sum_{t=1}^{r} \frac{L}{(1+r)^t} + \frac{Pr}{(1+r)^T} + Poa + S + \sum_{t=1}^{T} \frac{0}{(1+r)^t}, \tag{7.4}$$

where

L is the fee/rental cost

Pr is the the repurchase value of assets

Po is the the assets price given by the borrower

a is the fee percentage value for the SPV

o is the cost of operations (maintenance and insurance).

In the same vein, Yunita (2015) proposed a fair market value model of *sukuk mudaraba* price as follows:

$$Mudharabah\ price \sum_{t=1}^{T} \frac{I_T}{(1+r)^t} + \frac{P_T}{(1+r)^T} \tag{7.5}$$

where

I_T is the yield based on project profits of each period and
P_T is the capital which is returned at the due date.

Benefits and challenges of *sukuk*

Benefits of sukuk

There are varying perspectives on the values inherent in the utilisation of *sukuk* by corporate as well as public institutions. Some of the benefits have been highlighted as follows (Usmani, 2008):

1. The use of *sukuk* represents a way of raising financial resources for large companies including multinational corporations, multinational development institutions and government agencies requiring enormous resources that are difficult to be met by individual investors singly. *Sukuk* funds generation is a real vehicle in the drive for resource mobilisation that is consistent with Islamic legal injunctions and *maqasid al-shariah.*
2. For many investors, a major concern is whether there are diversified sources of income available from different investment outlets, which at the same time can be liquidated without difficulty to meet needs as they arise. This legitimate concern is addressed if *sukuk* are utilised, as there are openings in the secondary market for trading in the *sukuk* where investors can sell their current holdings in full or in part, for cash including earnings where it is a profitable one.
3. A major fault line usually associated with conventional financing is its unfair means of allocating returns from business efforts. This anomaly is effectively corrected by the use of *sukuk,* which carry a more equitable method of distributing wealth as all investors are carried along in fair manner and based on actual profits made. Note that there is a broader scale of wealth circulation in this arrangement as opposed to the restrictive conventional means of raising finance.
4. Islamic banks and other financial institutions sometimes have difficulty in managing their liquidity situations as they are limited by *shariah* constraints. With *sukuk* issuance by corporate entities, an avenue is created for them. For the corporate entities, their need for large-scale financing is met by the banks that may have vast resources trapped in excess liquidity.
5. Public–private partnership, which has been used in raising financing required for infrastructure provision and development, could have potential for its sustenance with the utilisation of *sukuk* as a source of finance. There are also many possible benefits of utilising *sukuk* financing to many parties. To the originators, the benefits are seen in respect of reduced cost of funds occasioned by higher ratings, access to capital markets, bringing in alternative and diversified funding sources, possibilities of reduction of risks, and possible tax relief on capital. Similarly, investors can derive benefits in terms

of provision of safe-harbour investment, an appropriate risk–reward relationship that ensues a fair profit-sharing arrangement and enhanced liquidity (Ismail, 2013)

6. Forward-lease *sukuk*, a not widely known and used source of funding, has the potential for uplifting economic developmental activities through infrastructure financing attributes it possesses.

Challenges of sukuk

1. Of course some challenges trail the issuance and utilisation of *sukuk* in corporate entities. The first challenge is related to the viability of an economy that involves the private sector in the production of public infrastructure and public goods. Thus where there are fault lines in the overall activities in the economic landscape, such as high interest rates and inflation rates, these permeates to the issuance and performance of *sukuk.*
2. Another challenge for full utilisation of the benefits associated with *sukuk* is concern about the capacity of the public sector to establish a sound legal framework that would attract private sector participation. From the perspective of the private-sector investor, the existence of a clear and consistent legal framework is a precondition for participation.
3. A further challenge facing *sukuk* in Islamic corporate entities is related to their use in a context regulated by conventional laws. An abundance of current evidence indicates that the majority of laws in various jurisdictions are at variance with *shariah* provisions and thus do not favour Islamic finance (Khan et al. 2015). Furthermore, a lack of consensus on *shariah* compliance, along with contingent matters that may surface with the application of conventional laws to *sukuk*, could have the combined effect of creating and enhancing apprehension among investors (Jobst et al. 2008).
4. Assets that are tradable in the secondary market for *sukuk* are limited in number. This is as a result of the fact that those assets are *shariah*-compliant and thus fresh issuers have a limited supply of underlying assets and have to wait for maturity of the underlying assets before new issuances can be made. This is unlike conventional bond issuances, which do not have underlying assets as a basis for issuance.
5. Again, there is the challenge of standardisation of *sukuk* in its documentation and structures, and also standardisation in *shariah* principles.

Differences in *shariah* explanations on *sukuk* issuance (i.e. schools of thought)

Far-reaching debates have been recorded and are still raging on in the Islamic scholars' community with regard to issues covering theories and laws of *sukuk*. Participants in the debate largely belong to the Shafi'i and Hanafi schools of thought. Note that the differences in opinion predate these schools of thought, going way back to the time of the companions of the Prophet. This is recorded in the two different pronouncements made by Umar *(radiyallah anhu)*, the second Caliph, who in one instance forbade the sale of food items until they are available, while in the other instance he asked Hakik bin Huzam to sell food items that were not availableThere was also a situation where Marwan, a companion of the Prophet, was charged by Abu Huraira, also a companion of the Prophet, with having justified the sale of food items that did not exist with *sukuk*, but retorted: 'I did not do it.'

As already mentioned, the accounts of differences of opinion on *sukuk* among the companions of the prophet predate the 'schools of thought' differences of opinion. The first opinion dismisses the concept of *sukuk* on the basis of Imam Shafi'i's *qiyas* (analogical) method. This position is anchored on the perceived fact that *sukuk* have similar features to conventional bonds with respect to risk (*gharar*) and gambling (*maisir*). By contrast, the second opinion approves *sukuk* on the basis of Imam Abu Hanifah's *ijtihad* method. Imam Shafi'i and Imam Abu Hanifah utilised different bases in building their positions on the validity or otherwise of *sukuk*: *istidlal al-hukm* (the inductive approach) and *instinbath al-hukm* (the deductive approach). Imam Abu Hanifah used the custom or tradition *('urf)* of the particular community with reference to social facts in building his position. For Imam Shafi'i, using the deductive approach, his conviction was that Allah is very much aware of the legitimate needs and rights of human beings, and thus determining these should not be on the basis of human judgment.

However, it should be noted here that many of the current trends in *sukuk* issuance show similarity to the structure of conventional bonds in terms of lack of ownership, right to a fixed return, and the guarantee of repayment of principal (Usmani, 2008). Furthermore, with the classifications of *sukuk* into asset-based and asset-backed categories, there are contentious *shariah* issues with respect to the actual ownership of the underlying assets under the asset-based *sukuk*. Although asset-backed *sukuk* appear to be better than asset-based *sukuk* in terms of compliance with *shariah* requirements, the number of issues of these *sukuk* remains limited due to the popularity of asset-based *sukuk*. One of the reasons for the greater interest in asset-based *sukuk* is lack of a proper regulatory framework for securitisation in the countries of the Gulf Cooperation Council (GCC). In the GCC, there is a major issue of handicap on foreign ownership of some classes of assets and this has implications for the structuring of *sukuk* (Dusuki & Mokhtar, 2010)

It is noteworthy that the important issue that remains not uncontroversial among Islamic scholars is whether there is actual ownership of assets under the asset-based *sukuk* in accordance with the spirit of Islamic law. In its true sense, ownership of an underlying asset is based on *qabd* which means taking possession, having a grip over a thing or having a hold on it, and this has been interpreted differently (with respect to the nature of the asset in the contract) by scholars of the schools of thought. Thus, in an Islamic sales contract there are divergent views on what constitutes *qabd* depending on the type and nature of goods being purchased or sold. There are of course two broad classifications of *qabd*, which are *qabd hissi*, i.e physical possession, and *qabd hukmi*, i.e legal possession. The distinction between the two forms of taking possession is that while the former means *explicit* taking of possession and is applied to movable and immovable assets, the latter means *implied* taking of possession.

Shariah scholars in the different schools of thought have established different views on the status of *qabd* in the sales contract. In the views of Hanafi, *qabd* does not constitute an essential part of a sales contract (thus can be postponed) unless it is in respect of transactions involving usury such as gold and silver, and where that is the case, *qabd* becomes an essential part of the contract. In the Maliki school of thought, non-food items are exempted from the purview of *qabd*, and this implies that taking possession of the items is not seen to be a requirement for their sale. For items that are liable to attract interest (*ribawi* food items), however, there are two opinions in the Maliki school of thought; while the first opinion allowsthe transaction, the second opinion disallows it. To the Shafi'is, possession is a requirement for all types of goods; the position taken by Imam Shafi'i is based on the Hadith of the Prophet. However, some scholars, specifically Ibn Qayyum, is of the opinion that what constitute *qabd* depends on the custom or *'urf* in the community.

Given the foregoing discussion on what constitutes *qabd* and its status in a sale contract, it becomes appropriate to evaluate *sukuk* transactions with respect to whether there is a real taking of ownership of the underlying assets by the subscribers. As found by Dusuki and Mokhtar (2010), analysis of the documents in respect of some issuances has revealed that *sukuk* holders especially in the unsecured asset-based *sukuk* structures have no interest in the underlying asset that they are supposed to own. The study found that, even for secured asset-based *sukuk* issuances, the holders are entitled to security interest in the assets only, which means that their status is confined to creditorship interest only and not ownership. Other issues that actually compromise the ownership status of subscribers to asset-based *sukuk*, as found through examination of several documents on issuances, are restrictions to disposal of the assets by subscribers in addition to purchase undertaking by originators at par and lack of financial due diligence on the assets.

Are *sukuk* comparable to conventional bonds?

Sukuk and conventional bonds have some features in common. These include similarities in terms of representating certificates of investment, in methods of raising capital and means of generating returns; both can be re-structured, and are both susceptible to default. All these similarities do not, however, preclude the existence of fundamental differences between *sukuk* and conventional bonds, which are as follows:

1. The relationship between the parties in *sukuk* is based on the specific type of contract that governs the issuance of the *sukuk*. The contracts can be based

on *musharakah, mudarabah, ijarah*, etc. Thus, profit or loss sharing of the proceeds from the *sukuk* performance is governed by the mode of contract agreed upon. For an *ijarah*-based contract, for instance, the issuer's liability is dependent on demand and supply for the leased asset in the market, whereas in the case of a bond the nature of the relationship is that of a lender and a creditor, in which situation incurring a loss is not recognised as a possibility.

2. Depending on the nature of contract, for example in the case of *sukuk al-ijarah*, there is the involvement of a special purpose vehicle (SPV) entity not owned by the originator who issues the *sukuk* to investors, but technically represents the *sukuk* holders, utilising the *sukuk* proceeds to pay the purchase price to the originator simultaneously. This arrangement does not exist under a conventional bond contract.
3. In *sukuk* issuance, subscribers or investors in *sukuk* lay claim to ownership of the underlying assets for which the *sukuk* issue is made. This means that the subscribers are part owners of the asset (which must be *shariah*-approved assets) and thus possess rights and obligations as owners of the asset. In contrast to this, bond holding does not confer right of ownership of the asset, but indicates a debt obligation on the issuer only.
4. A conventional corporate bond represents a contractual debt obligation in which the issuer is under an obligation to the bond holder for payment of principal and interest on specified dates irrespective of actual happenings (performance of the bond). This in in sharp contrast to the kind of obligation the issuer has to *sukuk* holders, who are entitled to receive an agreed share of the revenues generated by the asset underlying the *sukuk*. In addition, the holders are also entitled to receive an agreed share of the proceeds of the *sukuk* asset realisation.
5. Islamic corporate bond holders are not entitled to any guaranteed rate of return as either profits or losses can arise from its operations. In the case of conventional bond, by contrast, bond holders receive a pre-determined periodic interest payment in addition to repayment of the principal amount on maturity of the bond, i.e at the end of its life.
6. An important difference between *sukuk* and bonds is that the basis for face value determination of *sukuk* is the market value of the underlying asset upon which the *sukuk* are issued. The value of *sukuk* can thus increase with any increase in the market value of the assets underlying their issuance. For conventional bond issuance, by contrast, the face value is a function of the issuer's credit rating.

Conclusion

This chapter discussed the divergent shades of meanings, trends in issuances, valuation techniques, benefits and challenges, differences in *shariah* position as well as comparability or otherwise of *sukuk*. From the foregoing, it can be concluded that *sukuk* have become a veritable instrument for generation and subsequent utilisation of funds by large-scale fund users such as governments and corporate giants. Even though there are scores of unresolved issues associated with *sukuk*, their relevance to economies as a financing option remains significant.

References

Ahmad, N. 2009. *The parameters of forward* ijarah *and its application in financing services in Islamic financial institutions*. Available at: www.academia.edu/235360.

Dusuki, A. W., & Mokhtar, S. 2010. Critical appraisal of shariah issues on ownership in asset-based sukuk as implemented in the Islamic debt market. *ISRA* Research Paper No 8.

International Islamic Financial Market. 2016. *IIFM sukuk report: A comprehensive study of the global sukuk market* (6th ed). Available at: www.iifm.net.

Islamic Financial Services Board. 2009. *Capital adequacy requirements for sukuk IFSB 7*. Available at: www.ifsb.org/published.php.

Ismail, A. 2013. *Public private partnerships: Lesson from sukuk*. IRTI Working Paper 1435–04.

Jobst, A., Kunzel, P., Mills, P., & Sy, A. 2008. Islamic bond issuance: What sovereign debt managers need to know. *International Journal of Islamic and Middle Eastern Finance and Management*, *1*(4): 330–344.

Khan, T., Elsiefy, E., & Kyoung, L. E. 2015. Legal and regulatory issues in issuing sukuk in muslim-minority countries: Lessons from developed countries' experience. Available at: swfa2015.uno.edu/G_Islamic_Finance_I/p201.docx.

Naifar, N., & Mseddi, S. 2013. Sukuk spreads determinants and pricing model methodology. *Afro-Asian Journal of Finance and Accounting*, *3*(3): 241–257.

Nawawi, A., & Syarif, Y. 1992. *Sahih muslim bi Syarhi al-Nawawi*. Beirut: Daar Ihya' Al-Turath Al-Arabi.

Norton Rose Fulbright. 2018. *AAOIFI statement on Sukuk and its implications*. Available at www.nortonrosefulbright.com/knowledge/publications/16852/aaoifi-statement-on-sukuk-and-its-implications (accessed 4 May 2018).

Rohim, M., & Shereeza, M. S. 2013. Analysis on the thoughts of Imam Abu Hanifah and Imam Syafi'i on the ijtihad method for *sukuk* instrument. *Jurnal Teknologi*, *62*(1): 17–24. Available at www.jurnalteknologi.utm.my.

Usmani, T. 2008. *Sukuk and their contemporary applications* Available at http://Sukuk.net/library/education/MuftiTaqiSukukpaper.pdf.

Yunita, I. 2015. The development, scheme, risk and fair market value model of sukuk ijarah and mudharabah in Indonesia. *American Journal of Economics*, 5(2): 56–63.

Zulkhibri, M. 2015. A synthesis of theoretical and empirical research on sukuk. *Borsa I'stanbul Review*, 15(4): 237–248 Available at www.sciencedirect.com.

8

DIVIDEND POLICY

The case of *shariah*-compliant firms

Zaheer Anwer, Shamsher Mohamad Ramadili Mohamad, Mohamed Eskandar Shah Mohamed Rasid, M. Kabir Hassan and Andrea Paltrinieri

Introduction

Capital structure serves as an important device for mitigation of agency conflicts and, although firms combine debt and cash dividends to address the agency conflicts, debt is preferred as a bonding device by many managers due to its lower cost as compared to equity (John, Knyazeva, & Knyazeva, 2015). However, *shariah*-compliant firms[1] (SCF) cannot use this device due to prohibition of interest-bearing loans in Islam. In this scenario, the dividend payout policy becomes a highly important tool of corporate governance for *shariah*-compliant investors. Moreover, the managers of these firms cannot maintain stable dividends by issuing bonds and, therefore, the dividend policy of such firms would be different. This chapter highlights the dividend payout behaviour of SCF by comparing them to conventional firms.

Our argument of different dividend policies for SCF rests on the dividend–governance debate. The literature on payout and governance presents two divergent views. The substitute hypothesis indicates that good governance discourages dividend payout because firms with good governance will hold excess cash and invest in growth projects, while in the firms with weak governance managers are disciplined to distribute excess cash to shareholders instead of using it in wasteful projects (John & Knyazeva, 2006; Officer, 2011; John et al., 2015). Conversely, the complements hypothesis asserts that good governance encourages dividend payments as good managers would distribute excess cash to shareholders through payout or repurchases, whereas self-motivated managers would be constrained by strong governance to hold cash for investment in projects offering long-term benefits to the organization (La Porta, Lopez-de-Silanes, Shleifer, & Vishny, 2000; Hu & Kumar, 2004; Mitton, 2004; Michaely & Roberts, 2012). We argue that the relationship of governance and dividend assumes a different shape for

SCF as compared to their conventional counterparts, mainly due to their different corporate governance levels. We contend that SCF are better governed owing to multiple factors. Firstly, recent studies suggest that the two most important channels for disciplining managers and reducing agency cost, i.e. high debt[2] and good governance,[3] are in inverse relationship (Arping & Sautner, 2010). More formally, in addressing agency issues, high debt and good governance are substitutes, and low-debt firms are better governed (Jiraporn, Kim, Kim, & Kitsabunnarat, 2012). SCF are low-debt and in line with this argument are expected to be better governed. Secondly, the business activities of Islamic financial institutions are screened by a *Shariah* Board that serves as an additional layer of inspection and improves governance (Grassa, 2016; Hassan, Miglietta, Paltrinieri, & Floreani, 2018). Finally, *shariah*-compliant firms also face greater scrutiny from external institutions as well as investors to ensure that their business conduct is within *shariah* principles.

Moving further, we note that another strand of literature, which argues that governance and dividend payout can either be substitutes or complements depending upon the level of idiosyncratic risk, is also relevant in this case. It is argued that, if a firm faces high idiosyncratic risk, there are chances of underinvestment and good governance, discouraging payout to boost investments. The firms with low idiosyncratic risk would be tempted to overinvest and good governance would encourage payout to reduce overinvestment (Hoberg & Prabhala, 2009; DeMarzo, Fishman, He, & Wang, 2012; Panousi & Papanikolaou, 2012). Evidently, if SCF have different idiosyncratic risks, the relationship of governance and payout might be different for such portfolios.

Consequently, our research objective is to better address the agency issue for SCF and their linkage to firm-specific risk, dividend policy and grade of governance mechanism (weak or strong) for screened stocks.

The rest of the chapter is organized in the following manner: the literature review describes the theoretical background of the relationship between debt, dividend policy and corporate governance. This is followed by a section explaining data and research methodology. Summary statistics are then reported and the findings discussed. A final section gives conclusions from the study and offers suggestions for future research.

Literature review

A key challenge for financial economists is to devise an optimal dividend policy that can, simultaneously, ensure maximization of shareholders' wealth and utility for investors. For this reason, the dividend policy is a widely debated issue in corporate finance.[4] Most of the theories related to dividend policy literature in the pre-Miller and Modigliani (1961) period argued that higher dividends were associated with high value of the firm. This view was inspired from dividend discount models that said that the value of the firm was the sum of discounted dividends. Gordon (1959), however, took a different stand and asserted that investors' required rate of return *r* will increase with the retention of earnings as well as investments. He observed that even though the retention and increase in investment would result in higher dividends in future, this increase in dividends will be offset by greater uncertainty attached to the investments.

Miller and Modigliani (1961) identified the weaknesses of this view and introduced a more rigorous framework to analyse payout policy. In their opinion, a firm's investment policy plays a key role in explaining its payout behaviour. If investment policy remains unchanged, the firm's value will not be affected by a change in the mix of retained earnings and dividends. In other words, their framework deemed dividends irrelevant. Their seminal work paved the way for further research and development of theoretical models. For example, the later studies suggest that in addition to providing compensation to the investors, dividend payout policy is an important signal for investors (S. Bhattacharya, 1979; Miller & Rock, 1985) and also addresses the excess cash flow problem (Easterbrook, 1984; Jensen, 1986).

The payout policy is equally important from the view of *shariah*-compliant investors due to various reasons. The existing literature explains that the capital structure plays an important role in the selection of appropriate tools for minimizing agency conflicts. The firms can use either debt as a mechanism to address agency conflicts (Grossman & Hart, 1982; Jensen, 1986) or governance (Jiraporn et al., 2012) to ensure effective monitoring of managers. As already stated, *shariah* stocks have constraints on debt and their capital structure can be different from that of conventional stocks.

Another important issue that is specific for SCF portfolios is that investors cannot keep debt-based securities in their portfolios. Ordinary investors who need regular payouts from their investments to fulfil their daily needs usually keep a certain portion of debt-based securities (paying periodic coupons) or dividend-paying stocks for this purpose. *Shariah*-compliant investors cannot keep debt-based securities in their portfolios and dividends are their only source of payout.[5] Regular dividend payout is thus essential for such investors as an important source of income.

Moreover, as the selection of stocks for SCF portfolios is constrained due to religious implications, they are expected to have a higher idiosyncratic risk (in line with the arguments presented by Merton (1987) and Malkiel and Xu (2002), for which they may need risk-adjusted returns, at least at par with ordinary investors. This possibly higher firm-specific risk should be compensated by growth in size and profitability, and if the firm is not growing, faith-based investors may not be able to earn capital gains on their investments and a big source of investment returns will be compromised. Therefore, the retention of profits in order to utilize growth opportunities is equally important for such faith-based investors. In this scenario, an optimal dividend policy (having the objective of keeping a balance between payout and retention to ensure long-run benefit to the investors) becomes more important for these investors, and the corporate governance structure of the firms has to be effective in order to materialize the desired outcomes of the dividend policy.

In view of these arguments, it can be observed that the dividend policy decisions for faith-based firms may be different from those of conventional firms, owing to the difference in capital structure as well as the use of different devices to reduce agency conflicts. Some issues require detailed explanation to build an understanding of this difference.

The disciplinary role of debt

Contemporary knowledge states that debt can play an important role in mitigating agency risk and argues that high debt levels force managers to act in the organizational interest due to various reasons.

Firstly, the debt invokes the threat of bankruptcy in the event of non-payment of principal and interest. Managers seek continuity and stability of operations in order to keep on enjoying their salaries and perks. Bankruptcy would lead to the loss of their jobs and an uncertain future. Therefore, Grossman and Hart (1982) portray debt as the strongest bonding device available to the shareholders to regulate managers' behaviour. They indicate an 'incentive problem' in fragmented organizations[6] and posit that managers apparently have no incentive (except personal objectives like empire building or increasing personal wealth) to work for maximization of shareholders' wealth. The shareholders can overcome this problem by offering performance-related incentives to the managers or incorporating such clauses in the organization charter that can facilitate takeovers. These bonding mechanisms would constrain managers to work towards value maximization. However, another more powerful channel that can discipline managers more effectively is the threat of bankruptcy, which can deprive managers of their jobs and benefits. Therefore, debt emerges as a very powerful device to discipline managers' conduct. The issuance of debt also increases the market value of the firm, because investors know that the managers of leveraged firms are constrained and hence they put a high valuation on the firm. Managers also have incentives to increase the market value of the firm as their pay raises are mostly attached to a higher market value, and a higher market value of firm makes it lesser attractive target for takeover. Besides, higher market value can enable managers to issue new debt and equity. The higher amount of capital, in turn, would expand the managers' empire and increase their perquisites. The managers, therefore, would put their best efforts into maximizing profits in order to increase market value, avoid bankruptcy and to save their perquisites. Debt issuance is a pre-commitment, unlike dividends, and brings managers' incentives into line with those of shareholders. More formally, debt aligns managers' incentives with the shareholders' incentives and constrains them to work for profit maximization.

Secondly, organizations can use debt to maintain growing dividends and spend free cash flow on debt servicing. To explain this phenomenon, Jensen (1986) argues that, in a bid to expand their empire and resources under their control, managers prefer to initiate financing projects instead of distributing excess cash to shareholders. This strategy may not be in the best interest of shareholders, especially when these projects are expected to yield returns lower than the cost of capital. As a result, there arises a need to regulate managers' self-motivated behaviour. Jensen identifies that forces like product market competition, internal control and regulatory oversight can discipline managers, but their effectiveness over the years has become questionable. Jensen observes that payment of regular dividends instead of wasting resources on inefficient ventures is the best device for addressing agency conflict. These dividends are required to be kept at the same level or increased because dividend cuts are followed by an adverse response from capital markets that may lead to significant reductions in share prices. It is, nonetheless, not possible to distribute these growing dividends solely from earnings as markets are volatile and organizations cannot guarantee smooth earnings. In this scenario, debt enters into the picture and managers can fulfil the promise of paying 'permanent' dividends by relying on debt instead of putting their bet on future cash flows for the payment of dividends. Therefore, debt can be utilized as an effective tool for regulating managers' behaviour as it reduces the level of free cash flow available to self-motivated managers. Additionally, the high amount of debt makes the organization more efficient as, unlike dividends, the distribution to lenders in the shape of interest and principal is mandatory, and inability to service the debt may cause bankruptcy and loss of empire for the managers.

This control function of debt is more meaningful for large and seasoned companies having high book-to-market ratios as these firms generate a high amount of free cash flow and are more exposed to agency risk. It is easier for these firms to start 'below the cost of capital' projects, and regular dividends through debt creation discipline managerial conduct at these firms. Growing firms with no free cash flow, on the other hand, exhibit a smaller agency problem. These firms approach financial markets to fulfil their capital requirements for expansion projects. The capital providers assess the management and proposed projects extensively before extending capital and provide funding only when they consider the projects feasible for investment. Hence, due to reduced information asymmetry between providers and users of capital and strong monitoring by capital markets, there is alower probability that these firms will start wasteful projects.

In line with these arguments, Stulz (1990) asserts that, owing to information asymmetry, managers are better aware of the outcomes of projects than are shareholders. It is at their discretion to approve or reject any project upon the basis of the superior information they have. When they exercise this discretion, agency costs arise mainly due to two reasons: there may be overinvestment cost when managers spend too much, or else, in some circumstances, there may be an underinvestment cost when managers are unable to start a useful project due to lack of credibility. In this scenario, maintaining smooth dividends by issuing debt can help in addressing an overinvestment problem, because management would be bound to use free cash flow for the repayment of debt instead of spending on empire building projects. However, this practice would result in a worsening underinvestment problem because the firm would be unable to invest in positive net present value projects due to shortage of available resources. Similarly, the underinvestment problem can be managed by issuing equity as it would increase the investable funds, but this issue would exacerbate an overinvestment problem. Therefore, debt and equity offerings, when taken into account individually, decrease one source of agency cost and increase the other. This situation points to a unique underinvestment/overinvestment problem, and the solution can be found in the capital structure of the firm. Firms with high growth prospects would be required to maintain low debt and invest free cash flows in expansion projects, while seasoned firms should opt to issue higher debt and use free cash flows to service debt. Hence, the financing policy matters for mitigation of agency risk.

Moving further, Zwiebel (1996) suggests that instead of a stagnant financing mix, a dynamic capital structure would be more effective in curbing manager–shareholder conflict. In this structure, managers are not fully entrenched and voluntarily choose debt to restrict their empire building activities. This capital structure would change periodically in line with the needs of the organization and allow these partially entrenched managers to achieve a balance between empire building desires and organizational efficiency by choosing debt and maintaining smooth dividends. This structure does not require any discipliner in the shape of creditors, market forces or raiders to meet its objectives.

Governance as substitute for debt for minimizing agency conflict

The above discussion envisages that a higher debt level ensures a lower agency cost. Recent studies extend this argument and explore the role of debt in firms with good governance to reduce agency conflict. It has been observed that firms with good corporate governance do not need to build high debt levels to minimize agency cost. For example, Arping and Sautner (2010) observe that corporate governance reforms minimize agency conflicts between managers and shareholders by improving the monitoring and controlling mechanism. In the aftermath of these reforms, the companies reduce their debt levels because the value of debt as a disciplining device diminishes due to better governance.

Also, Jiraporn et al. (2012) argue that managers are motivated to maintain suboptimal debt levels that are inadequate to maximize shareholders' wealth and only enhance the private benefits of managers. Good governance ensures that managers maintain optimal debt levels. Their empirical findings reveal that firms manifesting weaker governance exhibit higher debt levels, and there is a significant negative relationship between governance quality and leverage.

In a similar manner, Hong and Kacperczyk (2009) argue that socially responsible investing (SRI) firms are better governed as they refrain from socially unacceptable business activities such as those involved with alcohol, tobacco, adult entertainment and firearms. Companies that deal in these businesses lack public acceptance, and for this reason institutional investors do not invest in these companies, and therefore the companies lose an important monitoring tool, i.e. institutional management. Furthermore, analysts also offer minimum coverage for these companies, resulting in lower visibility for these 'sin' stocks. By contrast,

SRI firms are targeted by institutional investors due to their good reputation. These firms also get adequate coverage from the analysts. These two channels provide better monitoring and, hence, SRI firms emerge as better governed entities. As SCF undergo negative ethical screening as SRI firms do, they are also expected to be better governed.

It is therefore apparent, in line with these arguments, that SCF need to exercise corporate governance in order to discipline managers, and they can use dividends to perform this function.

Governance and dividend policy

The existing literature asserts that an effective dividend payout framework is the key to addressing agency conflict. As Jensen (1986) posits, managers have incentives to adopt policies that can cause the firms under their control to grow beyond their optimal size, as such expansion would result in an increase in managers' powers, the resources under their control and their compensation. Therefore, self-motivated managers are inclined to use free cash flows for risky expansion projects. On the contrary, the shareholders prefer free cash flows to be used to pay regular dividends to discipline these managers. Corporate governance is instrumental in designing a dividend policy that can address this agency conflict (Balachandran & Faff, 2015).

There is, nevertheless, a continuing debate on the payout behaviour that the good governance practices should encourage in order to address agency issues. If governance and payout are deemed to be 'substitutes' to each other, good governance should discourage payout. For example, John and Knyazeva (2006) noted that firms with better governance had a tendency to avoid the costs attached to dividends in order to pursue a more efficient investment policy. They studied this relationship in the event of pre-commitment of dividends by management for a sample of 9,270 firm-year observations for the US market for the period 1993–2003. They used two governance indicators, namely internal governance (index of 12 governance-related characteristics) and external governance (G-index, comprising anti-takeover provisions developed by Gompers, Ishii, and Metrick, 2003) and found that the likelihood of dividend payout reduced with good governance. They also found that higher cash flow increased the propensity for payout. Conversely, weak governance is associated principally with dividend pre-commitment (instead of repurchases) as a part of total payout. Good-governance firms prefer using excess cash for investment in growth projects or repurchases. In general, dividends were found to be more effective in dealing with the agency problem, in the presence of free cash flow, as compared to the other forms of payout, owing to their pre-commitment attributes.

In a relevant study, John et al. (2015) observed that firms with weak governance had a higher payout ratio, and these firms used a combination of dividends and debt rather than debt alone for pre-commitment with external claim holders. They also found that dividends were more effective in addressing agency conflicts than were repurchases, and even implicit dividend commitments were deemed credible by investors. Dividend cuts by weak-governance firms are followed by adverse market reaction.

Officer (2011) supports the substitution hypothesis for dividend initiation as well and showed that managers of a firm with poor investment opportunities (low Tobin's *Q*) and abundant resources (high cash flow) are likely to waste available cash, and this visible agency problem can be reduced through higher dividends. He used outsider-dominated board, takeover defence and institutional ownership as proxies for governance.

Caton, Goh, Lee, and Linn (2016) had similar findings for a large sample of 53,523 US firms listed on different exchanges for the period 1991–2011, as they found that their governance indicator (i.e. anti-takeover law index) worked as a substitute for dividend payout and a complement for share repurchase. They asserted that companies having good governance had a tendency to manifest higher adjusted operating performance as well as abnormal stock returns (in comparison to weakly governed companies) in the first three years after completing a share repurchase programme announcement.

Finally, Chang, Kang, and Li (2016) found similar results for a large sample of 31,140 US firms for the period 1995–2009. They used institutional majority as a proxy for corporate governance and demonstrated that a higher presence of institutional investors in the firm discouraged payout.

The opposite view considers governance and dividends as 'complements' to each other and maintains that good governance reinforces dividend payout. La Porta et al. (2000) called dividends an outcome of effective legal protection of shareholders that gave minority shareholders an opportunity to extract dividends from corporate insiders. Their sample included 4,103 firms located in 33 countries, and they showed that in countries where shareholders had high protection rights, firms had paid higher dividends. Conversely, poorly protected shareholders may accept any dividends they can get, irrespective of investment opportunities, which can be presumed to be the agency cost arising out of weak legal protection.

Mitton (2004) tested for a governance–dividend connection in a sample of 365 firms from 19 countries and showed that firms with stronger corporate governance had higher dividend payout. He also noted that in common law countries, governance complemented payout, whereas in civil law countries, governance was a substitute for dividends. His control variable also had the expected signs, i.e. profitability and age had a positive sign and growth a negative sign, implying that, holding all else constant, firms with large size and profits but poor growth opportunities tend to pay higher dividends. Mitton used ratings developed by Credit Lyonnais Securities Asia as governance proxy.

Hu and Kumar (2004) looked at this relationship from the point of view of managerial entrenchment and observed that in the presence of weak governance, managers were disciplined to pay more dividends. They studied dividend payout as well as total payout behaviour of a sample of 2,081 US firms for the period 1992–2000. Their explanatory variables were related to managerial compensation as well as governance indicators. They found that, in general, a higher proportion of fixed emoluments in CEOs' salaries resulted in higher payout. However, higher stock options and other variable components of their compensation package decreased payout. The governance-related variables, including large shareholders and board independence, increased the payout ratio and thus dividends complemented governance. Firms that were older and had high tangible assets and lower investment opportunities paid higher dividends.

Jo and Pan (2009) investigated the relationship between managerial entrenchment and payout and found that there were higher odds of entrenched managers paying dividends. Their sample comprised large US firms for the period 1990–2003, and they used anti-takeover provisions as proxy for entrenchment.

Likewise, Petrasek (2012) demonstrated that when firms from countries with poor shareholder protection cross-listed in US exchanges, they increased their payouts by about 9 per cent of earnings. However, if external shareholder protection was already strong in the country of incorporation, no significant change in payout policy was observed. They concluded that transparency and enhanced shareholder protection were instrumental in higher corporate payout. Their sample comprised 755 foreign firms that cross-listed common shares on overseas exchanges from 1987 to 2006.

Michaely and Roberts (2012) studied the pattern of dividends of public and private firms for the period 1993–2002 and found that public firms had a smoother pattern of dividend payments as compared to private firms, due to better governance mechanisms of public firms and the presence of public capital markets that regulate the behaviour of listed firms. In a recent study, Liljeblom and Maury (2016) found the same results for the Russian market for the period 1998–2003.

Governance, dividends and idiosyncratic risk

The interplay of idiosyncratic risk with governance and its impact on the agency problem is extensively explored in contemporary literature seeking to unravel the 'disappearing dividend' puzzle, and as Hoberg and Prabhala (2009) explain, that risk explains 40 per cent of this puzzle. They analysed the dividend decisions of US firms from 1963 to2004 and found that higher idiosyncratic risk reduces the likelihood of payout. In effect, high idiosyncratic risk leads to an underinvestment problem owing to managers' risk aversion (DeMarzo et al., 2012). Good governance (in the shape of strong monitoring by institutional investors), in this scenario, can boost investments, or managers may be tempted to enhance investments if they are offered stock options (Panousi & Papanikolaou, 2012).

Kuo, Philip, and Zhang (2013) investigated the role of liquidity, risk and catering in explaining dividend policy for a sample of 18 countries (mostly developed markets) for the period from 1989 to 2011. They found that risk played a significant role in designing the dividend policy. In their final analysis, the propensity to pay dividends cannot be explained without discussing risk.

D. Bhattacharya, Li, and Rhee (2016) examined whether corporate governance serves as a complement or substitute to payout policy and observed that corporate governance is a substitute for the firm's payout in a firm with high idiosyncratic risk firm and a complement to the payout in a firm with low idiosyncratic risk.

The above review sheds some important insights. Firstly, dividends are an important source of payout and mitigate agency conflicts. Secondly, firms can use debt to maintain smooth dividends and use free cash flows to service debt instead of spending it on wasteful projects. Thirdly, firms with good governance use low levels of debt and governance as a substitute for debt as a controlling device to regulate managerial behaviour. Fourthly, there is ample evidence available that good governance affects dividend payout, but there is disagreement on the nature of this relationship. One view suggests that good governance substitutes for payout, i.e. in the presence of good managers and/or effective monitoring earnings are retained and invested in expansion projects. The opposite view, however, claims that governance complements payout as in countries with greater protection for shareholder rights, dividend payout is higher than countries where such laws are not in place or are weak. Moreover, at firm level, entrenched managers pay higher dividends instead of initiating unnecessary or risky projects aimed at increasing their personal wealth. Fifthly, there is an inverse relationship between idiosyncratic risk and payout. When idiosyncratic risk is high (low), there will be lower (higher) payout. Finally, the relationship between governance and payout can be further explained by the fact that when idiosyncratic risk is high (low), good governance serves as substitute (complement) and addresses the underinvestment issue (overinvestment), and good governance firms retain (release) cash.

Consequently, the differences in capital structure of SCF may result in a different linkage between dividend payout and governance. Also, the idiosyncratic risk of these portfolios may be different in a way that can affect the propensity for payout. Interestingly, Hayat and Hassan (2017), in line with the argument that debt and governance are complements, explored whether governance was different for SCF in comparison with conventional firms as SCF have constraints on debt. They found no evidence of any significant difference in the governance quality of the two kinds of firms for the majority of their governance proxies. Therefore, if governance structure does not differ between Islamic and conventional stocks, it is possible that their payout policies are similar. Our study investigated the dividend payout behaviour of SCF to ascertain whether investors interested in these portfolios would be compensated.

Research methodology

The broad objective of this study was to evaluate whether governance, risk and other specific variables are different for SCF as compared to conventional firms, as segregated/categorized by their dividend payout behaviour. In order to perform this evaluation, summary statistics and correlation matrices were used for different variables. The sample included representative SCF and market firms for the United States (US) market from 2006 to 2015. The SCF portfolio comprised constituent stocks of the Dow Jones Islamic Market Index US (DJIM-US) and the market portfolio was represented by the Dow Jones United States Index (DJUSI). The data, comprising lists of constituent stocks of both the indices, was purchased from Dow Jones S&P Indices as this information is not publicly available.[7] The motivation behind this selection was that both of them are among oldest such indices and Dow Jones is among the reliable vendors. Another advantage was frequent rebalancing by the service provider as the DJIMI-US is rebalanced quarterly while DJUSI is rebalanced once a year. Dow Jones finalizes the *shariah* screening by applying various qualitative and quantitative criteria,[8] and the screening done by Dow Jones is subsequently validated by an independent *shariah* supervisory board comprised of eminent scholars to ensure consistency with *shariah* law. The final sample included 11,795 observations for market firms and 4,520 for SCF firms. We retrieved the daily values for holding period returns, market capitalization and stock prices from the Center for Research in Security Prices (CRSP) database. The factor loadings (daily frequency) on market risk, small-minus-big, high-minus-low and momentum were sourced from Wharton Research Data Services (WRDS). The financial information including figures from financial statements was obtained from Compustat-Capital IQ. The governance indicators were collected from MSCI GMI Ratings available on WRDS.

The "difference of means" tests were performed using the following *t*-statistic as proposed by Dixon and Massey (1983):

$$t = \frac{\overline{x} - \overline{y}}{\left\{\frac{(n_x - 1)s_x^2 + (n_y - 1)s_y^2}{n_x + n_y - 2}\right\}^{1/2} \left(\frac{1}{n_x} + \frac{1}{n_y}\right)^{1/2}}$$

with a degree of freedom equal to $n_x + n_y - 2$.

The variables studied for both the SCF and the market sample were as described below.

Payer reflects the event that the firm has paid a dividend in the year under review.

Corporate governance highlights the level of corporate governance within a firm as a percentile score for each firm in the given year. This index is constructed in line with John et al. (2015) by taking into account board structure, ownership, internal governance committees and corporate audit. These traits are mainly related to the internal governance mechanism of the firm. Existing literature suggests that investor rights are better protected in firms where outsiders control the firm, the board is independent and performs effective monitoring with the assistance of its sub-committees and audit is effective (Grullon & Michaely, 2004; Bebchuk, Cohen, & Ferrell, 2009). Further details are given in Table 8.1.

TABLE 8.1 Governance index

	Internal governance mechanism
Board structure	
No insider control	Business ethics code available
Ownership diversity	Board meetings frequency
Outsiders majority	Outsiders board members meetings frequency
Outsider majority strict	Audit committee – independent
Directors active CEOs	Audit committee – fully independent
Presence of women directors	Compensation committee – independent
Audit quality	Compensation committee – fully independent
Auditor independence	Nomination & governance committee – independent
Big4auditors	Nomination & governance committee – fully independent
Auditor opinion	Company compensation plan approved
Auditor opinion – internal control	Formal governance policy approved

The table reports the constituents of the independent variable corporate governance index. It is developed in line with John et al. (2015). The variables in general take the value '1' if Yes and '0' otherwise. Owner Diversity takes the value "1' if ownership category is either 'Institutions Dominant' or 'Widely Held' or 'Indexed Stock' or 'Mixed Ownership. If Board Meetings Frequency is 4 or above, the value assigned is equal to '1' and otherwise '0'. Big4Auditors takes the value of '1' if the external auditor is among top four audit firms (or their subsidiaries) namely Deloitte & Touche LLP, Ernst & Young LLP, KPMG LLP and PriceWaterhouseCoopers LLP. Auditor Opinion (Compustat item no. 20) is assigned value '1' if it is 'unqualified (1)' or 'unqualified with additional language (4)' and '0' otherwise. Internal Control – Auditor opinion (Compustat item # 1) is '1' if opinion is 'Effective (1) and '0' otherwise. The governance score is converted into percentiles following Gompers et al. (2003).

Idiosyncratic risk is calculated in line with Hoberg and Prabhala (2009) and it is the firm specific risk that a firm faces. It is the standard deviation of residuals from a regression of the stock's excess return on Carhart (1997) factors.

Systematic risk is the standard deviation of predicted values from the above regression.

Free cash flow shows the extent of excess cash available to a firm and can be calculated as Operating Income (Compustat item no. 13) minus Total Income Taxes (Compustat item no. 16) plus ΔDeferred Taxes (Compustat item no. 35) minus Total Interest Expenses (Compustat item no. 15) divided by Total Assets (Compustat item no. 6).

The *KZ Index* of Kaplan and Zingales (1997) is used as a proxy for financial constraints. Kaplan and Zingales define unconstrained or less financially constrained firms as those who hold large amounts of liquid assets and high net worth and exhibit lower difference between cost of external and internal funds. The index calculations are shown in detail in Table 8.2.

The *market-to-book ratio of assets* is calculated as Total Assets (Compustat no. 6) minus Total Equity (Compustat no. 216) plus Market Value of Equity all

TABLE 8.2 KZ Index

KZ Index = −1.002(CF/K) − 39.368 (Div/K) − 1.315 (CA/K) + 3.139LEV + 0.283Q

Where

$$CF / K = \frac{Earnings\ before\ extraordinary\ items\left(18\right) + Depreciation\ and\ Amortization\left(14\right)}{lagged\ property,\ plant\ and\ equipment\left(8\right)}$$

$$DIV / K = \frac{Dividend\ Preferred\left(19\right) + Dividends\ Common\left(21\right)}{lagged\ property,\ plant\ and\ equipment\left(8\right)}$$

$$CA / K = \frac{Cash\left(1\right)}{lagged\ property,\ plant\ and\ equipment\left(8\right)}$$

$$Lev = \frac{Total\ Debt}{Tota\ Debt + Total\ Stockholders'\ Equity\ (216)}$$

where

$Total\ Debt$ = Debt in Current Liabilities (34) + Long − Term Debt − Total(9)

Q i.e. Market-to-book ratio of assets can be calculated as

$$Q = \frac{Total\ Assets\left(6\right) - Total\ Equity\left(216\right) + Market\ Value\ of\ Equity}{Total\ Assets\ 6)}$$

Where

Market value of equity = Closing Stock Price (Fiscal) x Shares Outstanding)

The table reports the detailed calculations of KZ Index developed by Kaplan and Zingales (1997). The detailed definitions of constituents are listed. The entries in parenthesis show Compustat annual data items.

divided by Total Assets (Compustat no. 6) where Market Value of Equity is equal to Closing Stock Price (Fiscal) times Shares Outstanding. It reflects whether a company is exposed to growth bias or value bias, as a high market-to-book ratio represents a growth bias while a low market-to-book is associated with a value bias (Fama & French, 1993). This is understandable because often the book value of assets does not account for the true value of the intangible assets of the company. These assets, such as brands, patents and copyright, are instrumental in the growth of the company, whereas companies having a high amount of book assets are mostly mature companies and may be categorized as value stocks. Theoretically, growing firms pay smaller dividends and invest more in expansion whereas mature firms possess fewer avenues of growth and distribute earnings to investors.

Asset growth is calculated as ΔTotal Assets (Compustat item no. 6) over Total Assets at year *t*-1. This variable was included to observe the influence of growth strategies on payout policy. Firms have a choice between investing their earnings in assets or paying dividends, and this variable has an important role in explaining propensity to pay dividends.

Profitability is also an important factor in deciding payout as loss-making firms are rarely expected to continue payments. Also, this measure partially reflects the stage of the dividend life cycle where a firm resides. Our Profitability measure is equal to Earnings before Extraordinary Items (Compustat item no. 18) plus Deferred Income Taxes (Compustat item No. 50) plus Interest Expenses (Compustat item no. 15) sdivided by Total Assets (Compustat item no. 6).

NYSE percentile represents firm size. Larger firms are mostly mature and expected to pay higher dividends, whereas smaller firms are mostly in their initial years and prefer to invest in expansion. We used two proxies for firm size. NYSE Percentile is the fraction of NYSE firms having a market capitalization equal to or smaller than firm '*i*' in year '*t*' as a proxy for firm size.

Equity/Assets is calculated as Stockholder's Equity (Compustat item no. 216) divided by Total Assets (Compustat item no. 6) and accounts for the capital structure of the firm. A firm's capital structure (shareholders' vs. creditors' stakes) can affect financing decisions (Stulz, 1990) and therefore has important implications for dividend policy decisions.

RE/TE can be calculated by Retained Earnings (Compustat item no. 36) divided by Stockholders' Equity (Compustat item no. 216). It is the amount of retained equity as a percentage of total equity. This metric was introduced by DeAngelo, DeAngelo and Stulz (2006), who posit that the mix of earned versus contributed capital is a proxy for the stage of dividend life cycle hypothesis at which a firm resides at time '*t*'. Firms with a low RE/TE would be in the growth stage while firms with high RE/TE would be seasoned firms. Therefore, this variable is also capable of measuring the extent to which a firm is either self-financed or relying on the external financing.

Results and discussion

The broad objective of this section is to investigate whether governance, risk, agency issues and firm performance measures are influenced by the dividend payment behaviour of the firms, and how idiosyncratic risk affects the variables. In the first part of analysis, we highlight the difference in size of variables in the two samples, while in the second part we split both kinds of firms in dividend payers and non-payers to obtain further insights.

Table 8.3 shows means of our variables of interest for the US market sample and SCF portfolios and evaluates how governance, performance and risk profile change with respect to the dividend payment behaviour of the firms. It can be seen that mean governance index, idiosyncratic risk and systematic risk are similar in magnitude across both kinds of firms. However, SCF show higher mean KZ Index and free cash flows. As a result, they may be more prone to have agency problems, since agency issues are aggravated in the presence of financial constraints and high free cash flows. Moreover, SCF have higher mean market-to-book assets ratio and asset growth and lower profitability and book value of assets. These figures reveal that SCF are younger firms that have high growth potential as compared to the

TABLE 8.3 Mean comparison with respect to type of firms and payout behaviour

	US portfolio				*SCF portfolio*			
	Total	*Non-payer*	*Payer*	*Difference*	*Total*	*Non-payer*	*Payer*	*Difference*
Governance index	44.750	37.540	48.800	−11.25***	44.190	37.772	49.220	−11.488***
Idiosyncratic risk	0.017	0.021	0.015	0.006***	0.017	0.020	0.015	0.005***
Systematic risk	0.015	0.016	0.014	0.002***	0.014	0.015	0.014	0.001***
KZ index	46.030	57.810	50.270	11.78***	50.485	60.117	42.929	17.188***
Free cash flow	0.086	0.085	0.086	−0.001	0.123	0.105	0.137	−0.032***
Market-to -book−assets	1.930	2.270	1.750	0.524***	2.448	2.694	2.256	0.438***
Asset growth	0.106	0.156	0.078	0.078***	0.121	0.171	0.082	0.089***
Profitability	0.058	0.043	0.067	−0.024***	0.081	0.058	0.099	−0.041***
NYSE percentile	0.244	0.178	0.280	−0.102***	0.277	0.206	0.332	−0.126***
Total assets	24,945	6,967	35,045	−28,077***	10,712	4,074	15,918	−11,844***
RE/TE	50.49	42.300	55.05	−12.75***	50.489	37.967	60.185	−22.22***
Equity/assets	0.406	0.468	0.372	0.096***	0.534	0.574	0.503	0.071***
N	11,882	7,608	4,274		4,559	2,555	2,004	

The table reports means of different variables of interest paying and non-paying companies for sample portfolios and difference of means tests. ***, **, * denote statistical significance at the 1%, 5%, and 10% level, respectively.

market sample. Finally, it is seen that SCF have a larger component of equity in their capital structure, mainly due to the restrictions on debt laid down by *shariah* rulings. Analysing the difference in payer/non-payer behaviour, we find that there is significant difference between payers and non-payers in terms of corporate governance. In general, the dividend-paying firms exhibit higher levels of corporate governance. Payers also experience lower idiosyncratic and systematic risk as compared to non-payers. Non-payers exhibit a higher level of financial constraints. In the market portfolio, payers and non-payers hold similar levels of free cash flow, whereas, in the SCF portfolio, payers possess higher free cash flows than do non-payers. We also notice that market-to-book assets ratio, asset growth and RE/TE are higher, and profitability and total size are lower, for non-dividend payers. These results are in line with conventional knowledge, which suggests that firms with growth potential prefer to invest in new projects instead of distribution, whereas mature firms pay higher dividends and display large asset size, higher profitability and a higher amount of retained earnings in their total equity.

As idiosyncratic risk plays an important role in shaping dividend decisions, we explored the impact of very high and very low idiosyncratic risk for payers and non-payers for firm-related variables in the sample portfolios. For this analysis, firms with extremely low idiosyncratic risk fall into the first quartile whereas extremely high idiosyncratic risk firms fall into the fourth quartile. The results are reported in Table 8.4 and Table 8.5.

We observe that, for the sample representing the US market (Table 8.4), firms with low idiosyncratic risk have better governance, total asset base, profitability, sales, debt and free cash flows while they have lower asset growth. In terms of payer/non-payer analysis, with low idiosyncratic risk, payers exhibit better governance and a higher asset base, total debt and sales while they show lower asset growth, profitability and free cash flows, in comparison with non-payers. The results are somewhat similar at the high idiosyncratic risk level. The statistics for SCF (Table 8.5) are not very different from those for the market. We can, therefore, infer that payout behaviour remains the same across both kinds of firms and in extreme cases of idiosyncratic risk.

The results suggest that investors with a preference for dividends need to look for companies with stronger corporate governance, lower idiosyncratic risk, lower exposure to financial constraints – mature companies with higher size and earned equity. For SCF investors, these statistics do not indicate any special disadvantage. Nevertheless, these findings are preliminary and further analysis is required to validate our conclusions.

Finally, a correlation analysis was performed among the variables of interest. For the market sample, Table 8.6 shows that dividend payout does not correlate with any of the variables of interest. Corporate governance has a negative correlation with idiosyncratic risk, market-to-book assets ratio, asset growth and KZ Index, while it has a positive correlation with profitability, size and free cash flow, implying that mature firms are better in governance This finding is understandable as these firms have experienced a higher level of regulatory insight. Likewise,

TABLE 8.4 Interplay of idiosyncratic risk and dividend payout: market portfolio

	Low idiosyncratic risk				*High idiosyncratic risk*			
	Total	*Non – payer*	*Payer*	*Difference*	*Total*	*Non -payer*	*Payer*	*Difference*
Governance index	49.374	43.828	49.92	−6.094***	43.478	37.472	52.201	−14.729***
Asset growth	0.073	0.141	0.066	0.075***	0.112	0.163	0.039	0.124***
Profitability	0.069	0.082	0.068	0.014***	0.020	0.008	0.037	−0.029***
Total assets	51,602	10,632	55,648	−45,015***	15,901	5,375	31,191	−25,816***
Total debt	12,180	2,727	13,097	−10,370**	4,835	1,589	9,493	−7,904***
Sales	15,566	9,430	16,161	−6,731*	4,877	3,321	7,109	−3,788***
FCF	0.079	0.104	0.076	0.028***	0.065	0.062	0.07	−0.008
N	2,971	267	2,704		2,970	1,759	1,211	

The table shows, for the US market portfolio, the means for variables of interest with respect to dividend payout and extreme levels of idiosyncratic risk and the results of difference of means tests are also reported. The extremely low idiosyncratic risk firms are considered those that fall in 1st quartile whereas the extremely high idiosyncratic risk firms fall in 4th quartile. ***,**,*denote statistical significance at the 1%, 5%, and 10% level, respectively.

TABLE 8.5 Interplay of idiosyncratic risk and dividend payout: SCF portfolio

	Low IR				*High IR*			
	Total	*Non-payer*	*Payer*	*Difference*	*Total*	*Non -payer*	*Payer*	*Difference*
Governance index	49.598	45.217	50.547	−5.331*	41.087	36.449	50.883	−14.434***
Idio risk	0.009	0.01	0.009	0.001***	0.028	0.028	0.027	0.001***
Asset growth	0.079	0.141	0.066	0.075***	0.147	0.178	0.083	0.095***
Profitability	0.104	0.104	0.105	−0.001	0.040	0.020	0.081	−0.061***
Total assets	22,462	8,724	25,438	−16,715***	3,282	2,254	5,454	−3,200***
Total debt	4,226	2,199	4,672	−2,473***	531	322	963	−641.1***
Sales	21,226	8,793	23,963	−15,170***	3,140	1,908	5,690	−3,782***
Free cash flow	0.136	0.135	0.136	−0.001	0.097	0.080	0.133	−0.053***
N	1,140	203	937		1,139	773	366	

The table shows, for the SCF sample, the means for variables of interest with respect to dividend payout and extreme levels of idiosyncratic risk and the results of difference of means tests are also reported. The extremely low idiosyncratic risk firms are considered those that fall in 1st quartile whereas the extremely high idiosyncratic risk firms fall in 4th quartile. ***,**,*denote statistical significance at the 1%, 5%, and 10% level, respectively.

TABLE 8.6 Market portfolio: correlation matrix

	Div. P/O	*Gov. Ind.*	*IR*	*SR*	*M/B*	*Asset*	*Profit.*	*NYSE*	*RE/TE*	*KZ Ind.*	*FCF*	*Eq/Asse*
Dividend payout	1											
Governance index	−0.01	1										
Idiosyncratic risk	−0.01	−0.03***	1									
Systematic risk	−0.01	0.11***	0.71***	1								
Market-book-assets	0.00	−0.13***	0.06***	−0.14***	1							
Asset growth	−0.01	−0.07***	0.01	−0.05***	0.09***	1						
Profitability	0.01	0.02**	−0.27***	−0.20***	0.18***	0.01***	1					
NYSE percentile	0.02	0.19***	−0.23***	−0.12***	0.10***	0.03***	0.15***	1				
RE/TE	0.01	0.02	−0.01	−0.01	0.01	−0.00	0.01	0.01	1			
KZ Index	−0.01	−0.01	0.01	0.02*	−0.02*	−0.02*	−0.10***	0.02*	0.00	1		
Free cash flow	0.01	0.03***	−0.15***	−0.15***	0.22***	0.06***	0.69***	0.14***	0.01	−0.05***	1	
Equity/assets	−0.01	−0.08***	0.01	−0.05***	0.14***	0.05***	0.10***	−0.06***	0.00	0.04***	0.21***	1

The table shows pair wise correlation between our variables of interest. The variable definitions are available in methodology section. ***,**,*denote statistical significance at the 1%, 5%, and 10% level, respectively.

TABLE 8.7 SCF portfolio correlation matrix

	Div. P/O	*Gov. Ind.*	*IR*	*SR*	*M/B*	*Asset*	*Profit.*	*NYSE*	*RE/TE*	*KZ Ind.*	*FCF*	*Eq/ Asse*
Dividend payout	1											
Governance index	0.00	1										
Idiosyncratic risk	−0.02	−0.05***	1									
Systematic risk	−0.01	0.11***	0.63***	1								
Market-book-assets	−0.01	−0.16***	−0.04**	−0.21***	1							
Asset growth	−0.01	−0.10***	0.06***	−0.02	0.13***	1						
Profitability	0.00	0.0324*	−0.27***	−0.14***	0.13***	0.08***	1					
NYSE percentile	−0.01	0.23***	−0.33***	−0.15***	0.09***	0.03*	0.21***	1				
RE/TE	0.00	0.01	−0.01	−0.024	0.02	0.00	0.06***	0.01	1			
KZ Index	−0.04*	0.05***	−0.02	0.05***	−0.07***	−0.03**	−0.05***	0.01	0.00	1		
Free cash flow	−0.02	0.0376**	−0.19***	−0.12***	0.24***	0.00	0.72***	0.16***	0.03*	−0.06***	1	
Equity/ assets	−0.03*	−0.10***	0.13***	0.06***	−0.03*	−0.01	−0.03*	−0.17***	−0.06***	−0.01	0.05***	1

The table shows pairwise correlation between our variables of interest. The variable definitions are available in methodology section. ***,**,*denote statistical significance at the 1%, 5%, and 10% level, respectively.

idiosyncratic risk has a positive correlation with market-to-book assets ratio and a negative correlation with profitability, size, RE/TE ratio and free cash flow, reflecting that younger firms possess higher idiosyncratic risk. Market-to-book assets ratio has positive correlation with asset growth, size and free cash flow while it has a negative correlation with KZ index, showing that young firms experience higher growth, hold more cash and are less exposed to financial constraints. We observe a very high correlation between free cash flow and profitability. The results for the SCF sample, as reported in Table 8.7, are similar to those for the market sample.

Conclusion

The existing literature suggests that higher debt disciplines managers. Additionally, total risk also affects the way managers of well-governed firms formulate dividend policy. As SCF cannot make use of debt above a certain threshold, they cannot use debt as a governance mechanism. Likewise, they are prone to have higher idiosyncratic risk that may affect their payout decisions. Finally, SCF are expected to be better governed, and therefore the relationship between governance and payout may differ for these firms. This connection is important from the investor's point of view because dividends are not only a device for payout, they also signal and mitigate agency risk.

We carried out a detailed review of the existing literature and also calculated descriptive statistics, using various specifications, in order to investigate if the dividend payout behaviour of SCF differs from that of the market. However, we did not find any notable difference. Our results also showed no difference in payout decisions at different levels of idiosyncratic risk. In summary, we observed that firms with good governance, large asset size, higher profitability, higher RE/TE and lower market-to-book ratio, lower idiosyncratic risk and lower financial constraints, on average, pay higher dividends. The results remain similar across both kinds of firms: SCF and the US market sample.

This research can be extended in many ways. Multiple regression techniques could be used to better understand the difference between the market and SCF in terms of dividend payout. Other forms of payout. e.g. repurchases, could also be included in the analysis. Finally, more countries could be added to the sample for better comparison.

Notes

1 *Shariah* does not allow investment in debt-based instruments like bonds, commercial papers and mortgage-backed securities or instruments based on notional assets or involving high risk, e.g., derivatives, and permissible equity instruments are mutual funds and common stocks (Hayat, Den Butter, & Kock, 2013). Dow Jones and other vendors employ two sets of criteria, namely 'line-of-business screens' and 'financial ratio screens' when deciding the investment universe. These screens are

subsequently used to constitute various *shariah* indices. These *shariah* screening results are endorsed by a board of highly renowned independent *shariah* scholars. The first criterion is qualitative and stipulates exclusion of impermissible businesses like interest (*riba*), pork, activities involving extreme risk taking (*gharar*), gambling (*maysir*), weapons and defence, pornography etc. The second filter excludes companies having

1) Revenues in excess of 5% from the impermissible business activities
2) Total debt and/or monetary assets accounting for 33% or more of market capitalization (24-month average)
3) Account receivable more than 33% of their total assets / market value of equity (24-month average)
4) Cash to market value of equity (24-month average) higher than 33%.

2 Grossman and Hart (1982) and Jensen (1986) propose that high debt can be used to discipline managers.

3 The finance theory discusses, at great length, the role of good governance in addressing agency conflict. Hart (1995) and Shleifer and Vishny (1997) provide with detailed overview of this discussion.

4 This introductory paragraph has benefited from Allen and Michaely (2003).

5 It is assumed that they do not intend to sell the stocks merely to meet household needs and instead they wish to keep them for their preferred investment period.

6 A structure resembling most opublic listed companies.

7 We are thankful to INCEIF-BNP Paribas Centre for Islamic Asset and Wealth Management, Malaysia for extending research grant for the purchase of this data.

8 The details of these *shariah* compliance screens are made available in the appendix and the complete screening methodology can be accessed at https://us.spindices.com/index-family/Shariah/all.

References

Allen, F., & Michaely, R. (2003). Payout policy. *Handbook of the Economics of Finance*, *1*, 337–429.

Arping, S., & Sautner, Z. (2010). Corporate governance and leverage: Evidence from a natural experiment. *Finance Research Letters*, *7*(2), 127–134.

Balachandran, B., & Faff, R. (2015). Corporate governance, firm value and risk: Past, present, and future. *Pacific-Basin Finance Journal*, *35*, 1–12. doi:10.1016/j.pacfin.2015.07.002

Bebchuk, L., Cohen, A., & Ferrell, A. (2009). What matters in corporate governance? *Review of Financial Studies*, *22*(2), 783–827.

Bhattacharya, D., Li, W.-H., & Rhee, S. G. (2016). *Does better corporate governance encourage higher payout? Risk, agency cost, and dividend policy*. Hitotsubashi Institute for Advanced Study, Hitotsubashi University. Tokyo.

Bhattacharya, S. (1979). Imperfect information, dividend policy, and "the bird in the hand" fallacy. *Bell Journal of Economics*, *10*(1), 259–270.

Carhart, M. M. (1997). On persistence in mutual fund performance. *The Journal of Finance, 52*(1), 57–82.

Caton, G. L., Goh, J., Lee, Y. T., & Linn, S. C. (2016). Governance and post-repurchase performance. *Journal of Corporate Finance*, *39*, 155–173. doi:10.1016/j.jcorpfin.2016.02.005.

Chang, K., Kang, E., & Li, Y. (2016). Effect of institutional ownership on dividends: An agency-theory-based analysis. *Journal of Business Research*, *69*(7), 2551–2559.

DeAngelo, H., DeAngelo, L., & Stulz, R. M. (2006). Dividend policy and the earned/contributed capital mix: A test of the life-cycle theory. *Journal of Financial Economics, 81*(2), 227–254.

DeMarzo, P. M., Fishman, M. J., He, Z., & Wang, N. (2012). Dynamic agency and the Q theory of investment. *The Journal of Finance, 67*(6), 2295–2340.

Dixon, W. J., & Massey, F. J. (1983). *Introduction to Statistical Analysis* (4th ed.). New York: McGraw-Hill.

Easterbrook, F. H. (1984). Two agency-cost explanations of dividends. *The American Economic Review, 74*(4), 650–659.

Fama, E. F., & French, K. R. (1993). Common risk factors in the returns on stocks and bonds. *Journal of Financial Economics, 33*(1), 3–56.

Gompers, P., Ishii, J., & Metrick, A. (2003). Corporate governance and equity prices. *The Quarterly Journal of Economics, 118*(1), 107–156.

Gordon, M. J. (1959). Dividends, earnings, and stock prices. *The Review of Economics and Statistics*, 99–105.

Grassa, R. (2016). Corporate governance and credit rating in Islamic banks: Does Shariah governance matters? *Journal of Management and Governance, 20*(4), 875–906.

Grossman, S. J., & Hart, O. D. (1982). Corporate financial structure and managerial incentives. *The Economics of Information and Uncertainty* (pp. 107–140): University of Chicago Press.

Grullon, G., & Michaely, R. (2004). The information content of share repurchase programs. *The Journal of Finance, 59*(2), 651–680.

Hart, O. (1995). Corporate governance: Some theory and implications. *The Economic Journal, 105*(430), 678–689.

Hassan, M. K., Miglietta, F., Paltrinieri, A., & Floreani, J. (2018). The effects of Shariah Board composition on Islamic equity indices' performance. *Business Ethics: A European Review, 27*, 248–259.

Hayat, R., Den Butter, F., & Kock, U. (2013). Halal certification for financial products: A transaction cost perspective. *Journal of Business Ethics, 117*(3), 601–613.

Hayat, R., & Hassan, M. K. (2017). Does an Islamic label indicate good corporate governance? *Journal of Corporate Finance, 43*, 159–174. doi:10.1016/j.jcorpfin.2016.12.012.

Hoberg, G., & Prabhala, N. R. (2009). Disappearing dividends, catering, and risk. *Review of Financial Studies, 22*(1), 79–116.

Hong, H., & Kacperczyk, M. (2009). The price of sin: The effects of social norms on markets. *Journal of Financial Economics, 93*(1), 15–36. doi:10.1016/j.jfineco.2008.09.001.

Hu, A., & Kumar, P. (2004). Managerial entrenchment and payout policy. *Journal of Financial and Quantitative Analysis, 39*(04), 759–790.

Jensen, M. C. (1986). Agency cost of free cash flow, corporate finance, and takeovers. *Corporate Finance, and Takeovers. American Economic Review, 76*(2).

Jiraporn, P., Kim, J.-C., Kim, Y. S., & Kitsabunnarat, P. (2012). Capital structure and corporate governance quality: Evidence from the institutional shareholder services (ISS). *International Review of Economics & Finance, 22*(1), 208–221.

Jo, H., & Pan, C. (2009). Why are firms with entrenched managers more likely to pay dividends? *Review of Accounting and Finance, 8*(1), 87–116. doi:10.1108/14757700910934256.

John, K., & Knyazeva, A. (2006). Payout policy, agency conflicts, and corporate governance. *Agency Conflicts, and Corporate Governance* (May 2006).

John, K., Knyazeva, A., & Knyazeva, D. (2015). Governance and payout precommitment. *Journal of Corporate Finance, 33*, 101–117. doi:10.1016/j.jcorpfin.2015.05.004.

Kaplan, S. N., & Zingales, L. (1997). Do investment-cash flow sensitivities provide useful measures of financing constraints? *The Quarterly Journal of Economics*, *112*(1), 169–215.

Kuo, J.-M., Philip, D., & Zhang, Q. (2013). What drives the disappearing dividends phenomenon? *Journal of Banking & Finance*, *37*(9), 3499–3514. doi:10.1016/j.jbankfin.2013.05.003.

La Porta, R., Lopez-de-Silanes, F., Shleifer, A., & Vishny, R. W. (2000). Agency problems and dividend policies around the world. *The Journal of Finance*, *55*(1), 1–33.

Liljeblom, E., & Maury, B. (2016). Shareholder protection, ownership, and dividends: Russian evidence. *Emerging Markets Finance and Trade*, *52*(10), 2414–2433.

Malkiel, B. G., & Xu, Y. (2002). *Idiosyncratic Risk and Security Returns*. Working Paper. University of Texas at Dallas.

Merton, R. C. (1987). A simple model of capital market equilibrium with incomplete information. *The Journal of Finance*, *42*(3), 483–510.

Michaely, R., & Roberts, M. R. (2012). Corporate dividend policies: lessons from private firms. *Review of Financial Studies*, *25*(3), 711–746. doi:10.1093/rfs/hhr108.

Miller, M. H., & Modigliani, F. (1961). Dividend policy, growth, and the valuation of shares. *The Journal of Business*, *34*(4), 411–433.

Miller, M. H., & Rock, K. (1985). Dividend policy under asymmetric information. *The Journal of Finance*, *40*(4), 1031–1051.

Mitton, T. (2004). Corporate governance and dividend policy in emerging markets. *Emerging Markets Review*, *5*(4), 409–426. doi:10.1016/j.ememar.2004.05.003.

Officer, M. S. (2011). Overinvestment, corporate governance, and dividend initiations. *Journal of Corporate Finance*, *17*(3), 710–724.

Panousi, V., & Papanikolaou, D. (2012). Investment, idiosyncratic risk, and ownership. *The Journal of Finance*, *67*(3), 1113–1148.

Petrasek, L. (2012). Do transparent firms pay out more cash to shareholders? Evidence from international cross-listings. *Financial Management*, *41*(3), 615–636.

Shleifer, A., & Vishny, R. W. (1997). A survey of corporate governance. *The Journal of Finance*, *52*(2), 737–783.

Stulz, R. M. (1990). Managerial discretion and optimal financing policies. *Journal of Financial Economics*, *26*(1), 3–27.

Zwiebel, J. (1996). Dynamic capital structure under managerial entrenchment. *The American Economic Review*, 1197–1215.

9

PROSPECTS FOR ISLAMIC DERIVATIVES IN BANGLADESH[1]

Md. Faruk Abdullah, M. Kabir Hassan and Asmak Ab Rahman

Introduction

Bangladesh, the third largest Muslim country by population, started Islamic banking in 1983. As of 2017, it has eight full-fledged Islamic banks and 16 Islamic banking windows of conventional banks. As of December 2015, the total deposits of the Islamic banking sector amounted to Bangladeshi taka (BDT) 1641.6 billion, representing approximately 20% of the total deposit of the banking sector in the country (Bangladesh Bank, 2017). However, Islamic banking in Bangladesh has not achieved substantial development yet due to a number of issues. A number of studies have stated that the lack of government support, absence of strong *shariah* regulation and governance and the lack of an Islamic capital market are the major challenges (Ahmad and Hassan, 2007; Abdullah and Rahman, 2017).

The scarcity of products is one of the major challenges for Islamic banks in Bangladesh. Lack of products may render the Islamic banking industry non-competitive with its conventional counterpart. Previous studies have shown that there are only a few classical products used by the Islamic banking industry. Therefore, product innovation is crucial for the development of Islamic banking industry in Bangladesh (Sarker, 2005; Ahmad and Hassan, 2007; Mohon, 2011; Sarker, 1999).

In general, product innovation is an essential element for the survival and growth of Islamic finance. Institutions that develop products and services corresponding to the needs and expectations of their prospective clients in an efficient and timely manner achieve important competitive advantage (Al-Salem, 2009). Particularly, Islamic finance lacks products in the area of risk management (Kok, Giorgioni and Laws, 2014).

Among new product innovations, Islamic derivative products are significant. Businesses which involve export and import of goods are in need of different derivative instruments, e.g. foreign exchange forward contracts (FX forwards) to hedge their currency risk. However, *shariah* approval is the first stage for introducing any Islamic banking product. *Shariah* scholars in Bangladesh have different opinions on the permissibility of these products. Therefore, this in-depth field study was carried out to interview the *shariah* scholars for their opinion on the issuance of Islamic derivatives in Bangladesh.

This article provides the opinions of the *shariah* scholars on the permissibility of Islamic derivatives in Bangladesh, followed by a discussion on their opinions. Finally, it offers some *shariah*-compliant structures of derivatives.

Overview of Islamic banking in Bangladesh

The Islami Bank Bangladesh Limited (IBBL) was the first Islamic bank in Bangladesh, launched in 1983 as a private commercial bank. From its establishment, Islamic banking in Bangladesh saw steady development due to the overwhelming response of the Muslims in Bangladesh. Following the success of IBBL, the second Islamic bank in Bangladesh was initiated in 1987, Al-Baraka Bank Bangladesh Limited. A number of conventional banks started to open Islamic banking windows from 1995 (Islam, 2010; Mohon, 2011; Mannan, 2010; Sarker, 2005; BMB Islamic, 2011). Currently, out of 47 banks in Bangladesh, eight full-fledged Islamic banks have more than 750 branches throughout the country. In addition, 16 conventional banks provide Islamic banking services through their Islamic banking branches.

Several acts govern the banks and financial institutions in Bangladesh: the Bank Companies Act 1991, the Bangladesh Bank Order 1972, the Securities and Exchange Commission Act 1993, and the Income Tax Ordinance 1984. However, there is no separate act for the operation of Islamic banks and financial institutions. Therefore, all Islamic banks in Bangladesh are required to follow the acts that govern the conventional banks and financial institutions. When Islamic banking was introduced in Bangladesh, no new act was passed, but some clauses were incorporated into the Bank Companies Act, and some amendments were made in the Income Tax Ordinance (Ahmad and Hassan, 2007).

The Bangladesh Bank (BB) is the central bank of the country and monitors, regulates, and supervises both Islamic and conventional banks. BB generally provides equal treatment to both Islamic and conventional banks. However, it has some special provisions for Islamic banks. Among the special provisions are that Islamic banks are permitted to keep their statutory liquidity requirement (SLR) with BB at the rate of 10% of their total deposit liabilities, whereas the conventional banks are required to maintain 20%. Islamic banks are independent to fix their profit and loss ratio as well as their mark-up rates based on their policy and banking situation (Ahmad and Hassan, 2007). BB does not have a separate section to monitor Islamic banking, but it has an Islamic Economics Division under the Department of Research to analyse the state of the Islamic finance industry in Bangladesh (BMB Islamic, 2011).

In 2009, BB issued guidelines on the operation and management of Islamic banks. The guidelines are considered a first attempt by BB to provide an operational framework for an Islamic bank. The guidelines include the mechanism of *shariah* and corporate governance, product definition and operational framework, alternative investment modes, and procedures for converting a conventional bank into an Islamic bank. However, these guidelines have some shortcomings. One of the major issues related to these guidelines is that under these guidelines, it is optional for an Islamic bank to have a *shariah* board, which is contradictory to global practice (BMB Islamic, 2011).

BB does not have a *shariah* advisory board to supervise Islamic financial institutions in Bangladesh. However, a private non-corporate body named the Central Shariah Board for Islamic Banks of Bangladesh (CSBIB) performs this function. Almost all the Islamic banks in Bangladesh are a member of CSBIB. CSBIB consists of a number of prominent *shariah* scholars in Bangladesh. It organizes regular meetings to discuss the *shariah* issues related to Islamic banking industry in Bangladesh. It also conducts timely research and publishes books and journals to serve its members (BMB Islamic, 2011).

Among the recent notable infrastructure developments in Bangladesh is the launch of the Islamic Interbank Money Market (IIMM). After a long period of waiting, Islamic banks in Bangladesh are now able to manage their funding crises through IIMM. However, Bangladesh still lacks a *sukuk* market. The government is about to make necessary amendments in *sukuk* regulation to develop a *sukuk* market in Bangladesh (Vizcaino and Quadir, 2012).

Research methodology

This study examines the possibility of Islamic derivatives in Bangladesh. It adopts a qualitative approach because determining the *shariah* status of Islamic derivatives requires rigorous analysis of the opinions of Islamic jurists (*fuqahā'*), which is very subjective in nature. In *shariah* research, the legal reasoning of the jurists (*ijtihād*) plays an important role in deciding the permissibility of a given issue (Faqir, 2011). For that reason, the study employs the qualitative approach to analyse the opinions of the *shariah* experts.

Library research was conducted as the first step to collect the expected data. For the field of Islamic jurisprudence (*fiqh*) it was necessary to collect opinions of the classical and contemporary Islamic jurists (Al-Sālih, 2002). Library research included reviewing the classical manuscripts of Islamic jurisprudence, contemporary literature, and *fatawa* (religious decrees issued by Islamic jurists) in the field of Islamic jurisprudence.

Secondly, qualitative interviews were conducted to learn the opinions of *shariah* scholars on this issue. The study employed semi-structured interviews as this is the predominantly practised interviewing technique for qualitative research. For this study, *shariah* scholars who were *shariah* committee members of Islamic banks and members of CSBIB were interviewed to acquire in-depth information on this issue. *Shariah* committee members have knowledge of and proficiency in Islamic law and jurisprudence. They advise banks on matters pertaining to *shariah*-compliant products and services. The *shariah* committee's approval is required before a product is introduced by an Islamic bank (Wardhany and Arshad, 2012; Rammal, 2010). Most importantly, *shariah* scholars who are members of CSBIB are the most respected and highest authority to issue *shariah* rulings pertaining to financial issues in Bangladesh. Therefore, it was necessary to interview the *shariah* committee members of the Islamic banks who are also members of CSBIB. The data gathered through interviews were analysed thematically. The scholars were classified according to their opinions as proponents and opponents of the Islamic FX forward.

The case regarding Islamic derivatives

There is an initiative by the CSBIB to develop the first Islamic derivative product in Bangladesh, which is the Islamic FX forward. However, the *shariah* scholars in Bangladesh have different types of opinions on the acceptability of an Islamic FX forward in the *shariah*. The view of one group of scholars is that an Islamic FX forward is not permissible in the *shariah*. They argue that *shariah* requires that currencies should be exchanged on the spot according to the price on the spot (Rafiq, 2014; Islam, 2014; Shamsuddoha, 2014, Uddin, 2014). On the other hand, some *shariah* scholars in Bangladesh are of the opinion that an Islamic FX forward should be allowed (Arif, 2014; Rahmani, 2014; Miah, 2014).

Arguments of the opponents

When interviewed, Rafiq (2014), a prominent *shariah* scholar in Bangladesh, stated that it is not possible to introduce Islamic derivative products in Bangladesh. In the case of the Islamic FX forward, he argues that there are several *shariah* violations. Firstly, Islamic *shariah* requires that currency exchange should be a transaction on the spot. He cites the following prophetic narration:

> Ubadah bin Al-Samit (RA) narrated that the Messenger of Allah (peace be upon him) said: Gold is to be paid for by gold, silver by silver, wheat by wheat, barley by barley, dates by dates, and salt by salt, like for like and equal for equal, payment being made hand to hand. If these classes differ, then sell as you wish if payment is made hand to hand.
>
> *Muslim, 1991, book: Al-Musaqat, chapter: Al-Sarf wa bay' al-dhahab bi al-waraq naqdan, Hadith no. 71*

Based on the above narration, different currencies should be exchanged based on the exchange rate at that day. It is not permissible to fix an exchange rate between two currencies three months earlier, for example, and then exchange those currencies after that on that fixed rate, ignoring that day's exchange rate in the market as this violates the rule of spot transaction prescribed in the above prophetic narration. The *shariah* only allows that the bank may promise that after three months it will sell to the customer USD 10,000, for example. Alternatively, the customer may promise that he will purchase USD 5,000 from the bank after three months. However, they are not allowed to fix the exchange rate beforehand. In reality, if an exchange rate cannot be fixed earlier, this type of promise is worthless for both the bank and the customer (Rafiq, 2014).

Furthermore, a FX forward involving *wa'd* (a promise) from one party may cause harm to the other party. For example, the customer promises to purchase USD 1,000 from the bank after three months at the rate of USD 1 = BDT 80. After three months, if the exchange rate of USD 1 = BDT 75 in the market, the customer is obliged to fulfil his promise. If the customer does not fulfil his promise, he is required to compensate the bank. On the other hand, after three months, if the exchange rate of USD 1 = BDT 85 in the market and the bank does not want to sell the USD 1,000 to the customer at the rate fixed earlier, then there is no liability on the bank. This type of arrangement allows the bank to take advantage and may cause harm to the customer. The *shariah* principle states: "Harm shall not be inflicted nor reciprocated" (Al-Asbahi, 2004, book: *Al-Aqdiyah*, chapter: *Al-Qada' fi al-Mirfaq*, hadith no. 2758). This means that both parties should be protected from harm in a transaction. Therefore, Islamic FX forward is not allowed in IBBL (Rafiq, 2014).

Similarly, Hannan (2014) holds the same position on Islamic derivatives. In regard to an Islamic FX forward, he argues that the practice of FX forward is not allowed because one cannot fix an exchange rate today and execute the transaction on a later date. He says one should be very cautious here because it is *bay' al-sarf* (currency exchange contract). Therefore, he takes the strict position even though the Accounting and Auditing Organization for Islamic Financial Institutions (AAOIFI) has allowed it.

Elahi (2014) acknowledges the need for Islamic derivative instruments in the export and import sectors. Nevertheless, he takes the strict position regarding their permissibility. He states that sometimes customers involved in export and import business ask a bank to fix the exchange rate of USD three months earlier than the transaction date. However, a bank cannot accept it because it is a violation of the *shariah* principle. This is *bay' al-sarf* and should be done on an on-the-spot basis as mentioned in the *hadith*. It is not permissible to decide an exchange rate today and execute the transaction another day. Likewise, Islam (2014) also agrees that FX forward is not allowed due to the *shariah* requirement of concluding the contract on the spot.

Arguments of the proponents

Contrary to this strict position, a group of scholars in Bangladesh opine that Islamic derivatives should be allowed in Bangladesh. Since the opinion of the previous group of scholars dominates the industry, this group of scholars can be described as the minority. In the case of an Islamic FX forward, Rahmani (2014) argues that in a FX forward, the customer first gives a *wa'd* to the bank to execute *bay' al-sarf* at a later date. The *shariah* ruling that states that the transaction should be on the spot is not applicable on *wa'd. Wa'd* is different from a contract (*'aqd*). *Shariah* principles relating to a contract (*'aqd*) are not applicable to *wa'd.* Therefore, even though *muwa'adah* is applied here, there is no issue from the *shariah* perspective. There are many differences between *muwa'adah* (mutual promise) and *al-bay'* (contract of sale).

Rahmani (2014) further explains that *muwa'adah* is just a promise to purchase or sell while *al-bay'* is a contract of sale. There are differences between these two expressions in Islamic jurisprudence, which are "I will purchase" and "I purchased". There must be *ijab* (offer) and *qabul* (acceptance) in *al-bay'* but this is not required in *muwa'adah.* In *muwa'adah,* the *'aqd* will be executed on a later date. On the mentioned date, there will not be any *'aqd* automatically but it will be executed through *ijab* and *qabul*. Finally, *muwa'adah* does not have any effect on changing the ownership of the subject matter. Thus, there are many differences between *muwa'adah* and *al-bay'*.

In addition, Rahmani (2014) points out that the *shariah* scholars in Bangladesh mainly follow the Hanafi school of jurisprudence (*madhhab*). Therefore, FX forward can be based on *muwa'adah.* This is because according to Hanafi scholars, *muwa'adah* can be used as binding on the promisor when there is a need. Khān (1892), a prominent Hanafi scholar cites: "Sometimes, a bilateral promise (*muwa'adah*) can be binding. Therefore, it can be made binding due to people's need." Therefore, a binding *muwa'adah* can be used in a FX forward due to public need (*hajah*).

Consistent with the above argument, Arif (2014) adds that Islamic banks in Bangladesh should start FX forwards first. Afterwards, if any mistake is found, it can be revised with the passage of time. There are amendments in every law around the world. It is natural to have amendments and revisions. *Shariah* rulings may change due to changes in situations and times. There are many instances in the *shariah* of something being lawful in some situations but unlawful in others. Besides, the scope for exercising juristic reasoning (*ijtihad*) in the field of commercial laws (*mu'amalat*) is wider than other areas. In this regard, it is not an obligation to confine oneself to one school of jurisprudence (*madhhab*). Wherever anything beneficial is found, it should be chosen.

Discussion of the arguments

Responding to the scholars' arguments prohibiting an Islamic FX forward in Bangladesh, Laldin (2014) argues that the *shariah* requirement for spot transaction (*yadan bi yadin*) is related to the period for executing the contract. This *shariah* principle is not applicable before the contract is executed. For example, A promises B that A will sell to B USD 100,000 on 5 June 2017. In this case, there is no problem from the *shariah* perspective if they fix the price of USD today. It does not violate the *shariah* principle of spot transaction (*yadan bi yadin*, hand to hand), because the contract is not yet concluded.

In addition, one can agree on the price today and execute the contract on the fixed future date. The buyer and seller are always free to decide the price. They are free to sell and purchase at any price even it is different from the market rate at that day. For example, on the day of executing the contract, 1 USD = Malaysian ringgit (MYR) 3.2, but both parties decide to exchange 1 USD for MYR 3.1; there is then no issue from the *shariah* perspective, as there is consent between the two contracting parties. Therefore, it is permissible to lock the exchange rate first; then when the time comes, both parties may enter into the contract, and possession (*qabd*) of the currency should be done at that point in time (Laldin, 2014).

Bangladesh's position in relation to FX forwards is contrary to the resolutions of some notable *shariah* authorities, namely those of AAOIFI (2010), Kuwait Finance House (1986), and Bank Negara Malaysia (BNM) (2010). In *shariah* standard no. 1 (2\9), AAOIFI (2010) states:

> A bilateral promise to purchase and sell currencies is forbidden if the promise is binding, even for the purpose of hedging against currency devaluation risk. However, a promise from one party is permissible even if the promise is binding.

AAOIFI does not allow binding *muwa'adah* in FX forwards but does allow *wa'd*. Likewise, BNM (2010) also allows *wa'd* in FX forwards. It resolves that:

> Islamic financial institutions are allowed to conduct forward foreign exchange transactions based on unilateral *wa'd mulzim* (binding promise) which is binding on the promissor. In addition, the party who suffers losses due to non-fulfilment of promise may claim compensation. The forward foreign exchange transactions may be carried out by the Islamic financial institutions with their customers, among Islamic financial institutions, or between the Islamic and conventional financial institutions.

Along with BNM, the Kuwait Finance House (1986) issued a resolution that it is allowed to exchange a currency for a rate agreed upon in advance with the condition that the contract is executed later where the delivery and the receipt of the subject matter is made on the spot.

In our opinion, the reason behind the prohibition of FX forward contracts in Bangladesh is that scholars have different understandings of the prophetic narration. It appears that according to their understanding, the "*yadan bi yadin*" concept requires the seller and purchaser to exchange the currency at that day's market price. However, the commentaries of this *hadith* mention that "*yadan bi yadin*" means that the transaction should be on a spot basis (Al-Nawawi, 1929; Al-Kirmani, 1981). This means that the delivery and possession of different currencies should be concluded immediately during the period of the contract.

However, there is no condition here to follow market price in sale and purchase. Instead, it is clearly mentioned in the *hadith* that both buyer and seller have the freedom to decide the price. It says: "If these classes differ, then sell as you wish if payment is made hand to hand."

When there is a transaction between two different items among the six types of items mentioned earlier in the *hadith*, it is not a requirement that both items should be equal. The purchaser and seller can freely exchange for whatever price they want. The only condition here is that it should be on a spot basis.

Therefore, we believe that there should be no problem accepting Islamic FX forward contracts in Bangladesh from the *shariah* perspective. Moreover, FX forwards are needed by customers who are involved in the export and import business. Foreign trade is increasing significantly in Bangladesh (Rahman and Ara, 2010; Jesmin, 2008). Therefore, Islamic banking should respond to the growing needs of the customer. Otherwise, customers may resort to conventional banking to fulfil their needs.

According to Rahman and Hassan (2011), Bangladesh needs to introduce derivative instruments to safeguard the foremost export sector. They argue that ready-made garments are the largest export sector in Bangladesh. Companies involved in exporting ready-made garments are exposed to currency rate risk for their foreign financial transactions. They have been employing two types of instruments to mitigate this risk: (a) selling the rights to letters of credit; and (b) forward contracts over the exchange rate. However, both these instruments have shortcomings. Transferring letters of credit may cost high processing fees, which can be from to 3% to 5% of the total amount. On the other hand, forward contracts can be problematic due to the rigid regulation of the central bank. Bangladesh Bank, the central bank of Bangladesh, does not permit derivative instruments on any asset except for some cases with special permission. Besides, when a forward contract is allowed by the Bangladesh Bank, the financial institution handling the whole contract is required to close the account on the maturity date. Therefore, the two instruments mentioned above do not truly serve the hedging purpose of the customers.

As for the export sector, so also derivatives are needed to mitigate risks in the leading import sector of Bangladesh. Bangladesh is a country that imports more than it exports. It has a growing negative balance in its current account. In 2008, the trade deficit was BDT 511 billion, which was nearly twice that of the previous years. This was due to increased importation of certain commodities, i.e. rice, wheat, fertiliser, cotton staple fibre, and edible oil. The political unrest in the world and the financial crisis in 2007–2008 were the primary reasons for the price hike in the market, particularly the edible oil and petroleum products. In the case of petroleum imports, the total volume imported increased from BDT 43 billion to 179 billion in 2009 compared with the previous five years. However, the total quantity of imports was reduced from 10 million metric tonnes to 7 million metric tonnes during the same period excluding the year 2005. Therefore, the government should consider mitigating the risks related to price instability and volatility in currency exchange rates through recourse to modern financial instruments.

Furthermore, Islamic derivatives could be viable instruments to hedge against the volatility in the capital market of Bangladesh. The capital market is the most important sector in the discussion about the establishment of derivatives. This is because derivatives on equities represent the largest portion of the international derivatives market. Rahman and Hassan (2011) have shown that the stock markets of Bangladesh are volatile. Basher et al. (2007) investigated the time-varying risk –return relationship as well as the effect of institutional factors on volatility for the stock market of Bangladesh utilising daily and weekly stock returns. They found that the Dhaka Stock Exchange (DSE) has negative skewness, excess kurtosis, and deviation from normality. Even though the volatility level did not reach the level of possible market collapse, the progressive rate of uncertainty and the spread indicated an alarming situation for the future. Therefore, Bangladesh needs a strong derivatives market to protect investors from loss in this volatile stock market.

Like abnormal volatility, unusual growth is a concerning factor. In the latter half of 2009, the DSE started to grow dramatically until in December 2010 it reached 8918.51 points. It grew at the rate of 103.47%, with approximately BDT 1.82 trillion in market capitalisation. Investors, policy makers, and market experts became afraid that the price bubble was going to explode in the near future, resulting in a big loss to the personal and institutional investors.

In December 2010, the DSE began to realise this fear on the part of the investors by falling nearly 147, 185, and 134 points in three consecutive sessions. Finally, on 19 December, the market recorded its biggest fall, losing 551 points, having lost 1264.10 points in nine business days. This collapse was marked as a "natural price correction" by the market authority. However, a number of investors lost valuable investments; individual investors, especially, in many cases lost everything. Taking into account the above scenario, derivatives may play a significant role through protecting investors by hedging their investments.

Finally, Islamic derivatives could be an additional investment source for local and foreign investors. As previously mentioned, there is enough volatility in the capital markets of Bangladesh to require hedging even when there is no threat of market collapse. As investors are getting decent return against risk, market capitalisation is rapidly growing and is currently greater than the supply of securities. As a consequence of this, the market is lacking efficiency and volatility is getting higher. To solve this issue, the market authority should ensure that there is enough supply of new good-quality securities. Derivative instruments can fulfil this need in the market, in addition to stocks and bonds.

Moreover, it is significant for a capital market that it should reflect the fair value of the securities. Due to the absence of this characteristic, a significant number of local and foreign investors are not paying attention to the Bangladeshi market. Foreign direct investment went down 36% in 2009 compared with 2008. The Bangladeshi capital market is mostly equity-centric as there is no viable bond market. Therefore, it would be more appropriate to issue derivatives to serve the needs of investors, rather than issuing new IPOs, which is quite difficult.

Considering the above factors, we would like to point out that Islamic *shariah* does not impose hardship on human beings. Islamic legal maxim reads "hardship begets facility" (*al-mashaqqah tajlub al-taysir*) (Laldin et al. 2013). What this means is that, whenever there is a hardship, *shariah* prescribes a way to remove that hardship. Allah (may He be glorified and exalted) says in the Qur'an: "Allah wants ease for you, and He does not want to make things difficult for you" (Baqarah: 185). In relation to this, Ibn Kathir (2000) stated that, though prayer (*salat*) is the second pillar of the *shariah*, it can be shortened for hardship, e.g. travel, fear, etc. The fundamental characteristic of the Islamic *shariah* is flexibility and ease. Therefore, in the exercise of *sadd al-dhara'i* scholars are recommended also to give consideration to public need (*maslahah*). Given the scenario of the export and import sector of Bangladesh, it is suggested that the *shariah* scholars might reconsider their opinions regarding Islamic derivatives.

In this juncture, we would like to mention that it is not acceptable to use conventional derivatives as they are prohibited in the *shariah*. Kunhibava (2010) has summarised the major objections of the *shariah* regarding conventional derivatives. Firstly, derivatives involve future sales where both subject matter of the sale i.e. price and commodity are deferred which is prohibited in the *shariah* as they come under the concept of *bay' al-kali bi al-kali* (selling debt for debt). Moreover, derivative transactions are basically a trade in non-existent items, which is forbidden in the *shariah*. In relation to conventional options contracts, scholars argue that options are simply "the right to purchase or sell", which cannot be the subject matter of a sale contract. Finally, the foremost criticism made by *shariah* scholars against derivatives is that these instruments involve excessive speculation, which is tantamount to *maysir* (gambling) and *gharar* (uncertainty).

Thus, leading Islamic banking practitioners around the globe are attempting to develop derivatives which fulfil the market need as well as at the same time meeting the criteria set by the *shariah* scholars. The initial aim of Islamic derivatives is to overcome the *shariah* objections outlined above. *Wa'd* and commodity *murabaha* (i.e. *tawarruq*: a deferred sale contract between two parties where the purchaser subsequently sells the asset to a third party for a cash price) are the two significant concepts to avoid: the prohibition on future sale and on the sale of the non-existent. However, the debate is ongoing on the issue of speculation as there is no precise criterion for prohibited speculative behaviours. Generally, *shariah* scholars resolve that Islamic derivatives should only be used for hedging purposes. The next section of this paper suggests several Islamic derivative instruments for Bangladesh.

Proposed Islamic derivative instruments

This paper suggests three Islamic derivative products for Bangladesh taking into account market need and *shariah* status. These derivatives are: (1) the Islamic FX forward contract; (2) the Islamic cross-currency swap, and (3) the Islamic FX option. Both the Islamic FX forward and the Islamic cross-currency swap are structured based on the concept of *muwa'adah,* while the Islamic FX option is based on the underlying concepts of *wa'd* and commodity *murabaha.*

Islamic FX forward contract

In order to hedge against currency risk, we would like to propose a *muwa'adah*-based Islamic FX forward contract. In the operation of this product, both bank and customer give *wa'd* that they will conclude *bay' al-sarf* (currency exchange contract) on a future date at a fixed exchange rate between two different currencies. On the transaction date, the bank and the client enter into a *bay' al-sarf* contract with a rate fixed before and instantly transfer the possession of the subject matter between them. Figure 9.1 shows the operational steps of the proposed *muwa'adah*-based Islamic FX forward contract.

Operational steps of the Islamic FX forward contract:

1. On 15 July 2017, the financial institution makes a promise (*wa'd*) to sell USD 500,000 to the customer on 5 September 2017 at the rate of BDT 80 per USD.
2. On the same day, the customer makes another promise (*wa'd*) to purchase USD 500,000 from the financial institution on 5 September 2017 at the rate of BDT 80 per USD.
3. On 5 September 2017, the financial institution and the client conclude the *bay' al-sarf* (currency exchange transaction) at the rate of 80 BDT per USD. The financial institution pays USD 500,000 to the client and the client pays BDT 40 million to the financial institution.

The above structure involves *muwa'adah* while one *wa'd* is used in a FX forward in normal circumstances. *Muwa'adah* is chosen because the Hanafi school of jurisprudence allows the use of *muwa'adah* as binding on both parties in the case of public need (Khān, 1892). The Hanafi school of jurisprudence is the leading school of Islamic jurisprudence in Bangladesh. Therefore, *muwa'adah* should be consistent with the *shariah* framework of Bangladesh. Furthermore, even though *muwa'adah* is binding on both parties, it is still not similar to a contract (*'aqd*). In the case of *muwa'adah,* there is no offer (*'ijab*), and acceptance (*qabul*) in the agreement, and these are the pillars of the execution of a contract (*'aqd*). Furthermore, there is no transfer of ownership in *muwa'adah,* whereas in a contract (*'aqd*) the ownership of the commodity is transferred to the purchaser and the purchase price becomes the

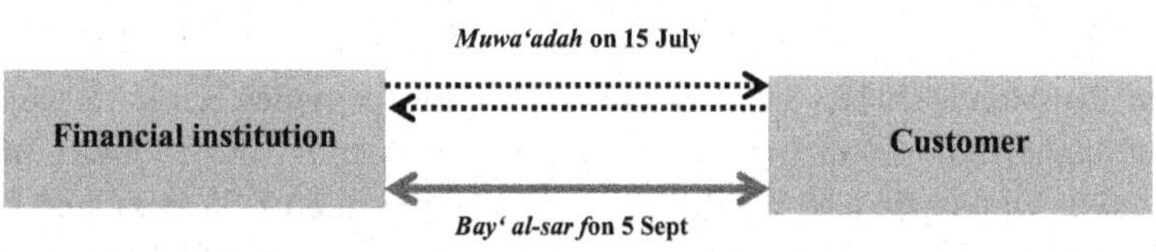

FIGURE 9.1 *Muwa'adah* Islamic foreign exchange forward contract

debt of the purchaser. In the case of *muwa'adah*, when the promisor breaches the promise without any valid excuse, he is obliged to compensate the promisee only for the amount of loss incurred due to the breach of the promise and not for the total contract price. This is very different to a contract (*'aqd*), where the full purchase price becomes a debt for the client (Abdullah and Rahman, 2015).

The *muwa'adah*-based Islamic FX forward provides more financial protection for the client. This is because the bank also provides *wa'd* that it will sell a certain amount of currency to the client on the fixed date. Therefore, if the currency exchange rate is against the interests of the bank, the bank is still obliged to fulfil its *wa'd* to sell the currency on the specified date. Hence, compared with the *wa'd*-based model, the *muwa'adah*-based model better serves the interests of both parties. Moreover, this *muwa'adah*-based model is more coherent with the *shariah* principle which states that harm should be eliminated from each individual in all Islamic transactions (Al-Asbahi, 2004, book: *Al-Aqdiyah*, chapter: *Al-Qada'fi al-Mirfaq*, hadith no. 2758).

Although *wa'dan* can serve the same interest of *muwa'adah, wa'dan* is more complicated than *muwa'adah*. As *muwa'adah* is accepted in the Hanafi school of jurisprudence, then it is better to choose the less complicated option. Islamic *shariah* encourages preferring the easier of two choices if both are lawful (Al-Bukhāri, 1980, book: *Al-Adab*, chapter: *Qawl al-nabi sallallahu 'alyhi wa sallam: yassiru wa la tu'assiru*, hadith no. 6126). Therefore, *muwa'adah* should be the best option. However, to minimize dispute among the scholars, a *wa'd*-based FX forward could be introduced instead of *muwa'adah*. This is based on the legal maxim which states that getting out of a dispute is desirable (Ismail, 1996). However, in this case, there would be no *wa'd* from the bank's side.

Islamic cross-currency swap (muwa'adah)

Like the Islamic FX forward contract, an Islamic cross-currency swap can be developed through *muwa'adah*. While the FX forward is structured to hedge against currency risk for a single time, the Islamic cross-currency swap is used to hedge against fluctuations of a currency for a longer period. In this product structure, the contracting parties execute a number of *bay' al-sarf* within a certain period. For instance, the bank and the customer fix an exchange rate of 85 BDT per 1 USD for a period of one year. Within this period, both parties exchange two different currencies every three months at the rate fixed. Figure 9.2 illustrates the operational steps of *muwa'adah*-based Islamic cross-currency swap.

Operational steps of the Islamic cross-currency swap:

1. On 20 March 2017, the financial institution provides *wa'd* to execute a number of *bay' al-sarf* transactions with the client at three-month intervals from 1 May until 1 November at the exchange rate of 80 BDT per 1 USD. The financial institution promises to sell a fixed amount of USD to the client every three months until the end of the tenure.

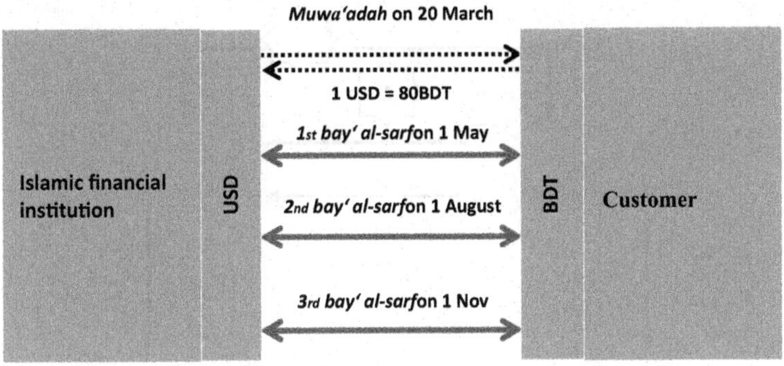

FIGURE 9.2 *Muwa'adah*-based Islamic cross-currency swap

2. On 20 March, the client provides *wa'd* to conclude a number of *bay' al-sarf* with the financial institution at three-months intervals from 1 May until 1 November at the rate of 80 BDT per one USD. The client promises to purchase a fixed amount of USD from the financial institution every three months until the end of the tenure.
3. On 1 May 2017, the financial institution and the client execute the *bay' al-sarf* contract based on the *wa'd* provided by both parties earlier. The financial institution sells for example USD 1 million to the client and the client purchases it for BDT 80 million. A similar *bay' al-sarf* takes place between the two parties every three months until the expiry of the swap.

Usually, Islamic banking practitioners use commodity *murabaha* for Islamic cross-currency swaps, but *muwa'adah* is suggested for Bangladesh as some *shariah* scholars in Bangladesh do not allow commodity *murabaha.* In addition to this, there is no developed commodity market in Bangladesh to exercise commodity *murabaha.* Since a binding *muwa'adah* is accepted in the Hanafi school of jurisprudence in the case of public need, it is preferable to use *muwa'adah. Muwa'adah*-based Islamic cross-currency swap holds a similar *shariah* ruling to FX forward. This is because making *wa'd* to execute a number of *bay' al-sarf* is similar to making *wa'd* for a single *bay' al-sarf.*

There are some benefits of using *muwa'adah* in an Islamic cross-currency swap. Firstly, it is less costly than commodity *murabaha* as there is no brokerage fee. Secondly, the product structure is less complicated than that of the commodity *murabaha.*

Islamic FX option

The Islamic option is a significant risk management tool. Globally, different models have been proposed for Islamic options. However, these models receive condemnation from the *shariah* perspective. Therefore, we propose a *wa'd*-based Islamic

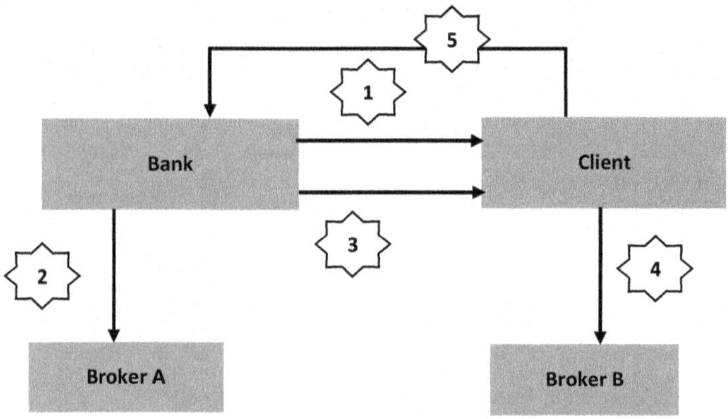

FIGURE 9.3 Islamic foreign exchange option based on *wa'd* and commodity *murabaha*

FX option. The Islamic FX option could be the future *wa'd*-based hedging instrument in Bangladesh. This model is based on *wa'd* with commodity *murabaha.* Figure 9.3 below describes the operational steps of the Islamic FX option based on *wa'd* and commodity *murabaha.*

Operational steps of the *wa'd*-based Islamic FX option:

1. On 23 February 2017, the bank promises to sell USD 1 million to the client at the rate of BDT 80 per one USD on any day from 1 April 2017 to 30 April 2017.
2. On the same day, the bank purchases a commodity from commodity broker A at a price of BDT 200,000.
3. At the same time, the bank sells the commodity to the customer at BDT (200,000 cost + 100,000 profit =) 300,000. BDT 100,000 is considered as the option premium for the bank.
4. On the above date, the customer appoints the bank as his selling agent to sell the commodity to commodity broker B at BDT 200,000.
5. After that, from 1 April 2017 to 30 April 2017, if the USD exchange rate is in favour of the customer, he may ask the bank to realise its *wa'd.*

From the *shariah* perspective, the above model is mostly recognised by *shariah* scholars as it has only one *wa'd* and a commodity *murabaha* which is based on *tawarruq*. There is no application of *tawarruq* in Bangladesh at present as it is not allowed by the *shariah* scholars. However, a group of *shariah* scholars in Bangladesh believe that *tawarruq* can be practised in Islamic financial instruments provided that there is a commodity market which facilitates the real *tawarruq* operation. *Tawarruq* is the most appropriate mechanism so far we have found to structure this product. Therefore, establishing a commodity market to facilitate the genuine practice of *tawarruq* should be among the future development agendas for Islamic banking in Bangladesh. In this respect, Malaysia's *suq al-sila'* (Commodity *Murabaha* House) can be taken into consideration. Even though there are some minor issues concerning its operation, it is a positive initiative to create a platform for practising genuine *tawarruq* (Dusuki, 2010).

Conclusion

This article discussed the opinions of prominent *shariah* scholars in Bangladesh on the permissibility of Islamic derivatives and particularly of the Islamic FX forward contract. It is found that the majority of the scholars heavily resort to the *sadd al-dhara'i'* principle to allow the practice of Islamic FX forwards and other Islamic derivatives. Moreover, they have a different interpretation of the *hadith* pertaining to the contract of *bay' al-sarf* comparing to the majority of the scholars around the world. This study suggests that scholars re-think the *shariah* permissibility of Islamic FX forwards and offers three suitable models for Islamic derivatives in Bangladesh. *Shariah* scholars should consider the fact that Islamic derivatives would be useful for Islamic banks in Bangladesh to fulfil the needs of their clients. This research focuses on the issuance of Islamic derivatives from the *shariah* perspective. Further research can be carried out on the financial and operational aspects of Islamic derivatives.

Note

1 This article is an extraction of the first author's doctoral thesis entitled "Application of Wa'd (Promise) in Islamic Banking Products: A Study in Malaysia and Bangladesh" submitted to University of Malaya, Kuala Lumpur in 2016. A significant part of the article is extracted from Chapters 4, 6 and 7 of the thesis.

References

Abdullah, M. F. and Rahman, A. A. (2015), "Is wa'dan any different to muwa'adah? Empirical evidence from Malaysia," *International Journal of Islamic and Middle Eastern Finance and Management*, Vol. 8, Iss. 3, pp. 310–328.

Abdullah, M. F. and Rahman, A. A. (2017), "Shari'ah governance of Islamic banks in Bangladesh: Issues and challenges", *Journal of Islamic Economics, Banking and Finance*, Vol. 13, No. 3, pp. 82–94.

Accounting and Auditing Organization for Islamic Financial Institutions (AAOIFI). (2010), *Shari'ah Standards for Islamic Financial Institutions*. Manama: Accounting and Auditing Organization for Islamic Financial Institutions.

Ahmad, A. U. F. and Hassan, M. K. (2007), "Regulation and performance of Islamic banking in Bangladesh," *Thunderbird International Business Review*, Vol. 49, Iss. 2, pp. 251–277.

Al-Asbahi, M. A. (2004), *Al-Muwatta'*, ed. Muhammad Mustafa Al-A'zami. Abu Dhabi: Zayed Bin Sultan Al-Nahayan Charitable and Humanitarian Foundation.

Al-Bukhāri, A. A. M. I. (1980), *Al-Jāmi'al-Sahih*, ed. Muhib al-Din al-Khatib. Al-Qāhirah: Matba'ah al-salafiyyah.

Al-Kirmani, S. D. (1981). *Al-Kawakib al-Dirari fi Sharh Sahih al-Bukhari*. Bayrut: Dar ihya' al-turath al-'arabi.

Al-Nawawi, M. D. A. Z. Y. (1929), *Al-Minhaj Sharh Sahih Muslim bin al-Hajjaj*, Al-Qarirah: Al-Matba'ah al-misriyyah bi al-azhar.

Al-Salem, F. S. (2009), "Islamic financial product innovation," *International Journal of Islamic and Middle Eastern Finance and Management*, Vol. 2, Iss. 3, pp. 187–200.

Al-Sālih, 'A. (2002), "Manāhij al-bahth al-mu'āsirah fi usul al-fiqh," *Majallat Jāmi'at Dimashq*, Vol. 18, No. 2, pp. 403–423.

Arif, A. Q. M. S. (2014), Secretary General, Central Shari'a Board for Islamic Banks of Bangladesh, interview with the first author, 16 April.

Bangladesh Bank. (2017), Annual Report 2015–16. Dhaka: Bangladesh Bank.

Bank Negara Malaysia. (2010), *Shariah resolutions in Islamic finance*. Kuala Lumpur: Bank Negara Malaysia.

Basher, S. A., Hassan, M. K. and Islam, A. M. (2007), "Time-varying volatility and equity returns in Bangladesh stock market", *Applied Financial Economics*, Vol. 17, Iss. 17, pp. 1393–1407.

BMB Islamic. (2011), *Global Islamic finance report (GIFR) 2011*. London: BMB Islamic UK Limited.

Dusuki, A. W. (2010). "Can Bursa Malaysia's Suq al-Sila' (Commodity Murabaha House) resolve the controversy over tawarruq?" Research paper no. 10, International shari'ah Research Academy for Islamic Finance, Kuala Lumpur.

Elahi, M. M. (2014), Member of the Shariah Supervisory Committee, Islami Bank Bangladesh Limited, interview with the first author, 10 April.

Faqir, S. 'A. (2011), "Khasā'is manhaj al-bahth fi al-fiqh al-Islāmi," available at: http://fiqh.islammessage.com/NewsDetails.aspx?id=4060 (accessed 6 May 2015).

Hannan, S. A. (2014), Member of the Shariah Supervisory Committee, Shahjalal Islami Bank Limited, interview with the first author, 20 April.

Ibn Kathir, A. F. I. U. (2000), *Tafsir al-Qur'an al-'azim*. Bayrut: Dar Ibn Hazm.

Islam, M. N. (2010), "Bangladeshe Islami bank protishthar andoloner itihash," *Amar Desh*, 21 April.

Islam, S. (2014), Member Secretariat, Central Shari'a Board for the Islamic Banks of Bangladesh, interview with the first author, 19 April.

Ismail, M. B. (1996), *Al-Qawa'id al-fiqhiyyah bayna al-asalah wa al-tawjih*. Heliopolis: Dar al-Manar.

Jesmin, R. (2008), "Maximizing the potentials of Bangladesh's export to the EU market," *Asia Europe Journal*, Vol. 6, Iss. 3–4, pp. 519–529.

Khān, Q. (1892), *Fatāwā Qādi Khān*, printed with Nizām al-Din al-Balkhi with others. *Al-Fatāwā al-Hindiyyah*. Bulaq: al-Matba'ah al-kubrā al-amiriyyah.

Kok, S. K., Giorgioni, G. and Laws, J. (2014), "Derivative products and innovation in Islamic finance: A hybrid tool for risk-sharing options," *International Journal of Islamic and Middle Eastern Finance and Management*, Vol. 7, Iss. 3, pp. 242–257.

Kunhibava, S. (2010), "Derivatives in Islamic finance", Research Paper No. 7, International Shari'ah Research Academy for Islamic Finance, Kuala Lumpur.

Kuwait Finance House. (1986), "Al-Fatawa al-Shar'iyyah fi al-Masa'il al-Iqtisadiyyah," Fatwa no. 171, available at: http://iefpedia.com/arab/ (accessed 7 July 2015).

Laldin, A. (2014), Deputy Chairman, shari'ah Advisory Council of Bank Negara Malaysia, interview with the first author, 14 October.

Laldin, M. A., Khir, M. F. A., Bouheraoua, S. and Ansary, R. (2013), *Islamic legal maxims & their application in Islamic finance*, International shari'ah Research Academy for Islamic Finance: Kuala Lumpur.

Mannan, M. A. (2010), *Islami Bank Babostha*. Dhaka: Central Shariah Board for Islamic Banks of Bangladesh.

Miah, A. (2014), Member of the Shari'ah Supervisory Committee, Islami Bank Bangladesh Limited, interview with the first author, 10 April.

Mohon, I. K. (2011), *Islami Orthoniti*. Dhaka: Zerin Publishers.

Muslim, A. H. (1991), *Sahih Muslim*, ed. Muhammad Fu'ād 'Abd al-Bāqi. Bayrut: Dār al-kutub al-'ilmiyyah.

Rafiq, A. B. (2014), Member, Central Shari'a Board for Islamic Banks of Bangladesh, interview with the first author, 4 May.

Rahman, M. M. and Ara, L. A. (2010), "Bangladesh trade potential: A dynamic gravity approach", *Journal of International Trade Law and Policy*, Vol. 9, Iss. 2, pp. 130–147.

Rahman, S. and Hassan, M. K. (2011), "The potential of derivatives market in Bangladesh" *Journal of Economic Cooperation and Development*, Vol. 32, No. 4, pp. 97–144.

Rahmani, S. (2014), Member of the Shariah Supervisory Committee, Shahjalal Islami Bank Limited, interview with the first author, 10 April.

Rammal, H. G. (2010), "Corporate governance in the Islamic banking system in Pakistan: The role of the shari'ah supervisory boards." Doctorate thesis, University of Adelaide, Adelaide.

Sarker, A. A. (2005), "Islamic banking in Bangladesh: Achievements and challenges," *Journal of Islamic Economics, Banking and Finance*, Vol. 1, No. 1, available at: www.ibtra.com/pdf/journal/v1_n1_article5.pdf (accessed 8 March 2017).

Sarker, M. A. A. (1999), "Islamic banking in Bangladesh: Growth, structure, and performance." Proceedings of the Third Harvard University Forum on Islamic Finance: Local Challenges, Global Opportunities, pp. 271–290.

Shamsuddoha, M. (2014), Vice President, Shariah Secretariat, Research Unit, Islami Bank Bangladesh Limited, interview with the first author, 7 April.

Uddin, M. F. (2014), Junior Assistant Vice President & Muraquib, Shahjalal Islami Bank Limited, interview with the first author, 13 April.

Vizcaino, B. and Quadir, S. (2012), "Bangladesh launches Islamic interbank money market." *Reuters*, 5 June.

Wardhany, N. and Arshad, S. (2012), "The role of Shariah board in Islamic banks: A case study of Malaysia, Indonesia and Brunei Darussalam." Paper presented in Second ISRA Colloquim, Bank Negara Malaysia, Kuala Lumpur, 27 November.

10

IMPACT OF DERIVATIVE USAGE ON THE VALUE OF *SHARIAH*-COMPLIANT FIRMS IN MALAYSIA

Mamunur Rashid, Lim Li Chern and Cheong Jiunn Yan

Introduction

Derivatives are financial instruments often used to reduce transaction exposures. Nonetheless, researchers have long concurred that derivative usage is one of the sources of the financial crises in the past two decades (Paligorova & Staskow, 2014; Alam & Afza, 2017). Success in a derivative contract largely depends on taking the right position, which depends on a near-perfect estimation of the future expected value (i.e. stock price, currency rate, etc.). Despite the risks behind the usage of derivatives, many non-financial firms are still utilising derivatives to mitigate firm risks. Although risk management objectives are generally synonymous, the impact of using derivatives in handling firm risks differs from study to study.

Past studies have done research on developed markets, so an insight into the impact of derivative usage in risk management activities in the context of a developing country may provide new perceptions. Information from Malaysia was the chosen data set for this study, because this country not only is recovering steadily from the oil shock economic event in 2014, it also has a sizeable number of firms which are consistently maintained to be *shariah*-compliant as overseen by the Securities Commission's Shari'ah Advisory Council (Colton, 2016; Securities Commission Malaysia, 2017).

Two major theories are discussed in recent studies to explain the relationship between the use of derivatives and financial performance. Overall, if used properly, the use of derivatives should reduce cash flow volatility to stabilise a firm's financial condition (Lookman, 2004). This view stands against the classical theory. In the context of a perfect capital market, Modigliani and Miller (1958) theorised that corporate risk management will not maximise firm value as shareholders can diversify and manage risks by investing in well-performing portfolios. On the other hand, higher expected cash flow volatility may trigger underinvestment. Hence, the two major angles on the derivatives–performance connection are the financial distress (risk management) theory and the underinvestment theory. Financial distress, according to Bartram, Brown and Fehle (2009), is when a firm is unable to meet its fixed payment obligations on time because it is facing some cash flow volatility that affects the firm's liquidity. The likelihood of encountering such problems and the cost associated with financial distress could be reduced with proper financial risk management. According to Charumathi and Kota (2012), the underinvestment problem arises when a firm is unable to raise enough capital expenditure because it is too costly to raise capital externally and simultaneously there are not enough internal funds. With financial risk management, firms can increase shareholder value through coordination of their financial and investment policies.

In general, firms with financial (liquidity) constraints and high leverage tend to use derivatives to manage risks (Smith & Stulz, 1985; Carter, Rogers & Simkins, 2006). Derivative usage is also found to be positively related to size and growth opportunities (Alam & Afza, 2017; Lau, 2016). Much of the recent risk management literature examines the impact of derivatives usage on firm value in the context of developed countries, mainly in the United States. Such research was pioneered by Allayannis and Weston (2001) in the context of usage of foreign currency derivatives on market value. The impact of derivatives usage on firm financial performance has also been researched in various other industries such as the US airline industry (Carter et al., 2006), oil and gas (Jin & Jorion, 2006), and gold (Callahan, 2012). A mixed bag of results has been obtained in research studying the benefits of using derivatives outside of the United States. Nguyen and Faff (2010) claimed that derivatives usage among Australian firms led to a decrease in firm value. By contrast, research done in Asian countries (Ameer, 2009; Allayannis et al., 2003) generally showed that derivatives usage improves firm value.

Arnold et al. (2014), using meta-analyses, further reinforce the suggestion that firms that were at the brink of bankruptcy or facing financial distress would find hedging more valuable. However, different types of leverage would affect the use of derivatives differently; the probability of using derivatives will decrease as firms hold more long-term debt (Bartram et al., 2009).

Larger firms may have the economies of scale to afford a hedging programme, hence they are more likely to be in greater need of derivatives. On the flip side, smaller firms might experience challenges in raising external capital and their assets might not be diversified enough. This would make smaller firms more likely to default than bigger firms, and this would give them more incentives to hedge their risk using derivatives (Warner, 1977). Dolde (1993) found that smaller firms showed relatively larger hedging activities than did larger firms, while Bodnar, Consolandi, Gabbi and Jaiswal-Dale (2013) found evidence that supported both reasons for hedging when they studied risk management practices among Italian non-financial firms, where both large and small firms were more likely to use foreign currency derivatives.

Berkman and Bradbury (1996) stated that when firms were presented with investing opportunities, they would most often face a conflict of interest between their debtholders and their shareholders. Myers (1977) argued that shareholders will tend to forgo positive net present value (NPV) projects whenever the gains were added onto the debtholder, which is an example of underinvestment. Nance, Smith and Smithson (1993) then added that hedging will be able to control the likelihood of a firm defaulting on bond payments. Therefore, firms that possess more growth opportunities will opt for hedging programmes to reduce volatility of firm value. The decision to hedge, according to Froot, Scharfstein and Stein (1993), is due to the fear of not being able to capitalise on growth opportunities because of short-term financial challenges. Geczy, Minton and Schrand (1997) discovered in their study that heavily leveraged firms with high growth opportunities will have a higher probability of using derivatives. Malaysia firms' participation in the use of derivatives motivated a few studies on the determinants of derivative usage by Malaysian firms (Ameer, 2009; Ahmad & Haris, 2012; Isa, Ismail & Rahman, 2017).

Despite the presence of contradictory findings, general empirical evidence shows that use of derivatives impacts firm value positively: a positive (negative) relationship between the use of derivatives and a firm's value (risk) indicates that derivatives are used for risk management purposes. Firms from emerging economies with faster growth, from volatile economies, and of relatively smaller size would opt for derivative use. Islamic firms are relatively smaller in their global footprint, and these firms are often listed in volatile but emerging economies. Islamic firms, therefore, should use derivatives to reduce higher expected volatility. It should be noted here that the way Islamic finance operates is slightly different from the way Islamic firms operate. Islamic firms are *shariah*-compliant and thus include a significant portion of debt in their capital structure (Rashid, Hassan, Amin & Samina, 2017). Theoretically, Islamic firms should not engage in excessive and known risk. Since, Islamic firms engage in transactions with other firms, irrespective of their religious identity, the demand for derivatives in Islamic firms should be similar to that in conventional firms.

This study contributes to the literature on derivatives use by *shariah*-compliant firms by taking a sample from Malaysia. Extending from existing studies, this study added analysis on the impact of derivatives use during the periods leading up to and the end of a crisis. It will provide an insight into the effect of derivatives usage on firm performance during different phases of the economic cycle.

Analysis and data

To investigate the relationship between the impact of derivatives use and firm value, this study identified 200 *shariah*-compliant non-financial firms from a list compiled in 2016 by Malaysia's Securities Commission Shari'ah Advisory Council. Financial firms were excluded from the sample as they are considered to be both users and traders of derivative instruments, and incorporating them into this study might have resulted in biased results. Firms listed on the Main Market of the Bursa Malaysia were selected as the sample for this study.

The data was retrieved from Bursa Malaysia website and the Datastream financial database. The annual reports of these firms were also manually examined for disclosures of derivatives usage. Among the 582 listed *shariah*-compliant firms, approximately 23% of the firms had disclosed derivatives usage in their annual reports.

Based on the aims of this study, non-missing firm data as well as disclosures on derivatives spanning the years 2011 to 2016 were collected respectively from Datastream and annual reports. A sample of 100 firms was collected and classified as the 'treatment group' of derivative users. Another sample of 100 firms were selected separately from the remaining 77% of firms who had no disclosures of derivative usage in their annual reports, and these formed the control group of non-derivative users. Both groups contained similar numbers of firms from the different sectors in their sample: technology (5), construction (3), plantation (15), services (27), consumer products (25) and industrial (25).

According to Alam and Afza (2017), one of the methods for empirically examining the role of derivatives in mitigating firm risks and maximising firm value along with other firm-specific factors is to use the ordinary least squares method (2-stage least squares method to address potential endogeneity). Thus, this study aimed to analyse the relationship between derivatives use and firm value by using the following model for estimation:

$$\begin{aligned} LnTobinQ = \alpha &+ B1SIZE + B2ROA + B3GROWTH + B4LEV + \\ &B5LIQ + B6DIVD + B7DERIVD + BBPRECRISIS + \\ &B9CRISIS + B10POSTCRISIS + \varepsilon \end{aligned}$$

The dependent, independent and controlled variables are defined in Table 10.1.

In this study, the dependent variable of the model is the firm value measured using the natural logarithm transformation of Tobin's *Q* ratio. Past research (Ayturk, Gurbuz & Yanik, 2016; Bashir et al., 2013; Lau, 2016) has shown that Tobin's *Q* ratio is a good proxy for firm value measurement. Furthermore, Ayturk et al. (2016) proposed that the natural logarithm of the ratio poses better statistical distribution properties. The usage of derivatives is taken as the independent variable in this study. This variable is measured through a dummy variable whereby the value of 1 is taken if a firm uses derivatives, and 0 if a firm does not use derivatives.

In line with past research, this study incorporated firm size, return on assets (ROA), growth opportunities, leverage, liquidity and dividend as controlled variables. Studies have shown that larger firms are more likely to hedge due to the larger fixed cost in running the firms as well as greater economies of scale (Ahmed et al., 2014; Lau, 2016; Bashir et al., 2013). Researchers used ROA to assess the impact of derivatives use on firm value. As ROA is a proxy for profitability, the more profitable firms are, the higher the their value.

TABLE 10.1 Definition of variables used in the analysis of derivatives useage by *shariah*-compliant firms

Variable	*Definition*
LnTobinQ	Natural logarithm of the sum of equity market value and liabilities book value, divided by equity book value and liabilities book value
SIZE	Natural logarithm of total assets
ROA	Net income over total assets
GROWTH	Inverse of market-to-book value
LEV	Book value of total debt over book value of total equity
LIQ	Current ratio
DIVD	Dummy variable with value of '1' if firm paid a dividend in the year, otherwise '0'
DERIVD	Dummy variable with value of '1' if firm uses derivatives, otherwise '0'
PRECRISIS	Dummy variable with value of '1' if firm is in pre-crisis years of 2011 and 2012, otherwise '0'
CRISIS	Dummy variable with value of '1' if firm is in crisis years of 2013 and 2014, otherwise '0'
POSTCRISIS	Dummy variable with value of '1' if firm is in post-crisis years of 2015 and 2016, otherwise '0'

According to the literature, the growth opportunities of a firm also affect the firm's value (Ayturk et al., 2016). Due to the lack of data, the variable to estimate growth opportunities will be defined using the inverse of market-to-book value, as proposed by Goldberg et al. (1994). Highly leveraged firms are more likely to hedge as hedging increases debt capacity, which can ultimately lead to increased tax shield advantages (Bashir et. al, 2013). However, Titman and Wessels (2012) noted that too much debt may lead to financial distress and can decrease firm value.

High liquidity can indicate that firms are sufficiently able to undertake projects without relying on external funds. Firms with liquidity constraints are more likely to use derivatives to hedge and maximise firm value (Alam & Afza, 2017). In this study, the dividend dummy is to illustrate firms' access to financial markets as firms with better access are able to undertake projects which may not result in positive NPV values. A lower *Q* value may be the consequence of such action. Therefore, according to Allayannis and Weston (2001), firms which pay dividends, are most likely not capital constrained, will see a positively change in value. It is well noted in the existing literature that a problem of endogeneity may exist in research on derivatives use and firm value. This study uses a two-stage least squares (2SLS) model to estimate parameters for the model.

Results

Table 10.2 shows the descriptive statistics of derivatives usage variables for the full sample, for *shariah*-compliant firms with derivatives, and for *shariah*-compliant

TABLE 10.2 Descriptive statistics of the study sample of *shariah*-compliant firms

Variables	*N*	*Mean*	*Median*	*Std. dev.*	*Min.*	*Max.*
Full sample of *shariah*-compliant firms						
Tobin's *Q* ratio	1,200	5.7681	5.5756	0.8070	4.3233	8.2134
Size	1,200	5.7771	5.6378	0.7162	4.3452	8.1234
Return on assets	1,200	0.0411	0.0389	0.1758	−0.9370	5.2805
Growth	1,200	1.3903	1.1764	1.0397	−3.0303	10
Leverage	1,200	47.9927	28.515	111.701	−1395.21	1664.72
Liquidity	1,200	2.9031	1.84	4.2905	0.03	65.3
Dividend dummy	1,200	0.6683	1	0.4710	0	1
Pre-crisis dummy	1,200	0.3333	0	0.4716	0	1
Crisis dummy	1,200	0.3333	0	0.4716	0	1
Post-crisis dummy	1,200	0.3333	0	0.4716	0	1
Shariah-compliant firms using derivatives						
Tobin's *Q* ratio	600	6.0987	5.9936	0.85563	4.5841	8.2134
Size	600	6.0657	5.9867	0.7664	4.6949	8.1234
Return on assets	600	0.0627	0.0484	0.2228	−0.31064	5.2805
Growth	600	1.2529	0.9523	1.0311	0.0498	7.6923
Leverage	600	49.7762	37.755	54.1627	0	407.52
Liquidity	600	2.3628	1.665	2.3688	0.27	26.8
Dividend dummy	600	0.76	1	0.4274	0	1
Pre-crisis dummy	600	0.3333	0	0.4717	0	1
Crisis dummy	600	0.3333	0	0.4717	0	1
Post-crisis dummy	600	0.3333	0	0.4717	0	1

(*continued*)

TABLE 10.2 (Cont.)

Variables	*N*	*Mean*	*Median*	*Std. dev.*	*Min.*	*Max.*
Shariah-compliant firms not using derivatives						
Tobin's Q ratio	600	5.4375	5.3646	0.5939	4.3233	7.5630
Size	600	5.4886	5.4562	0.5220	4.3452	7.2524
Return on assets	600	0.0194	0.0283	0.1061	−0.9370	0.4711
Growth	600	1.5276	1.3698	1.0309	−3.0303	10
Leverage	600	46.2088	19.875	148.4421	−1395.21	1664.72
Liquidity	600	3.4434	2.03	5.5364	0.03	65.3
Dividend dummy	600	0.5766	1	0.4945	0	1
Pre-crisis dummy	600	0.3333	0	0.4717	0	1
Crisis dummy	600	0.3333	0	0.4717	0	1
Post-crisis dummy	600	0.3333	0	0.4717	0	1

firms without derivatives, respectively. As can be seen in the entries for the full sample, the mean value of Tobin's Q is 5.768156. To prevent the sample from being skewed, the natural log value of Tobin's Q is taken. Bashir et al. (2013) showed that skewness is under control when the median value does not differ distinctly from the mean value. From the entries for the *shariah*-compliant firms that use and those that do not use derivatives, it can be seen that both type of firms have similar firm values, with means of approximately 5.4–6.1. This is consistent with the findings that if firms can manage risks efficiently, investors will value the firms more highly.

Firms using derivatives are observed to be larger and have higher profitability and higher leverage than firms that do not use derivatives. On the other hand, firms that do not use derivatives have higher growth opportunities, higher liquidity levels, and generally pay lower dividends on average than firms that do use derivatives. The mean value for growth of firms that use derivatives is smaller than the mean value of those that do not, indicating that the decision to use derivatives results in negative growth for a firm. Firms that use derivatives pay more dividends on average, because by paying dividends firms can avoid financial distress even without using derivatives (Bashir et al., 2013).

A *t*-test was applied to test for significant differences between derivatives users and non-derivatives users with respect to firm differences. Table 10.3 shows that there exists statistically significant difference for all variables except leverage between firms that use and those do not use derivatives. The variables which show statistically significant differences in means are size, ROA and dividend dummy. The presence of a positively related and statistically significant dividend dummy variable is in line with the study by Ayturk et al. (2016), in which the authors claimed that easy access to financial markets tends to increase firm value.

The correlation coefficients between independent variables are reported in Table 10.4. The Pearson correlation illustrates whether the problem of

TABLE 10.3 Comparison of *shariah*-compliant firms that use and those that do not use derivatives

	With derivatives	*Without derivatives*	*Differences*	*T-statistics*
Tobin's Q ratio	6.0987	5.4375	0.6611***	−15.5485
Size	6.0657	5.4886	0.5770***	−15.2424
Return on assets	0.0627	0.0194	0.0433***	−4.3001
Growth	1.2529	1.5276	−0.2747***	4.6156
Leverage	49.7766	46.2087	3.5678	−0.5531
Liquidity	2.36288	3.4434	−1.0805***	4.3954
Dividend dummy	0.76	0.5766	0.1833***	−6.8704

Source: Compiled by authors.

Note: ***,** and * denote statistically significant levels of 1%, 5% and 10% respectively.

Figures for crisis-related dummies are not shown.

TABLE 10.4 Pearson correlation coefficients among independent variables

	Tobin's Q ratio	*Size*	*Return on assets*	*Growth*	*Leverage*	*Liquidity*	*Derivative usage*
Tobin's Q ratio	1						
Size	0.9689	1					
Return on assets	0.1125	0.062	1				
Growth	−0.3845	−0.242	−0.11	1			
Leverage	0.1692	0.193	−0.063	0.0094	1		
Liquidity	−0.1381	−0.132	0.116	−0.0272	−0.1497	1	
Derivative usage	0.4098	0.403	0.123	−0.1322	0.016	−0.126	1
Dividend dummy	0.3755	0.359	0.213	−0.2629	−0.0825	0.1103	0.1947
Pre-crisis dummy	−0.0682	−0.055	0.064	0.0139	−0.0278	−0.018	0
Crisis dummy	0.0004	−0.007	−0.015	0.0657	0.0036	0.0076	0
Post-crisis dummy	0.0678	0.062	−0.05	−0.0797	0.0243	0.0103	0

TABLE 10.5 Variance inflation factor (VIF) test for independent variables for the crisis, pre-crisis and post-crisis periods

Variable	*VIF*	*1/VIF*
Crisis		
Firm size	1.46	0.6859
Dividend dummy	1.29	0.7762
Derivatives use	1.23	0.8139
Growth	1.12	0.8967
Leverage	1.09	0.9209
Liquidity	1.08	0.9250
Return on assets	1.07	0.9316
Crisis dummy	1.01	0.9947
Mean VIF	1.17	
Pre-crisis		
Variable	VIF	1/VIF
Firm size	1.47	0.6819
Dividend dummy	1.29	0.7728
Derivatives use	1.23	0.8139
Growth	1.11	0.9006
Leverage	1.09	0.9208
Liquidity	1.08	0.9234
Return on assets	1.08	0.9288
Pre-crisis dummy	1.01	0.9859
Mean VIF	1.17	
Post-crisis		
Variable	VIF	1/VIF
Firm size	1.47	0.6817
Dividend dummy	1.3	0.7698
Derivative use	1.23	0.8137
Growth	1.12	0.8940
Leverage	1.09	0.9209
Liquidity	1.08	0.9240
Return on assets	1.08	0.9300
Post-crisis dummy	1.02	0.9782
Mean VIF	1.17	

multicollinearity exists among the independent variables. As a further check on the probable problem of multicollinearity, the variance inflation factor test (VIF) was conducted. As shown in Table 10.5, the VIF values of all the independent variables for all three phases of the crisis lie from 1 to 2, which is below the threshold of 10 that indicates the presence of multicollinearity amongst independent variables.

In all three phases of the cycle, most of the controlled variables are shown to be statistically significant, which can indicate that the variables can significantly affect firm value. Based on the table, only the dummy variables are statistically insignificant in affecting firm value. Firm size is found to be positively and significantly related to firm value, and this is in line with the literature (Bashir et al., 2013). However, this relationship is in contrast with the relationship shown by Ayturk et. al. (2016) whereby firm size is shown to be negatively related to firm value. Regardless of the economic cycle, firm size plays an important role in affecting firm value.

ROA is shown to have a positive relationship with firm value, which indicates that the higher the profitability of the firm, the higher the firm's value. Lau (2016) and Alam and Afza (2017) showed similar results with ROA being statistically significant in their respective research.

The negative growth variable shows that firms with future investment opportunities have lower firm value. This result contrasts with the findings of Fauver and Naranjo (2010) and Alam and Afza (2017), who have found that growth has a positive relationship with firm value in a Malaysian context.

Leverage can be seen to be statistically significant in affecting firm value, which is supported by the trade-off theory (Alam & Afza, 2017). However, Allyannis et. al (2003) found that leverage has a positive relationship with firm value. Lau (2016) also found contrasting results, whereby leverage is not statistically significant in affecting firm value.

Based on the literature, higher liquidity indicates higher ability of firms to fund for their own investments without sourcing external funds. In this study, liquidity is found to be statistically significant and negatively affects firm value, which is in contrast with the results of Bashir et al. (2013).

According to prior studies, a firm's ability to pay dividends indicates the firm's access to financial markets. As firms which pay dividends are not likely to be capital constrained, this should affect firm value in a positive manner. However, although the dividends dummy is not statistically significant, the findings from the table indicate that, no matter which phase of the economic cycle, firms are not viewed favourably when they pay dividends. This finding is not in line with the findings of Bashir et al. (2013) and Alam and Afza (2017), who both found that dividends have a positive relationship to firm value, although the latter's findings also indicated that dividends do not statistically affect firm value in Malaysia.

As an innovative contribution to the literature on the impact of derivatives use on firm value, it can be seen that in this study firms are valued negatively in the pre-crisis phase. This can perhaps be construed as investors being pessimistic about the well-being of a firm in the face of an oncoming recession. Longis and Ellis (2016) showed that market sentiment tends to deteriorate in the oncoming presence of an economic slowdown. Interestingly, firms are valued in a positive manner in the midst of a crisis. Investors tend to be more confident in the recovery phase of an economic cycle, hence firms are valued in a more positive manner with production and employment increasing nearing the end of the crisis period (Longis & Ellis, 2016).

Lastly, based on the results in Table 10.6, although derivatives use has a positive relationship with firm value, the regression analysis shows they are statistically

TABLE 10.6 Regression outputs: firm value in different crisis-related periods

	Firm value (Tobin's Q ratio)		
	Pre-crisis period	*Crisis period*	*Post-crisis period*
Intercept	−0.0585	−0.0864	−0.0779
	(−1.40)	(−2.08)	(−1.87)
Size	1.0409***	1.0428***	1.0428***
	(140.92)	(141.60)	(140.50)
Return on assets	0.1896***	0.1859***	0.1847***
	(7.36)	(7.22)	(7.14)
Growth	−0.1214***	−0.1227***	−0.1217***
	(−27.43)	(−27.67)	(−27.27)
Leverage	−0.0001*	−0.0001*	−0.0001*
	(1.72)	(1.72)	(−1.69)
Liquidity	−0.0048***	−0.0047***	−0.0047***
	(−4.57)	(−4.46)	(−4.41)
Derivatives use	0.0154	0.0148	0.0150
	(1.59)	(1.53)	(1.55)
Dividend dummy	−0.0081	−0.0114	−0.0106
	(−0.76)	(−1.08)	(−1.00)
Pre-crisis dummy	−0.0312***		
	(−1.40)		
Crisis dummy		0.0314***	
		(3.38)	
Post-crisis dummy			−0.0005
			(−0.05)

Source: Author's own compilation from Stata14.

Note: ***, ** and * denotes statistically significant levels of 1%, 5% and 10% respectively.

insignificant in affecting firm value. In the context of *shariah*-compliant firms in Malaysia, the results above indicate that, regardless of the different phases in the economic cycle, the use of derivatives for risk management purposes is not statistically significant enough to increase firm value. This is in line with the research done by Alam and Afza (2017), who studied the impact of derivatives use on firms in Pakistan and Malaysia. They posit that Malaysian firms are sounder operationally as well as geographically (Alam & Afza, 2017) . Hence, the value of derivatives use is quite limited in the country.

To detect endogeneity, the two-step least squares estimation method was used to re-examine the relationship between use of derivatives and firm value. The two-step least squares method first analyses the ordinary least squares model for a firm's value in the first stage. The error terms collected are then regressed in the second stage, from which the results (not reported here) indicate that the parameters used in the estimation model are exogenous. This allows the model to be run using the ordinary least squares method without any concerns of endogeneity issues between firm value and derivatives use.

Conclusion

This study investigated the relationship between the impact of mitigating firm risks using derivatives and firm value by employing data from 200 Malaysian *shariah*-compliant non-financial firms for the period spanning the oil shock, which was from 2011 to 2016. Firm value was measured through Tobin's *Q* and the independent variable was measured using derivatives use in the form of a dummy variable.

Prior studies generally show that derivatives use affect firm value both positively and negatively. In this study, the empirical findings suggest that firms are able to reduce firm risk by employing derivative instruments. This study also attempted to discern the different impacts of derivative use on firm value during different phases of the economic cycle, and found that only during phases prior to a crisis and in the midst of the crisis will firm value be significantly affected.

Despite the fact that risk reduction is achieved through the use of derivatives, the use of derivatives did not maximise Malaysian *shariah*-compliant firms' values significantly. This result is different from those of similar studies carried out the developed markets, such as the United States, but is in line with research carried out the context of Asian firms. Published studies have suggested that one of the reasons for this disparity is a less liquid derivatives market and weaker institutional governance in Asian countries.

One of the implications behind this finding is that, prior to and during an economic recession, firms should take extra caution in attempting to mitigate firm risks using instruments that are considered highly volatile in the financial markets. Particularly in the context of *shariah*-compliant firms, which are required to abide by the more stringent rules of Islamic finance to ensure that the status of being *shariah*-compliant can be upheld, perhaps the use of derivatives use is not well documented to the extent where investors feel comfortable knowing the company is not put at further risk by using derivatives. In addition, before the oncoming of a recession, perhaps the regulatory body of the Malaysian financial markets can configure certain regulations on utilising derivatives to ensure minimal impact on the firm when the crisis hits.

Hence, future studies can consider investigating dividend using notional amounts, not as dummy variable, to observe the extent of its impact on firm value/performance. Another interesting aspect to consider is comparing derivative use and the extent of derivative use on the firm value of *shariah*-compliant firms and non-*shariah*-compliant firms in the context of multiple countries. On another note, since the sectors covered in this sample ran to six types, perhaps future studies can focus on a specific sector to further reduce the endogeneity problem.

References

Ahmad, N., & Haris, B. (2012). Factors for using derivatives: Evidence from Malaysian non-financial companies. *Research Journal of Finance and Accounting*, *3*(9), 79–87.

Ahmed, H., Azevedo, A., & Guney, Y. (2014). The effect of hedging on firm value and performance: Evidence from nonfinancial UK firms. In: *European Financial Management*. Conference paper, United Kingdom.

Alam, A., & Afza, T. (2017). Impact of derivative usage on firm's risk and value: A comparative analysis of Pakistan and Malaysia. *Argumenta Oeconomica*, *1*(38), 221–242.

Allayannis, G., & Weston, J. P. (2001). The use of foreign currency derivatives and firm market value. *Review of Financial Studies*, *14*(1), 243–276.

Allyannis, G., Lel, U., & Miller, D. P. (2003). Corporate governance and the hedging premium around the world. Darden Business School Working Paper No 03-10, University of Virginia, Charlottesville, VA.

Ameer, R. (2009). Value-relevance of foreign exchange and interest rate derivatives disclosure: The case of Malaysian firms. *The Journal of Risk Finance*, *10*(1), 78–90.

Arnold, M. M., Rathgeber, A. W., & Stockl, S. (2014). Determinants of corporate hedging: A statistical meta-analysis. *The Quarterly Review of Economics and Finance*, *54*, 443–458.

Ayturk, Y., Gurbuz, A. O., & Yanik, S. (2016). Corporate derivatives use and firm value: Evidence from Turkey. *Borsa Istanbul Review*, *16*(2), 108–120.

Bartram, S. M., Brown, G. W., & Fehle, F. R. (2009). International evidence on financial derivatives usage. *Financial Management*, *38*(1), 185–206.

Bashir, H., Sultan, K., & Jghef, O. K. (2013). Impact of derivative usage on firm value: Evidence from non-financial firms of Pakistan. *Journal of Management Research*, *5*(4), 108–127.

Berkman, H., & Bradbury, M. E. (1996). Empirical evidence on corporate use of derivatives. *Financial Management*, *25*(2), 5–13.

Bodnar, G., Consolandi, C., Gabbi, G., & Jaiswal-Dale, A. (2013). Risk management for Italian non-financial firms: Currency and interest rate exposure. *European Financial Management*, *19*(5), 887–910.

Callahan, M. (2012). To hedge or not to hedge…that is the question: Empirical evidence from the North American gold mining industry 1996–2000. *Financial Markets, Institutions & Instruments*, *11*(4), 271–288.

Carter, D. A., Rogers, D. A., & Simkins, B. J. (2006). Does hedging affect firm value? Evidence from the US airline industry. *Finance Management*, *35*(1), 53–86.

Charumathi, B., & Kota, H. B. (2012). On the determinants of derivative usage by large Indian non-financial firms. *Global Business Review*, *13*(2), 251–267.

Colton, N. A. (2016). Oil prices and the Malaysian economy. Retrieved from http://wimnet.org.my/wp-content/uploads/2016/09/Inspire-31-C-1-pg30-31-OilPrice.pdf (accessed 13 April 2018).

Dolde, W. (1993). The trajectory of corporate financial risk management. *Journal of Applied Corporate Finance*, *6*(3), 33–41.

Fauver, L., & Naranjo, A. (2010). Derivative usage and firm value: The influence of agency costs and monitoring problems. *Journal of Corporate Finance*, *16*, 719–735.

Froot, K. A., Scharfstein, D. S., & Stein, J. C. (1993). Risk management: Coordinating corporate investment and financing policies. *The Journal of Finance*, *48*(5), 1629–1658.

Goldberg, S. R., Godwin, J. H., Kim, M. S., & Tritschler, C. A. (1994). On the determinants of corporate hedging with financial derivatives. Purdue CIBER Working Papers. Paper 99.

Geczy, C., Minton, B. A., & Schrand, C. (1997). Why firms use currency derivatives. *The Journal of Finance*, *52*(4), 1323–1354.

Isa, M. A. M., Ismail, N., & Rahman, N. H. A. (2017). The use of derivatives to hedge risk for plantation and property companies in Malaysia. *e-Academia Journal*, *6*(1), 38–47.

Jin, Y., & Jorion, P. (2006). Firm value and hedging: Evidence from US oil and gas producers. *The Journal of Finance*, *61*(2), 893–919.

Lau, C. K. (2016). How corporate derivative use impact firm performance? *Pacific-Basin Finance Journal*, *40*, 102–114.

Longis, A. D., & Ellis, D. (2016). Market sentiment and the business cycle: Identifying macro regimes through investor risk appetite. Retrieved from www.oppenheimerfunds.com/investors/doc/Market_Sentiment_and_the_Business_Cycle.pdf?dig_asset_metrics=done (accessed 15 April 2018).

Lookman, A. (2004). Does hedging increase firm value? Evidence from oil and gas producing firms. In EFA 2004 Maastricht Meetings, Working Paper (No.5174).

Modigliani, F., & Miller, M. H. (1958). The cost of capital, corporation finance and the theory of investment. *The American Economic Review*, *43*(3), 261–297.

Myers, S. C. (1977). Determinants of corporate borrowing. *Journal of Financial Economics*, *5*, 147–175.

Nance, D. R., Smith, C. W., & Smithson, C. W. (1993). On the determinants of corporate hedging. *The Journal of Finance*, *48*(1), 267–284.

Nguyen, H., & Faff, R. (2010). Does the type of derivative instrument used by companies affect firm value? *Applied Economic Letters*, *17*(7), 681–683.

Paligorova, T., & Staskow, R. (2014). The use of financial derivatives by Canadian firms. Bank of Canada Review, 47–54.

Rashid, M., Hassan, M. K., Amin, N., & Samina, Q. S. (2017). Shari'ah compliant companies in Bangladesh. *Journal of Islamic Economics, Business and Finance*, *13*(2), 129–143.

Securities Commission Malaysia (2017). Islamic capital markets. Retrieved from www.sc.com.my/general_section/islamic-capital-market/ (accessed 10 April 2018).

Smith, C. W., & Stulz, R. M. (1985). The determinants of firm's hedging policies. *Journal of Financial and Quantitative Analysis*, *20*(4), 391–405.

Titman, S., & Wessels, R. (2012). The determinants of capital structure choice. *The Journal of Finance*, *43* (1), 1–19.

Warner, J. B. (1977). Bankruptcy costs: Some evidence. *Journal of Finance*, *32*(2), 337–347.

INDEX

Note: Page numbers in **bold** refer to tables and in *italics* to figures.